I0819932

THE
BALLAD REPERTOIRE
OF
ANNA GORDON,
MRS BROWN OF FALKLAND

The Scottish Text Society
Fifth Series
no. 8

THE
BALLAD REPERTOIRE
OF
ANNA GORDON,
MRS BROWN OF FALKLAND

Edited by
Sigrid Rieuwerts

The Scottish Text Society

2011

First published 2011 by The Scottish Text Society

ISBN 978–1–89797–632–6

A Scottish Text Society publication
Published by The Boydell Press
an imprint of Boydell & Brewer Ltd
PO Box 9, Woodbridge, Suffolk IP12 3DF, UK
and of Boydell & Brewer Inc.
668 Mt Hope Avenue, Rochester, NY 14620, USA
website: www.boydellandbrewer.com

A CIP catalogue record for this book is available from the British Library

Papers used by Boydell & Brewer Ltd are natural, recyclable products made from wood grown in sustainable forests

Printed in Great Britain by
CPI Antony Rowe, Chippenham and Eastbourne

Contents

Illustrations

Figures

For my daughter
Marijke Saskia

Preface and Acknowledgements

Anna Gordon (1747–1810) is generally known to ballad scholars as Mrs Brown of Falkland since she resided at Falkland in Fife at the time when the ballads she sang were first being discussed. "No Scottish ballads are superior in kind to those recited in the last century by Mrs Brown, of Falkland" according to Francis James Child's introduction to his monumental ballad collection, *The English and Scottish Popular Ballads* (1882–98) (*ESPB* 1: vii–viii).

From the time that her repertoire was recorded in the late eighteenth century, literary scholars like Thomas Percy, Joseph Ritson, Robert Jamieson, Walter Scott, "Monk" Lewis and Francis James Child were eager to see it. More recently, David Buchan, David Fowler, Holger Nygard, William Montgomerie and Marianne Solbach devoted their research to Mrs Brown's ballads. And yet none of her manuscripts has ever been published as an entity. Her repertoire has been dispersed through various printed collections and has been difficult to grasp as a whole.

What makes her ballad repertoire so special is partly the size – it consists of one song and thirty-four ballads in fifty-two versions – but above all, the fact that it is a genuinely female repertoire at a time when women were not given a voice in the public sphere of polite society (see Rieuwerts, "Anonymity" and "Mainly through Women"). The quality and age of her ballad texts, tunes and stories are indeed remarkable and this edition testifies to this.

More than two hundred years later, it is a great honour and joy to be the first to publish Mrs Brown's repertoire. Twenty of her ballads were first recorded about 1781–83 (in the lost source of manuscript A) and then fifteen ballads were written out with music, in 1783 (manuscript B). In 1800 another nine ballads followed, in this case written by Anna Brown herself (manuscript C), and her letters, written between 1800 and 1802, enclosed three more ballads taken down by her husband the Rev. Dr Andrew Brown (manuscript D). Robert Jamieson recorded more ballads from her and these were published in his *Popular Ballads* in 1806 (E).

I am particularly pleased that in the Homecoming Year, created and timed to mark the 250th anniversary of Robert Burns, the Scottish Text Society has agreed to honour the female Robert Burns and to publish her repertoire to mark the bicentenary of Mrs Brown's death in 2010.

I would like to thank the owners and keepers of the manuscripts for making this possible, in particular the owners and the National Library of Scotland for permission to publish Acc 10611 (1–2) and all letters associated with it and the University of Edinburgh for permission to publish from MS La.III.473.

It has been a great pleasure to work at the Centre for Research Collections at Edinburgh University Library and I would like to thank Tricia Boyd and her team. I am also grateful to Sheila Mackenzie and her colleagues at the National Library of Scotland for providing a wonderful service. Thanks are also due to the University of Aberdeen for giving permission to publish a portrait of Robert Eden Scott and to Andrew MacGregor and Laura Castle for supplying it; to Paul Barnaby of the Corson Collection / Walter Scott Digital Archive for providing an image of Alexander Fraser Tytler and to Bonn University Library for tracing Marianne Solbach's Doctoral Dissertation on Mrs Brown. I would also like to express my appreciation to the staff at the Advocates Library, Abbotsford; Library and Historic Collections at the University of Aberdeen; the Mitchell Library, Glasgow; Register House, Edinburgh; the National Archives of Scotland; the library of The Society of Antiquaries of Scotland and Houghton Library at Harvard University, as well as to my colleagues and friends at the University of Edinburgh, Harvard University, Siegen University and the University of Mainz.

I am very grateful to Holger Nygard, who contemplated preparing an edition of Mrs Brown's ballads in the 1970s, for kindly encouraging me to proceed and for making available his notes on the manuscripts that were formerly at Aldourie Castle and Old Clune House. Thanks are also due to Ruth Perry for sharing her material and thoughts on Mrs Brown in the early phase of this project, to the late Ian MacKenzie for technical support, to James Porter for musical advice, to Walter Duncan for introducing me to the world of Old Machar and to Ian Olson for his continuing interest. A big thank-you goes to Frances Fischer for giving me a home in Edinburgh and for doing much more than I could possibly have asked for. I have very much appreciated my attachment to the department of Celtic and Scottish Studies at the University of Edinburgh as an Honorary Fellow.

I would like to acknowledge gratefully the financial and moral support I received from the Johannes Gutenberg University of Mainz and particularly from Bernhard Reitz. I would also like to thank my student researchers Frauke (Joy) Katzmarzik, Inga Surges, Frauke Jung, and above all Theresa von Helden and Elaine Keenan, for being such a wonderful team and for sharing my love for Mrs Brown's repertoire, even if it meant proof-reading from back to front or tackling unintelligible words in eighteenth-century Scots. I am extremely grateful to Katherine Campbell for giving generously of her time in setting all the music in this edition and for advising me in musical matters. From the very beginning Emily Lyle at Edinburgh has been a great promoter of this project and it has been a great privilege and pleasure to work with her throughout the preparation of this book. Her determination to see Mrs Brown's ballad repertoire published at last, and to get it done right, has given me the strength to go on even at difficult times. This edition benefited greatly from her enquiring approach, her thoroughness in proof-reading and, above all, her time and energy and I am deeply grateful to her. For advice on the contents and layout of this edition I would also like to thank Sally Mapstone and Nicola Royan as well as the Council and Editorial Committee of the Scottish Text Society.

Without the support and tolerance of my family, however, this book would not have come about. Thanks to Marijke Saskia and Frederick James for sharing my love for Scotland and to Hans for holding the fort in my absence and for joining me in the quest for Mrs Brown and her ballads.

Sigrid Rieuwerts
Zotzenheim, October 2010

Abbreviations

A	Brown A manuscript (Robert Jamieson's Brown manuscript in the David Laing Papers) in EUL: La.III.473, ff. 10–43
Adv.	Advocates Library, Abbotsford
AFT	Alexander Fraser Tytler
APL	Aberdeen Public Library
AUL	Aberdeen University, Special Libraries and Archives
B	Brown B manuscript (William Tytler's Brown manuscript) in NLS: Acc 10611 (1)
BL	British Library, London
C	Brown C manuscript (Alexander Fraser Tytler's Brown manuscript) in NLS: Acc 10611 (2)
D	Brown D manuscript (letters including Andrew Brown's transcript of ballads) in EUL: La.III.473, ff. 1–9
DgF	*Danmarks gamle Folkeviser* (12 vols, 1853–1976), edited by Svend Grundtvig; *DgF* type = DgF
E	Brown E (Mrs Brown's ballads in *Popular Ballads*, edited by Robert Jamieson)
ESPB	*The English and Scottish Popular Ballads* (5 vols, 1882–98), edited by Francis J. Child
EUL	Edinburgh University Library
GD	*The Greig-Duncan Folk Song Collection* (8 vols, 1981–2002) edited by Patrick Shuldham-Shaw and Emily B. Lyle; *GD* type = GD
JR	Joseph Ritson
MSB	*Minstrelsy of the Scottish Border* (3 vols, 1802–03), edited by Walter Scott
NAS	National Archives of Scotland, Edinburgh
NLS	National Library of Scotland, Edinburgh
PB	*Popular Ballads* (2 vols, 1806), edited by Robert Jamieson
RES	Robert Eden Scott
RJ	Robert Jamieson
SL	*The Letters of Sir Walter Scott* (12 vols, 1932–37), edited by Herbert Grierson
TG	Thomas Gordon
TSB	*The Types of the Scandinavian Medieval Ballad* (1978), edited by Bengt R. Jonsson; *TSB* type = TSB

TT	*The Traditional Tunes of the Child Ballads* (4 vols, 1959–72), edited by Bertrand H. Bronson
VHS	Virginia Historical Society, Richmond
WS	Walter Scott
WT	William Tytler

Introduction

Description of the Manuscript and Printed Sources

Brown A

Brown A is an interleaved manuscript consisting of (a) a copy made by Robert Jamieson in 1799 of a manuscript containing twenty ballad texts written by Robert Eden Scott some years prior to Brown B (1783) and of (b) Jamieson's annotations on the interleaved pages. It has been referred to in the literature as Robert Jamieson's Brown manuscript.

In 1799, Robert Jamieson (1772–1844) was a classical assistant at a grammar school in Macclesfield, Cheshire, in England. He was, however, a Scotsman who came from Morayshire and had received his education at King's College, Aberdeen (see Harvey Wood, *Letters to an Antiquary*; Rieuwerts, *In the Footsteps of Herder*). Brown A is in the David Laing Collection in Edinburgh University Library and forms the greater part of MS La.III.473, running from folio 10 to the end.

The earlier folios of La.III.473 were bound up with Brown A at a later stage and contain four letters to Jamieson (see Brown D). The original covers are no longer extant apart from a fragment glued onto the first page which has "Popular Ballads" written on it in large letters in Jamieson's hand. He wrote out the following description on folio 1v:

> A faithful transcript of Popular Ballads, written from oral recitation, for his amusement by Mr R. Scott, Professor of Greek in King's College, Aberdeen, and favoured, and transmitted to me by Dr. Gilbert Gerard, Professor of Theology, Aberdeen. July 29, 1799. Robert Jamieson.

Later, there was a deletion of "oral" before recitation and the addition of extra wording in an unidentified hand so that this section reads: "written from the recitation, of his aunt Mrs Brown of Falkland for his amusement".

La.III.473 measures about 20.5 cm x 23.5 cm (8 in. x 9.3 in.) and has fifty sheets in total in a late nineteenth-century leather binding. There are forty-six folios numbered in pencil and blank unnumbered binding sheets at front and back. The folio numbering of all pages, including letters and interleaves, was added at the time of rebinding. As to its custodial history, Adam Sim Coulter's book plate and the name and date "D. Laing, 1869" are still visible. Apart from his name, David Laing also left the following note on folio 1r: "Purchased at the Sale of the late Mr Pitcairn's / 19 December 1855. / Mr Laing of the Signet Library

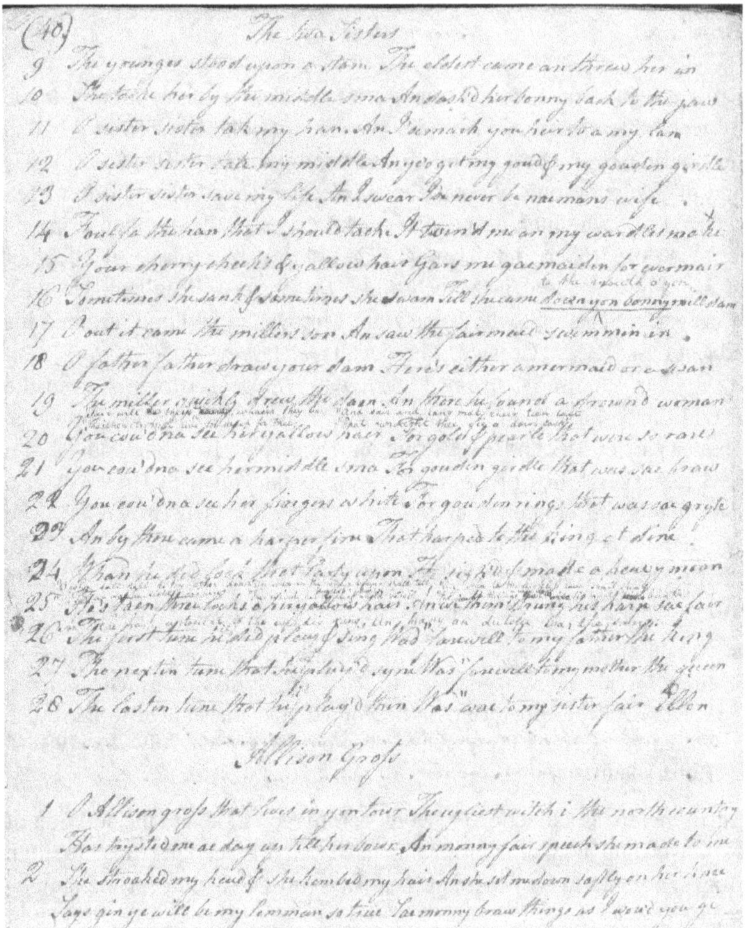

(40) The twa Sisters

9 The younges stood upon a stan The eldest came an threw her in
10 She took her by the middle sma An dash'd her bonny back to the jaw
11 O sister sister tak my han An I'se mak you heir to a my lan
12 O sister sister tak my middle An ye'se get my goud & my gouden girdle
13 O sister sister save my life An I swear I'se never be nae mans wife
14 Foul fa the han that I should tak It twin'd me an my wardles make
15 Your cherry cheeks & yallow hair Gars me gae maiden for evermair
16 Sometimes she sank & sometimes she swam Till she came down yon bonny mill dam
17 O out it came the millers son An saw the fair maid soummin in
18 O father father draw your dam There's either a mermaid or a swan
19 The miller quickly drew the dam An there he fand a drown'd woman
20 You cou'dna see her yallow hair For gold & pearle that were so rare
21 You cou'dna see her middle sma For gouden girdle that was sae braw
22 You cou'dna see her fingers white For gouden rings that was sae gryte
23 An by there came a harper fine That harped to the king at dine
24 When he did look that lady upon He sigh'd & made a heavy moan
25 He's taen three locks o her yallow hair An wi them strung his harp sae fair
26 The first tune he did play & sing Was farewell to my father the king
27 The nextin tune that he play'd syne Was farewell to my mother the queen
28 The lasten tune that he play'd then Was wae to my sister fair Ellen

Allison Gross

1 O Allison gross that lives in yon towr The ugliest witch i the north country
Has trysted me ae day up till her towr An monny fair speech she made to me
2 She stroaked my head & she kembed my hair An she set me down saftly on her knee
Says gin ye will be my lemman so true Sae monny braw things as I would you gi

Figure 1:
Facsimile of page 40 of A
in Robert Jamieson's hand

seemingly desired it. / Bought at the Sale of the Library of Mr Adam Sim of Coulter / £ 3.15 o / D. L.".

Robert Pitcairn (1793–1855), a ballad collector and a member of the Bannatyne Club in Edinburgh, was not only a friend of David Laing and Walter Scott (see Hewitt), but also a friend and colleague of Robert Jamieson at the General Register House, where Jamieson worked as a clerk from 1809 to 1840s. It is therefore quite possible that Pitcairn obtained Brown A directly from Jamieson before he left for London in 1844. After Pitcairn's death in 1855, the manuscript went to Adam Sim of Coulter (1805–1868), a councillor of the Society of Antiquaries, and it was then bought at the auction of Coulter's library in 1869 by David Laing (1793–1878) (see also Laing's letter to Child, 13 January 1873, in MS Am 2349, vol. 11: f. 98 at Houghton). It came into Edinburgh University Library in 1879 as part of the David Laing Collection.[1]

The primary use of A by Jamieson was to have a copy of the songs recorded from Anna Gordon by Robert Eden Scott in another (now lost) manuscript. As Jamieson explained in the preface to *PB* (1: iv–v), he was glad to obtain from "professor Scott [...] a transcript of a large collection of upwards of twenty pieces, which that gentleman had written down a good many years ago, when he was very young, from the recitation of his aunt, Mrs Brown of Falkland". As the number of ballads in Brown A confirms, Jamieson did not add any ballads to the twenty texts taken down from Mrs Brown. But nevertheless Brown A is not only a "faithful transcript". It also had a secondary use since Jamieson took the Brown texts in it as the base for his own developments of the Brown ballads that were intended for publication and which eventually appeared in his *Popular Ballads* in 1806.

In *PB*, the following six of Anna Brown's ballads appeared with additions and revisions by Jamieson: Brown 10 ("Burd Ellen"), Brown 11 ("Lady Maisery"), Brown 14 ("King Henry"), Brown 15 ("Sweet Willy"), Brown 18 ("The twa Sisters") and Brown 20 ("The Bonny Birdy"). Most of these changes are already indicated in A. In Brown 12 ("Fair Anny") Jamieson draws a few slight revisions from Mrs Brown's C text through Walter Scott and an insertion point is indicated in A where *PB* includes two verses given from Jamieson's own memory.

1 Because of its importance to ballad studies and thus to Harvard, F. J. Child had offered what he considered a great sum of money for Brown A in 1878 (Child's letter to Murdoch, 11 November 1878, in MS Am 1319/*53m–101, f. 36, at Houghton; see Reppert 294–97).

The dual function of this manuscript is also underlined by the variety of papers used. Light paper with the mark CPATCH 1797 is used for the texts from page 10 to 24. This paper came from the Carshalton Mills in Surrey, and the trading dates for Christopher Patch, a paper-maker and retailer, are listed in Shorter (237) as 1780–1801. From page 25 onwards, a watermark is clearly visible – similar to the one printed below, only having the date 1797 on it instead of GR (see Shorter 264 for image). Patch was said to have been one of the "best writing paper makers" in Britain (Shorter 395), but the interleaved sheets (between 11 and 30) are of an even higher quality. The paper is finer and heavier and truncated letters of ALLEE are visible as watermarks on four of the interleaved sheets (ff. 37, 39, 42, 44). Despite the fact that this type of paper is known as best-quality Dutch paper, William Allee was a paper-maker from the Hustbourne Mills in Hampshire, England, whose trading dates are given as 1791–1803 (Shorter 168). Other interleaved pages (ff. 11, 14, 16, 18, 20, 22, 24, 26, 30) bear a "horn" watermark (see below; Churchill ccliii; No. 323) and are indeed made by a Dutch paper-maker.

Although the paper for the ballad texts can clearly be dated to 1797, no exact date can be given for the interleaved paper for this was a very common watermark, used for his London prints from 1776 onwards by the Dutch papermaker L. V. Gerrevink (see Churchill 80). There can be no doubt that all the papers were roughly of the same period, but given the variety of paper used, it seems that Jamieson probably worked from loose sheets and had them bound up afterwards.

Jamieson makes full use of the paper by having up to twenty-six lines filling one page, and by running the ballads straight on from each other. Furthermore, he writes across the full width of the page. Each line takes two lines of verse but he indicates where a new verse line begins by capitalising a word in the middle. The verses are numbered, but since the numbers sometimes fall between lines or are lacking, Jamieson must have added them later; this is also suggested by the different size and ink of the numbers. There is some see-through but not so much as to interfere with the reading of the text except that sometimes heavily written letters leave visible dots on the reverse side that have to be carefully distinguished from punctuation marks. All the texts are in Jamieson's hand and not, as Montgomerie has suggested, in Robert Eden Scott's (see Montgomerie, Part VI, 64). Jamieson has added some remarks on the interleaves which apply to the ballad texts on the facing pages (see Notes for details), and these are often indicated by a manicule:

At three points, the loss of an interleaf is shown by the presence of indications for insertions on the text pages and the absence of the material to be inserted. These points come between pages 20 and 21, 28 and 29 and 42 and 43 and are treated in the notes to Brown 9 "Lady Jane", Brown 12 "Fair Anny" and Brown 20 "The bonny birdy". There is no indication of the removal of these leaves from the binding, and it appears that they were missing before the current binding was done. This being so, we can probably understand the erratic make-up of A, which sometimes has an interleaf between pages and sometimes not, as resulting from the loss or removal of some of the interleaves which had been present in all cases between the pages.

Jamieson normally uses ink in the manuscript but the pencil note on "witch knots" in Brown 15 "Sweet Willy" appears to be his. It may be a different hand that makes other additions in pencil. These consist of: large asterisks before the titles of Brown 1 ("Rose the red & White Lilly"), Brown 13 ("Kempion") and Brown 16 ("Gil Brenton") and before the heading of Brown 7 ("Brown Adam") that occurs at the top of the page before the second verse; textual revisions to Brown 3 ("Willy o Douglass dale"), Brown 12 ("Fair Anny") and Brown 15 ("Sweet Willy"); and a note to Brown 19 ("Allison Gross").

The following are the ballads (with page numbers) as they appear in A. In this edition, A is used as a base and so the ballads in it are to be found here in their original order:

		Brown No.
1.	Rose the red & White Lilly (1–5)	1
2.	Jack the little Scot (5–8)	2
3.	Willy o Douglass dale (8–10)	3
4.	Young Bekie (11–13)	4
5.	Young Bicham (14–15)	5
6.	The gay goss hawk (15–17)	6
7.	Brown Adam (17–19)	7
8.	Lady Elspat (19–20)	8
9.	Lady Jane (20–21)	9
10.	Burd Ellen (22–24)	10
11.	Lady Maisry (24–27)	11
12.	Fair Anny (27–29)	12
13.	Kempion (29–31)	13
14.	King Henry (31–33)	14
15.	Sweet Willy (33–34)	15
16.	Gil Brenton (34–37)	16
17.	Brown Robin (37–39)	17
18.	The twa Sisters (39–40)	18
19.	Allison Gross (40–41)	19
20.	The bonny birdy (42–43)	20

Brown B

Brown B is a manuscript containing the texts and tunes of fifteen ballads written in the hand of Robert Eden Scott (1769–1811), Mrs Brown's nephew. The manuscript is on long-term deposit in the National Library of Scotland (Acc 10611 (1)). The original title page gives the date as 1783 and runs:

A Collection / of / Old Songs. / M.DCC.LXXX.III –.

It is known to be later than the original of A, having been prepared when it was realised that music was required as well as words. It was communicated to William Tytler of Woodhouselee by Anna Brown's father,

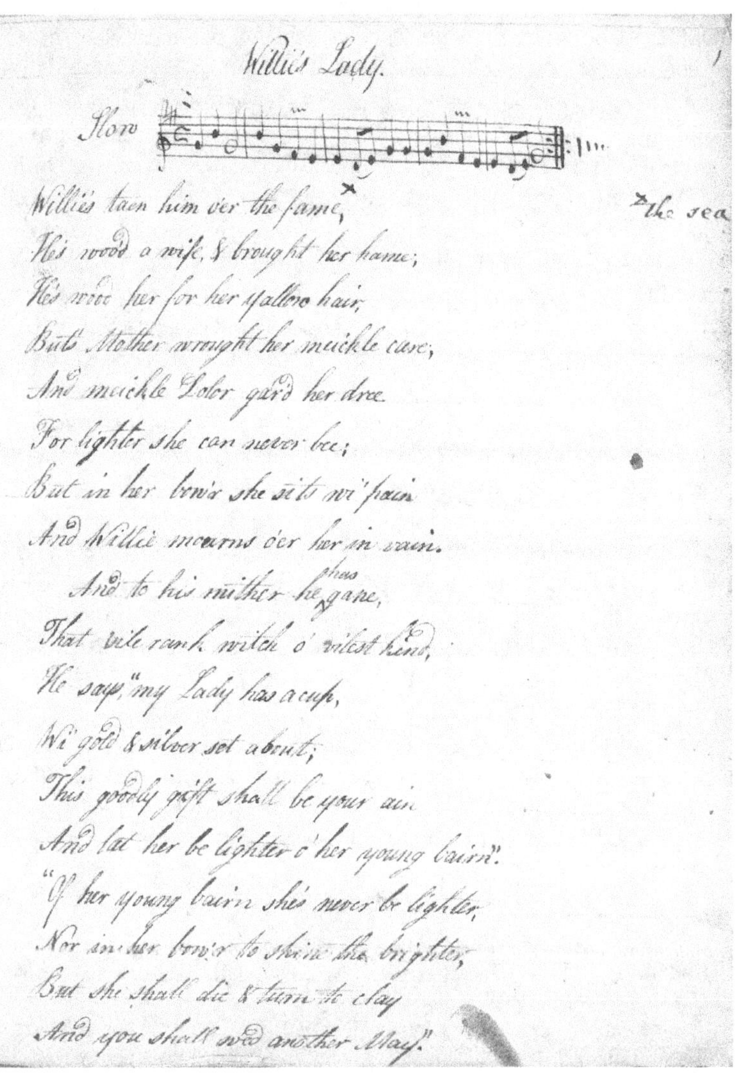

Willie's Lady.

1

Slow

Willie's taen him o'er the fame, x the sea
He's woo'd a wife, & brought her hame;
He's woo'd her for her yallow hair,
But's Mother wrought her meickle care;
And meickle Dolor gar'd her dree.
For lighter she can never bee;
But in her bow'r she sits wi' pain
And Willie mourns o'er her in vain.
And to his mither he has gane,
That vile rank witch o' vilest kind,
He says, "my Lady has a cup,
Wi' gold & silver set about;
This goodly gift shall be your ain
And let her be lighter o' her young bairn".
"Of her young bairn she's never be lighter,
Nor in her bow'r to shine the brighter,
But she shall die & turn to clay
And you shall wed another May."

Figure 2:
Facsimile of page 1 of B
in Robert Eden Scott's hand

Professor Thomas Gordon, and has been referred to in the literature as William Tytler's Brown manuscript.

William Tytler (1711–92), a lawyer and historian, was "a well-known member of Edinburgh's polite, literary society" (Couper) who showed a keen interest in the music of Scotland.[2] The manuscript he obtained from Thomas Gordon was first kept at Woodhouselee, his home near Edinburgh at the foot of the Pentland Hills, and was later moved to the family seat of the Fraser Tytlers, Aldourie Castle near Inverness. During the latter part of the nineteenth century and the first half of the twentieth century, the Brown B manuscript was missing.[3] Not even the complete and accurate copy (with music) of Brown B that Joseph Ritson had made in 1793–94 could be located; the Houghton Library at Harvard University only received the Joseph Ritson Brown manuscript in 1920 (now: MS Eng 1486.1; see Kittredge, "Lost Manuscript"; for Ritson see Barczewski).

And thus, F. J. Child's definitive collection of *The English and Scottish Popular Ballads* (1882–96) and the T. F. Henderson edition of Scott's *Minstrelsy of the Scottish Border* (1902) had to be published without knowledge of the original manuscript. Some items from B had found their way into Scott's manuscripts at Abbotsford (see below) and two ballads from Brown B, "Willie's Lady" (Brown 15) and "Clark Colven" (Brown 21), were found at Aldourie Castle. Mary Fraser Tytler discovered them in 1881 in an old manuscript entitled *Poems* that had belonged to William Fraser Tytler (1777–1853).

She had them copied and sent to Child at Harvard (see MS Eng 1486.4 and MS Am 2349, vol. 10, ff. 58–59, Mary Fraser Tytler's Letter to Child, 5 June 1881 at Houghton), not knowing, however, that these were in no way accurate copies of the texts in Brown B. While "Willie's Lady" varied "in small particulars in nearly every stanza", even bigger

[2] For more details on William Tytler of Woodhouselee see Couper; Mackenzie and Anon. ("Short Characteristical Notices" and "Memoirs of William Tytler").

[3] Despite numerous attempts by the Fraser Tytler family at the request of David Laing, William Macmath, William and James Curtis and others, the manuscript was not to be found, nor could a mysterious manuscript called "An Album containing numerous Ballads and Songs, in an old hand, 4to, from the Woodhouselee Library" (Lot 2300, Sale of C. K. Sharpe's Library, 30 January 1852) ever be traced. See MS Am 1922–1922.2; MS Am 2349, vol. 10, ff. 51–53 at Houghton; Acc 3639 at NLS. More details are given in Lyle, *Fairies and Folk* 218–19.

changes were made in "Clark Colven": "Professor Child accepted Mary Fraser Tytler's copy of the two ballads as identical with the originals in WT-B [Brown B] (which he never saw) and was misled therefore about Scott's copy of *Clark Colven*" (Montgomerie, Part VI, 71; see also *ESPB* 1: 371–72; 387–88).

Child was also misled about the exact nature of Brown B. The contents of the manuscript and the first verse of each ballad were given in Robert Anderson's letter to Bishop Thomas Percy in January 1801 (see below; *Percy Letters* 9: 53–55). Anderson's list, however, was not accurate and the confusion he caused by inadvertently renaming ballads[4] and giving the second and third items in the manuscript ("Clark Colven" and "Brown Adam") as the thirteenth and fourteenth, can only now be cleared up with this edition of Mrs Brown's repertoire in hand.

Mrs Christian Fraser Tytler (1897–1995) of Aldourie Castle eventually recovered Brown B "sometime in the 1930s". As she explained to the American ballad scholar Holger Nygard in 1979, she had the practice of allowing no one else to clean the books and had thus spent many days sitting on top of a ladder reading marginalia. "And that's how I found the manuscript. It was bound in with a lot of pamphlets and papers" she recalled in a conversation with Nygard ("Reminiscence"). Ever since she had married into the Fraser Tytler family in 1919, she had been asked to search for Mrs Brown's ballad manuscripts and their failure to find them had been a burden to her.[5] About 1927, she had located Brown C in a safe in the wine cellar but Brown B still eluded her, and thus she was more than relieved and filled with a "sense of rejoicing" when she found it. It was the only manuscript bound into a volume of pamphlets and papers marked "G" on the spine which belonged to a set of alphabetically lettered quarto volumes, and it was item eight in the volume (Alexander Fraser Tytler's index to his *Miscellany* collection).[6] The

4 Brown 4 "Young Bekie" becomes "Young Betrice" (*Percy Letters* 9: 51; see also La.IV.Chi at EUL for Macmath's desperate attempt to find this ballad), and Brown 22 "Thomas Rymer & Queen of Elfland" becomes "Thomas Rhymer & Queen of England" (*Percy Letters* 9: 54).

5 After William Montgomerie in the early 1950s, Emily Lyle (April 1966), Dorothy Laughlin Mircowich (June 1966), David Fowler (May 1970) and Holger Nygard (June 1979) are also on record as having contacted Mrs Christian Fraser Tytler about the two Brown manuscripts (Nygard, "Reminiscence").

6 David Herd had inspected Brown B in November 1804 "pr. favour of Mr Constable" when it was already bound up in this way and had then wondered about the wisdom of *William* Tytler's Brown ballad manuscript being "bound

volume was taken to the National Library of Scotland so that Brown B could be removed and separately bound, and it was then returned to the library at Aldourie Castle.

When Christian Fraser Tytler moved to Old Clune House, Aldourie, c. 1948, the manuscripts went with her and were kept in a black folder (see Nygard, "Reminiscence"), presumably the one in which they are now contained in the NLS. The two manuscripts were deposited temporarily in the NLS in May 1982 and placed on long-term deposit in 1992 (Acc 10611 (1) and (2)).[7]

Brown B measures 24.5 cm x 19 cm (or 9.6 in. x 7.5 in.) and is in perfect binding. The pages have been restored and rebound in blue cardboard by the National Library of Scotland; there is no trace of a contemporary cover. The paper is of fine quality and all the sheets are lightly ruled with nine lines per page. There are no other watermarks apart from lines for pages 1–10 and 75–81. The top of an elaborate watermark – an open crown – is to be found at the point of binding on pp. 11–44, starting with page 11, "John the Little Scot", changing to a different one from p. 45 until p. 74.

This suggests that the watermark must be seen as being in the centre of the sheet and thus the first six sheets and the last four sheets form one unit and the middle ones (seventeen top sheets, fifteen bottom sheets on either side) too. The elaborate watermark is the so-called "Strasburg Lilly" (Churchill cccvi; No. 411), used from 1766 onwards by Lubertus van Gerrevink from "Egmond a/d Hoef, Phoenix mill" in the Netherlands (Churchill 18; 84). Paper from his mills was used in all three surviving manuscripts.

The name of the writer of the manuscript is not given, but the handwriting, clearly identifiable through its distinct crossing of the letter "t", is that of Robert Eden Scott. The handwriting is very even and unpretentious; hardly any corrections were made. It is clearly the handwriting of a young person; his later hand is far less careful and tidy.

up in a Collection of Pamphlets belonging to *Alexander Fraser* Tytler, Esq." [emphasis mine]. He must have sensed that this might create problems in the future and accordingly left a note, stressing the importance of the manuscript: "To any future Collector of Old Scotish Songs for Publication this M.S. might be of great service" (La.IV.25.47, f. 118).

7 Microfilms of the two volumes were made in 1953 (Mf MSS 29) and Xerox copies in 1964 (Acc 3640). See Bibliography for full details of NLS photographic and microfilmed copies obtained by the National Library of Scotland before the deposit of the originals.

Alexander Fraser Tytler has written his name at the top right of the title page. He gives an account of the origin of the manuscript in ink on the back of this page and signs his statement. He explains how his father "got the following songs from an old friend, Mr Thomas Gordon Professor of Philosophy in King's College Aberdeen", and quotes at length from Professor Gordon's letter to his father of 19 January 1793 (see below). Set apart from this text, he made the following note, which relates to Brown C:

> On the hint contained in the foregoing letter from Professor Gordon I wrote to Mrs Brown of Falkland very lately (February 1800) & requested that if her memory could furnish any more ballads of the same nature, she would be so kind as to write them & send them to me. In consequence I received from her *nine* other ballads, some of them extremely curious & all of considerable antiquity, together with the music to which they are sung.

Alexander Fraser Tytler also indicates in B 4 (Brown 2) that the heavy writing is that of Thomas Gordon (Anna's father) and adds a gloss in B 1 (Brown 15). Gordon, whose contributions in dark ink are clearly identifiable, has made small corrections and has offered glosses in B 1, 4, 6, 7 and 8 (Brown 15, 2, 6, 4 and 1), and in one case, Brown 4 "Young Bekie", he has added an entire stanza. Other additions made in pencil were written by Joseph Ritson who had the manuscript in his hands in

1793–94. His contributions relate to B 1, 2, 4, 14 and 15 (Brown 15, 21, 2, 11 and 18). He refers to himself by his initials in his note at the end of B 15 (Brown 18) "The Cruel Sister" (see also Walter Scott's *Scottish Songs*, which has "Note by Ritson" added to the "JR" text copied). A list of contents was added at the end (p. 82).

B is a very neat and tidy manuscript, with pages numbered in the upper right- or left-hand corner. By contrast with A, each of the fifteen ballads in B starts on a new page and above the text the title of the ballad is given, followed by one line of music in all but the last case (see below). Robert Eden Scott has sometimes drawn a line at the end of a ballad and, in seven of the ballads, he has used one or more such lines as internal division markers, as shown below in the notes to the individual ballads. Similarly, he has used indenting to indicate transitions at three points in Brown 18 "The Cruel Sister".

The following list gives the ballads in B in order along with their page numbers, and shows their Brown numbers in the present edition on the right.

		Brown No.
1.	Willie's Lady (1–4)	15
2.	Clark Colven (5–7)	21
3.	Brown Adam (8–10)	7
4.	Jack the Little Scot (11–17)	2
5.	Chil Brenton (17–23)	16
6.	The Gay Goss-Hawk (24–29)	6
7.	Young Bekie (30–36)	4
8.	Rose the Red, & White Lilly (37–46)	1
9.	Brown Robin (47–50)	17
10.	Willie o' Douglass-Dale (51–57)	3
11.	Kempion (58–62)	13
12.	Lady Elzpat (63–65)	8
13.	King Henry (66–70)	14
14.	Lady Maisery (71–77)	11
15.	The Cruel Sister (78–81)	18

Brown C

Brown C is a manuscript containing nine ballads written out by Anna Brown between February and April 1800 and sent to Alexander Fraser Tytler. The tunes of these ballads were also taken down at the time but neither the original music nor any copy of it is to be found. Brown C has been known as Alexander Fraser Tytler's Brown manuscript.

Like his father William Tytler, Alexander Fraser Tytler (1747–1813) was not only in the law profession – he became an advocate in Edinburgh in 1770 and was raised to the bench in 1802 – but he also devoted much of his time to literary pursuits. He took the name "Fraser Tytler" in 1776 on his marriage to an heiress, Anne Fraser of Balnain and Aldourie (see Du Toit; Alison; Lamont).

Brown C was formerly at Aldourie Castle, then at Old Clune House and is now in the National Library of Scotland (Acc 10611 (2)). Unlike Brown B, manuscript C was available to Child since it was copied for him by Mary Fraser Tytler (1849–1939) in 1881 (see MS Eng 1486.4 at the Houghton).

When other scholars wanted to inspect the manuscript at the beginning of the twentieth century, however, it had gone missing, but c. 1927 Mrs Christian Fraser Tytler found it in a safe in the wine cellar that was used to store items of value: "It was in the wine-safe, up high" and was "wrapped in an old newspaper & tied with string", as she recollected in July 1979 ("Reminiscence"). After she also found Brown B, the two manuscripts were kept together and their history is the same (see above under Brown B).

Brown C is a notebook, measuring 22.5 cm x 19 cm (or 7.5 in. x 9 in.), in its original worn grey cardboard cover which has nothing inscribed on it and consists of one gathering. The paper is cream in colour and the sheets have been folded, sewn and trimmed. Ten chain lines are parallel to the sheet's short edge and a not over-refined pen with brown ink has been used. Clear watermarks of a "horn" above the initials GR – very similar to the interleaved paper used by Jamieson for A – are to be found on all sheets and pp. 23–24 reveal the full set (see also Churchill ccliii and cclvii; Nos. 323 and 329).

At the front of the notebook a double sheet has been tipped in, on which is mounted a letter about the ballads sent to Alexander Fraser Tytler by Thomas Gordon on 19 January 1793. The ballad texts begin on the left-hand page of the first opening and the page numbering in pencil, in the hand of Alexander Fraser Tytler, begins there. On the blank last page of the notebook, Tytler has added in pencil the heading "Contents"

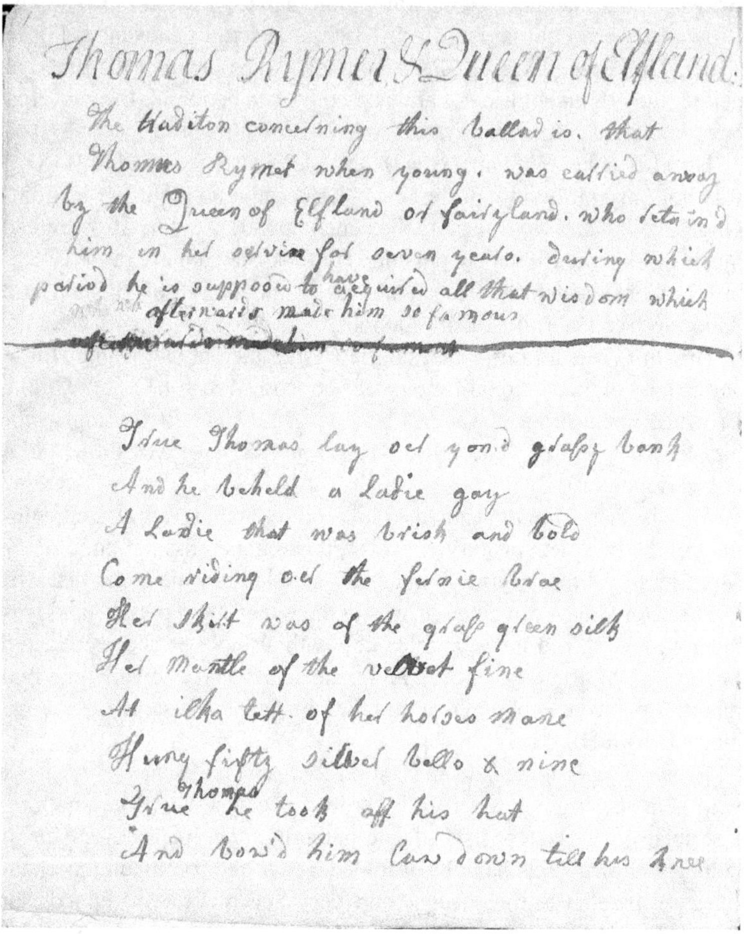

Thomas Rymer & Queen of Elfland

The tradition concerning this ballad is. that Thomas Rymer when young. was carried away by the Queen of Elfland or fairyland. who detain'd him in her service for seven years. during which period he is supposed to have acquired all that wisdom which afterwards made him so famous

~~afterwards made him so famous~~

True Thomas lay oer yon'd grassy bank
And he beheld a ladie gay
A ladie that was brisk and bold
Come riding oer the fernie brae
Her skirt was of the grass green silk
Her mantle of the velvet fine
At ilka tett of her horses mane
Hung fifty silver bells & nine
True Thomas he took off his hat
And bow'd him low down till his knee

Figure 3:
Facsimile of page 1 of C
in Anna Brown's hand

and has given a numbered list of the ballads with the opening page numbers. A few pencilled annotations to the texts, including two words in Greek, are probably also in Tytler's hand (Brown 27; p. 35). Other pencilled additions – a partial stanza numbering of one ballad (Brown 24; pp. 18–10) and variant readings in another (Brown 10; p. 43) – are in a different hand.

Anna Brown's writing, in brown ink throughout, is generally large and is distinct in one sense although poorly shaped letters and blotting sometimes make it difficult to read. Punctuation is sparse and, when present, is not always fully formed. In particular, there is a sign which appears solely after "O" that is evidently intended as an exclamation mark but is normally a line without a dot below it and may even be simply a vestigial tick in the same position.

Brown has sometimes written over her script with a view to clarifying the writing. She has also inserted a number of words into the original texts (sometimes marking them with small crosses); these are generally not revisions but simply corrections of obvious slips. (It may be noted that insertions of this kind also occur in her letters.) She has added three glosses (in Brown 22 "Thomas Rymer, & Queen of Elfland" (p. 3); Brown 23 "Fa'se Footrage" (p. 11); Brown 27 "Bonny Foot-Boy" (p. 32)), which are indicated by crosses or asterisks and has marked the two occurrences of six-line stanzas by brackets (in Brown 10 "Lord John and Bird Ellen", p. 45). The ballad headings are large and, in six of the nine cases, occur at the tops of pages.

Since Mrs Brown had been sent a list of ballads from B, there is no overlap between B and C. Two of the ballads of C, namely Brown 10 "Lord John and Bird Ellen" and Brown 12 "Love Gregor", have parallel texts in A. These are also the only two where the titles of parallel versions differ greatly from each other. The following list gives the ballads in C in their manuscript order and shows their numbers in the present edition on the right.

	Brown No.
1. Thomas Rymer, & Queen of Elfland (1–4)	22
2. Love Gregor (5–10)	12
3. Fa'se Footrage (11–18)	23
4. Jellon Grame and Lillie Flower (18–22)	24
5. The bonny Earl of Livingston (23–25)	25
6. Bonny Bee Ho'm (26–28)	26
7. Bonny Foot-Boy (28–35)	27
8. Cruel Brother Or The Bride's Testament (35–38)	28
9. Lord John and Bird Ellen (39–46)	10

Brown D

Brown D is a separate small collection consisting of four letters to Robert Jamieson dated 1800–05, with their enclosures, which has been bound in at the beginning of MS La.III.473 preceding Brown A. They are:

ff. 2–3	letter from Robert Eden Scott, 9 June 1805;
ff. 4–5	letter from Anna Brown, 2 December 1802;
ff. 6–8	letter from Anna Brown, 18 June 1801;
f. 9	letter from Anna Brown, 15 September 1800.

This material includes three ballads in Andrew Brown's hand, which form a distinct part of the Mrs Brown corpus.

		Brown No.
1.	Bonny Baby Livingston (f. 8)	29
2.	The Baron of Braikly (f. 6)	30
3.	Allan O Maut (f. 6v)	31

While Brown 29, "Bonny Baby Livingston", is written on the same sheet as Anna Brown's letter of 15 September 1800, Brown 30, "The Baron of Braikly", and Brown 31, "Allan O Maut", which were sent with her letter of 18 June 1801, are written on a separate sheet of paper which bears the watermark of Buttanshaw, a British paper-maker of the 1780s (see Churchill 49).

Brown E

Another separate corpus within the repertoire of Mrs Brown consists of her ballads in Robert Jamieson's *The Popular Ballads*, published in two volumes in 1806. Thus Brown E is a printed source. Jamieson clearly identifies five of the ballad versions as being from Mrs Brown and these are included here as Brown 29 (also found in Brown D) and Brown 32–35. He recorded some of these ballads in Dysart in the summer of 1800, among them "Bonny Baby Livingston" and "Hugh of Lincoln", but "Lamkin" was evidently sent later for he mentions in a letter to Percy of 11 November 1800 that he is expecting to get a complete copy of this ballad from Mrs Brown (Nichols 8: 339). It can be suggested that some other material gathered at the meeting in Dysart in early August 1800 might have been incorporated without ascription in his published

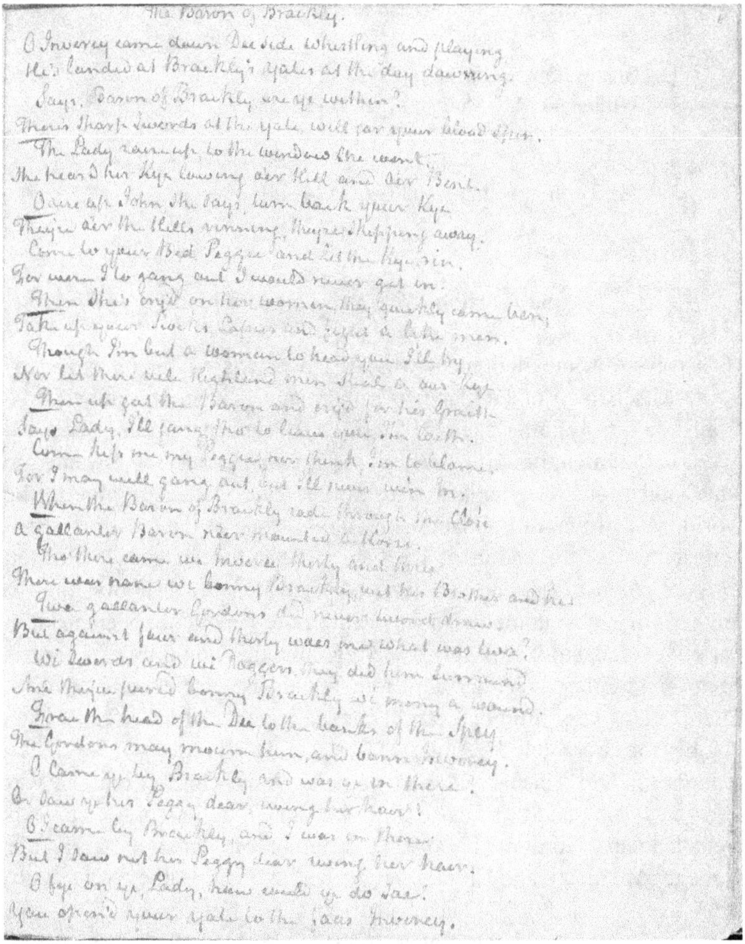

The Baron of Brackly.
O Inverey came down Dee side whistling and playing
He's landed at Brackly's yates at the day dawning.
Says, Baron of Brackly are ye within?
There's sharp swords at the yate will bar your blood spin.
The Lady rase up, to the window she went,
She heard her kye lowing o'er hill and o'er bent.
O rise up John she says, turn back your kye
They're o'er the hills rinning, they're skipping away.
Come to your bed Peggie and let the kye rin,
For were I to gang out I would never get in.
Then she's cry'd on her women, they quickly came ben;
Take up your rocks Lasses and fight a' like men.
Though I'm but a woman to head you I'll try
Nor let these vile Highland men steal a' our kye.
Then up gat the Baron and cry'd for his graith—
Says Lady, I'll gang tho to leave you I'm laith.
Come kiss me my Peggie, nor think I'm to blame,
For I may well gang out, but I'll never win in.
When the Baron of Brackly rade through the Close
A gallanter Baron ne'er mounted a horse.
Tho there came wi Inverey thirty and three
There was nane wi bonny Brackly but his Brother and he.
Twa gallanter Gordons did never sword draw,
But against four and thirty wae's me what was twa?
Wi swords and wi daggers they did him surround
And they've pierc'd bonny Brackly wi' mony a wound.
Frae the head of the Dee to the banks of the Spey
The Gordons may mourn him, and bann Inverey.
O came ye by Brackly and was ye in there?
Or saw ye his Peggy dear, riving her hair!
O I came by Brackly, and I was in there
But I saw not his Peggy dear riving her hair.
O fye on ye, Lady, how could ye do sae!
You open'd your yate to the fause Inverey.

Figure 4:
Facsimile of folio 6r of D
in Andrew Brown's hand

collections but only the ballad versions specifically identified as Mrs Brown's are included here.

		Brown No.
1.	Bonny Baby Livingston (*PB* 2: 135–43)	29
2.	Willie and May Margaret (*PB* 1: 135–38)	32
3.	Hugh of Lincoln (*PB* 1: 139–56)	33
4.	Lamkin (*PB* 1: 176–81)	34
5.	The Birth of Robin Hood (*PB* 2: 44–48)	35

Anna Gordon, Mrs Brown of Falkland

"[A] privete acknowledgment was all I ever wish'd for or expected" wrote Mrs Brown of Falkland to Robert Jamieson in December 1802 (La.III.473, f. 4v) after she was horrified to learn that Walter Scott had given her name in his *Minstrelsy of the Scottish Border*. She wanted to stay anonymous. Her ballads were all she ever wanted to give to the world. Mrs Brown of Falkland is, no doubt, "one of the most important contributors to the canon of English and Scottish balladry" (Fowler, *Literary History* 298) and two hundred years after her death it is time to tell her story in an unmediated way. Until now she has not been heard in her own voice and it is deeply to be regretted that no portrait of her has been found either – she has until now remained voiceless and faceless. There is also very little that can be pieced together of her life.

She was born on 24 August 1747 in Old Aberdeen. The church records for Old Machar give her name as Anne Gordon but she was known as Anna and this is also how she signed her letters. Her parents were Thomas Gordon (1714–97), Professor of Humanity at King's College, Aberdeen, and Lillias, daughter of William Forbes of Disblair. They were married in 1742 and had six children, but George (1743–43), Diana (1749–51) and Alexander Henry (1755–55) died very young, leaving only three girls: Elizabeth (1745–1802), Margaret (1746–97), and Anne (1747–1810). Their mother Lillias died in May 1764 while Anna was still at home in Humanity Manse, located on the High Street in Old Aberdeen, and her father was married again on 27 May 1772 to Elizabeth, *née* Innes (1714–99), widow of James Walker, minister of Peterhead (see OPR 168 B/3 for Old Machar).

Anna Gordon herself married late in life, at the age of forty-one in December 1788 (see OPR 168 B/8 for Old Machar). Her husband Andrew was three years her senior. Born in 1744, he first worked as a tutor in the family of John Cadell of Cockenzie, was licensed by the Presbytery of Haddington in July 1773 and was ordained chaplain to the 21st Foot Regiment, the Royal North British Fusiliers, in April 1777, serving during the American War of Independence. He returned to Scotland in November 1783, took up the post of minister in the parish of Falkland in Fife and obtained his Doctor of Divinity degree from King's College, Aberdeen, on 27 November 1794 (Anderson, *Officers* 104). In April 1802 he and his wife Anna moved to Tranent near Edinburgh. There he died in his sixty-first year on 25 April 1805 (see Scott, *Fasti* 1: 397; OPR 722 for Tranent). Anna Brown returned to Old Aberdeen where she died on 11 July 1810. She was buried three days later in her father's tomb in the Gordon Aisle in St Machar's Cathedral.

Apart from her own sisters Margaret and Elizabeth, Anna's mother and her aunts Elizabeth and Anne play an important role. "The Ladies of Disblair" (see Alexander Walker), as Lillias, Elizabeth and Anne Forbes were called, came from a very musical family (see Johnston, "Musical Traditions"). Their father William Forbes possessed a musical library and valuable musical instruments and he composed and wrote poetry (MS 500 at AUL; MacFarlane MSS at the NLS). Their mother, Elizabeth Bateman, was "an English Woman [...] of Ordinary Condition and bred to wig-making for a livelihood" (MS 500 at the AUL). While Elizabeth and Lillias had both married professors from the Gordon "dynasty" in Old Aberdeen, Anne had married Joseph Farquharson, a small landed proprietor from Allanaquoich, a remote place on Upper Deeside which had seldom more than twenty inhabitants, including children (see Ewen 330). Anna claimed that her ballads were mainly derived from her mother's side. By the time she was twenty-five, these relatives had all died: her mother Lillias in 1764, her aunt Anne in 1767 and her aunt Elizabeth in 1772 (see OPR 168 B/10 for Old Machar).

Another important family member in Anna Brown's story is Robert Eden Scott (1769–1811), her nephew. His mother was Anna's sister Elizabeth and his father was the Rev. John Scott (1747–84) of Virginia who had come to Aberdeen to study theology. John Scott graduated in 1768, was ordained in 1769 and took up a post as minister in Maryland (Anderson, *Roll of Alumni* 247). Robert Eden Scott was born on 13 April 1769 in Old Machar but his parents moved shortly afterwards to America, leaving him to grow up in his grandfather's family. His aunt Anna served as a mother substitute and, when Thomas Gordon married again in 1772, his second wife Elizabeth Gordon shared the responsibility. Robert Eden's father John Scott died in Virginia at the age of thirty-seven in 1784. His mother was left in straitened circum-

Figure 5:
Robert Eden Scott
(1769–1811)

stances but she, her two daughters (Elizabeth Brown Scott (1773–1842) and Margaret Christian Scott (1783–1843)) and her son John Scott (1781–1850) stayed on in America. Robert Eden Scott remained with his grandfather's family while pursuing his studies at Aberdeen (see Peyton Papers at the VHS). He was enrolled in King's College in 1781, graduated and received his M.A. on 30 March 1785, was tutor to Lady Erroll's sons in 1785–86 and became Regent on 8 May 1788. Before he took up the position of Professor of Moral Philosophy at King's College in 1796 (see Anderson, *Roll of Alumni* 98; Anderson, *Officers* 259), he stayed for some time in 1791–92 with his family in Virginia. He married Rachel Forbes in 1797 and died of a fever on 14 January 1811 (see Creffield; Ogilvy 24–33; CC1/6/74 at the NAS).

The Recording and Reception of her Ballads

Mrs Brown of Falkland has been called "the greatest informant encountered by any collector of traditional ballads" (Friedman, *Ballad Revival* 57) and the story of her discovery by other ballad collectors in her lifetime certainly testifies to this. Needless to say, these collectors of traditional ballads were all men. In eighteenth-century Scotland music-making was strictly divided along gender lines. Women were excluded from membership of the Musical Societies of Edinburgh and Aberdeen (founded respectively in 1728 and 1747) and, although they were sometimes allowed to participate as singers or listeners, they were not allowed to perform on musical instruments at these gentlemen's concerts. In a private setting or at public tea-tables, however, women were active in music-making and publications like Allan Ramsay's *Tea-table Miscellany* (4 vols, 1723–37) or George Thomson's *Select Collection of Original Scottish Airs* (5 vols, 1793–1818) were catering for this female, middle-class demand (see Rieuwerts "Allan Ramsay" and "Anonymity").

It was through one of the directors of the Edinburgh Musical Society, William Tytler of Woodhouselee (1711–92), that Mrs Brown's ballad repertoire was first encountered. Tytler had published a highly interesting "Dissertation on Scottish Music" in Hugh Arnot's *History of Edinburgh* (1779). He was taking issue with the notion of the superiority of German and Italian compositions in general, and the notion that "David Rizzio was either the composer or reformer of the Scottish melodies" (486) in particular, and argued instead for the high quality and the remote age of Scots melodies and songs:

Figure 6:
William Tytler of Woodhouselee
(1711–92)

> The Scottish music does no less honour than its poetry, to the genius of the country. The old Scots songs, or melodies, have always been admired, for that wild pathetic sweetness which distinguishes them from the music of every other country. [...] From their artless simplicity, it is evident, that the Scots melodies, or songs, are derived from a very remote antiquity. (486)

Tytler, himself a harpsichordist and flautist (see Couper), was one of the first to write on the history of Scots melodies and songs and his article was to set the tone for the collecting and editing of Scots songs and ballads at the end of the eighteenth century.

Robert Burns in particular echoed his friend's sentiments, when he spoke of "a wild happiness of thought and expression" that set the old Scots songs apart from English songs or from the songs of his day (see his letter to the Rev. John Skinner of 25 October 1787; Ferguson, *Letters of Burns* 1: 167; letter no. 147). Just like Burns, Tytler gave his whole-hearted support to the making of *The Scots Musical Museum* (1787–1803) and his "Dissertation" might have even given James Johnson the idea for this project of preserving Scottish "National Music and Song". The decision of the editors to retain the original simplicity of the Scottish songs and to refrain from elaborate accompaniments was certainly taken in light of Tytler's argument that

> the proper accompaniment of a Scottish song is a plain, thin, dropping bass, on the harpsichord or guitar. The fine breathings, these heart-felt touches, which genius alone can express in our songs, are lost in a noisy accompaniment of instruments. (498)

Only if thus performed, Tytler insisted, a Scots song "is among the highest entertainments to a musical genius" (640; see Johnson for a critical view 148–49). Together with James Beattie and Thomas Blacklock he presided over the collecting of old poetry and thus Tytler came to be the first to encourage writing down traditional songs from memory. The difficulties he encountered are summed up by Burns in a letter to William Tytler (Aug. 1787), accompanying fragments of traditional songs:

> Inclosed I have sent you a sample of the old pieces that are still to be found among our Peasantry in the West. I once had a great many of these fragments and some of these here entire; but as I had no idea then that any body cared for them, I have forgot them.
>
> (Ferguson, *Letters of Burns* 1: 147, letter 126)

If Robert Burns had forgotten "the old pieces" because nobody cared for them, Anna Brown of Old Aberdeen had not. Her memory could at least furnish her with some of the old Scottish songs and ballads.

Tytler first heard of Anna Gordon, as she was then still called, through her father Professor Thomas Gordon. Just like Tytler in Edinburgh, Gordon was one of the members of the Musical Society in Aberdeen and, as his friend later recalled in a letter to his son Alexander Fraser Tytler, the question of old songs had come up in conversation. "I mentioned them [Mrs Brown's ballads] to your Father, at whose request, my Grandson Mr Scott, wrote down a parcel of them as his aunt sung them." (C, f. 1r) This is how Anna Brown's ballads were first recorded for William Tytler at the request of her father and with the help of her young nephew.

Whatever the exact date, the significance of this event cannot be overestimated. After all, this was still the age of enlightenment which laid stress on the bettering of oneself and society; progress and improvement were the key words. In the Scottish musical societies of the time, the emphasis was clearly on new compositions. Turning to old Scottish ballads instead, and thus to tales from oral tradition full of ghosts and superstition, revealed a different mindset. The Romantic era was beginning to dawn.

Again, it has to be borne in mind that women had always been singing these ballads – aunts, nurses and old women in the neighbourhood are named as tradition bearers for Mrs Brown's repertoire – but despite their antiquarian interest in music, men were only then discovering these female activities. Thomas Gordon and William Tytler knew nothing about these "very peculiar" ballads and their focus was not on contemporary ballad-singing but on ballads and old songs. William Tytler in particular had a historical and antiquarian interest in Scots songs and his enthusiasm encouraged not only James Johnson and Robert Jamieson but also George Thomson to begin their respective collections of Scottish songs.

While he received only fragments of traditional songs from Robert Burns, William Tytler must have been very pleased with the substantial collection he received from Anna Brown: fifteen ballads with up to thirty-five verses. After William Tytler's death in 1792, Thomas Gordon was asked to explain to his son Alexander how this ballad collection had come about and this letter, pasted into one of Mrs Brown's ballad manuscripts (C), is here printed in full. It is addressed to Alexander Fraser Tytler; Esquire, Advocate; Edinburgh.

[f. 1r]

Kings College 19 January 1793

Dear Sir

You are exceedingly welcome to make what use you think proper of the old songs which I recollect sending to your father several years ago. If Mr Ritson approves of them I believe I could send you better than a dozen more than those you mention in your postscript.

An Aunt of my children, Mrs Farquherson now dead, who was married to the proprietor of a small estate near the sources of the Dee, in the division of Aberdeenshire, called Braemar, a sequestered romantic, pastoral country, if you ever went to your estate by the way of the castle of that name, you are not such a stranger to it as need a description. This good woman, I say, spent her days from the time of her marriage, among flocks & herds at Allanaquoich her husbands seat, which, even in the country of Braemar is considered as remarkable for the above circumstances. She had a tenacious memory, which retained all the songs she had heard the nurses & old women sing in that neighbourhood. In the latter part of her life she lived in Aberdeen; & being mater- [1v] ternally fond of my children when young, she had them much about her, & was much with us. Her songs & tales of chivalry & love were a high entertainment to their young imaginations. My youngest daughter, Mrs Brown at Falkland is blessed with a memory as good as her aunts, & has almost the whole store of her songs lodged in it. In conversation I mentioned them to your Father, at whose request, my Grandson Mr Scott, wrote down a parcel of them as his aunt sung them. Being then but a meer novice in musick, he added in his copy such musical notes as he supposed, notwithstanding their incorrectness, might give your father some imperfect notion of the airs, or rather lilts, to which they were sung. Both the words & strains, were perfectly new to me, as they were to your father, & proceeded upon a system of manners & in a stile of composition, both words & music, very peculiar & of which we could recollect nothing similar. I have, but cannot at this moment lay my hands on it, the paper book, in which many more were taken down than were sent; & Mrs Brown, I am persuaded, can recollect many more than these. I can not pretend to say with certainty, that they had their origine in that part of the coun [2r] try, but I believe Mrs Farquhersen learned them there. Mrs. Farquhersen, I am sure invented nor added nothing herself.

My kindest & best compliments attend Mrs Fraser, your brother the Captain

Yours sincerely

Thos Gordon.

This letter provides valuable information about Mrs Brown's repertoire and its context and much could be said about that (see my book *Mrs Brown of Falkland* [forthcoming]). At this point, however, it is important to understand how the manuscripts came about. Robert Eden Scott is credited with writing down "a parcel of them as his aunt sung them". No mention is made of the fact that the ballads were first recorded without music although Thomas Gordon was certainly aware of two manuscripts, the now lost source of A, "a paper book" and manuscript B which was "sent", for he speaks of "a paper book, in which many more were taken down than were sent". If, in 1793, Professor Gordon thought that the larger ballad collection, the lost source of our manuscript A, was still with him, then the first manuscript made out for William Tytler was certainly never sent (see also Montgomerie, Part VI, 70).

This is also suggested by the fact that Anna Brown believed that this manuscript "had been destroyed". Her letter to Alexander Fraser Tytler dated 23 December 1800 (quoted below) gives the details. She speaks only of "the intention" of sending the original of Brown A to William Tytler, not of actually having sent it. For "upon his additional request of having the tunes of the ballads noted down", they started all over again and Robert Eden Scott appears to have kept the first manuscript. He was the one who was "ordered" by his grandfather "to try to do it", she explained, and he set to work with his aunt. For the second manuscript, Brown B, they selected "what we thought the best of the ballads" and this manuscript was sent to William Tytler in Edinburgh.

Neither of them would have known at the time of the significance of these first recordings although they were aware of the shortcomings in setting down the music, Robert Eden Scott being just "a novice in musick". As Tytler, however, had argued in his "Dissertation", the text alone would not give the full character of a song. "The Scots melodies contain strong expression of the passions, particularly of the melancholy kind, in which the air often finely corresponds to the subject of the song" (496).

In the authoritative edition of *The English and Scottish Popular Ballads* by Francis J. Child it is stated at one point that Tytler had received this manuscript of Mrs Brown's ballads "about 1783" (*ESPB* 5: 397) but I have not found any documents supporting this date. The manuscript itself has not survived, and nor have any letters acknowledging its receipt. According to Child's more cautious statement elsewhere, this first recording took place "in 1783, or shortly before" (see *ESPB* 1: 62).

Robert Jamieson suggests an earlier date than 1783. In his discussion of Brown 12 he compares his version of "Fair Anny" from A with "Mr Scott's copy, dictated also by Mrs Brown, at a distance of near twenty years" (A, f. 32v) when Robert Eden Scott was "very young" (*PB* 1:v). Since we have March–April 1800 as the exact date of "Mr Scott's copy" (C), the first manuscript (A) must have been "near" to 1780. Even given that "near" is rather vague, 1781 and 1782 (Robert Eden Scott would have been a boy of twelve or thirteen) are more likely dates than 1783 and the earlier years; besides according better with Jamieson's comment, this would also bring the date of the first recording closer to the original impetus received by Tytler's publication of his "Dissertation" in 1779.

In 1792 Alexander Fraser Tytler received, a couple of months after his father's death, the following letter from the Englishman Joseph Ritson who was preparing an edition of Scots Songs (NLS: Acc 3639, vol. 1, f. 53).

[1: 53r] Grays Inn, 20th Decemr 1792.

Sir,

Though a stranger to you, I have had the honour of several letters from your late father, whose character as well literary as personal I reflected and esteemed. On enquiring after his health, when last in Edinburgh, I understood it to be in so declining a state that a visit from any person not in habit of intimacy with him would be scarcely acceptable: which prevented my having the pleasure of waiting upon him. I am, however, exceedingly sorry to learn that he should know I had been in ~~Edinburgh~~ Scotland without seeing him; as it was owing much more to delicacy than to want of respect. Mr. Allan informs me that you have "a great many old rare Scotish Songs," and that, if there be any of them not in my catalogue, you are willing to give me them to print. As I am almost enthusiastically fond of such things, which formed the subject of my correspondence with Mr. Tytler, who favoured me with two or three specimens of what he judged most ancient in respect of both poetry & music, I shod [53v] esteem myself under the greatest obligation ~~for~~ to you for a communication of whatever you may have curious in this way: having employed myself for many years passed in collecting everything of the kind I could meet with; and intending to publish a selection to which, I flatter myself, you will not regret to have contributed your assistance.

I am,

Sir,

Your most obedient

& very humble Servant,

J Ritson

Ritson was unaware of the fact that William Tytler had died on 12 September 1792. Thus his son Alexander Fraser Tytler did not know what to make of Ritson's request to publish the "great many old rare Scotish Songs" he had inherited. He turned to his father's friend Thomas Gordon for advice and this is what prompted the letter quoted above.

"You are exceedingly welcome to make what use you think proper of the old songs which I recollect sending to your father several years ago" was Professor Gordon's response in January 1793 and, although Fraser Tytler's reply to Ritson is not to be found, he obviously granted him permission to print material from the requested manuscript. He must have even given Ritson to understand that there might be "a dozen more" ballads from Mrs Brown, if he approved of them. Surprisingly though, Ritson did not approve of them. He made a copy (MS Eng 1486.1 at Houghton) of Mrs Brown's manuscript B and wrote a few comments in B itself (see Notes for details), but he did not use any of these fifteen ballads for his two-volume collection of *Scotish Songs* that appeared shortly afterwards in 1794. Instead, he presents a very sceptical view on Scottish ballads "preserved by tradition among the country people":

> There are in Scotland many ballads, or legendary and romantic songs, composed in a singular style, and preserved by tradition among the country people, […] some of these will be found in Mr. Herds collection of *Scots songs*, and for a collection of others,[8] not hitherto published, the editor of these volumes is indebted to the liberality and politeness of Alexander Fraser Tytler, esquire. It must however be confessed, that none of these compositions bear satisfactory marks of the antiquity they pretend to while the expressions or allusions occurring in some, would seem to fix their origin to a very modern date. (*Scotish Songs* 1: lxxx–lxxxi)

While Ritson has accepted some texts from Herd's manuscripts he rejects Mrs Brown's ballads as being too modern ("none … bear satisfactory marks of the antiquity") and too vulgar ("a performance of genius and merit … may in time be degraded to the vilest jargon"), thus blaming tradition for converting gold into lead (*Scotish Songs* 1: lxxxi). His rather unfavourable view of the Brown ballad manuscript on loan was also expressed in his letter to Fraser Tytler when he returned the manuscript on 17 July 1800 (NLS: Acc 3639, vol. 1, f. 95) through Fraser Tytler's friend George Chalmers at the Office for Trade in Whitehall:

[8] Here Ritson inserts a footnote, giving the titles of the fifteen ballads in B.

> From the introduction to my recently published collection of "Scotish Songs" […] you will perceive that I do not consider the publication of these pieces as tending to enhance the reputation of your lyric poetry. I certainly conceive them to be genuine & in many respects curious, but by no means ancient, not equal in point of merit to those few productions of a similar nature which have already appeared in print. – It is highly probable, at the same time, that in the "better than a dozen more" which professor Gordon obligingly offers to send, I might discover something of more importance than is, perhaps, to be found in this manuscript. But having already trespassed too far upon your liberality, I should be ashamed to ~~req~~ solicit any further favours.

Fraser Tytler cannot have been too pleased with Ritson's response and the treatment his father's ballad manuscript received. His father's writings on Scottish songs and ballads, his *Dissertation*, fared no better:

> A very ingenius writer, in an express, *Dissertation on the Scottish music*, has tried to fix the æra of the most ancient Scotish melodies, and to trace the history of the Scotish music down to modern times: an attempt in which, as he has been guided rather by fancy and hypothesis than by argument or evidence, it is almost unnecessary to say that he has not succeeded. (*Scotish Songs* 1: lxxxiii)

Given Ritson's outright attacks also on Bishop Thomas Percy, the much-admired editor of the *Reliques of Ancient English Poetry* (see Friedman, *Ballad Revival* 216–20; Hustvedt, *Ballad Criticism* 189–91) he certainly had no more favour to expect from Percy's friend Fraser Tytler despite having published an excellent edition of Scots songs.

Alexander Fraser Tytler, best known today for his pioneering work on the art of translation from foreign languages, had a legal as well as an academic career and pursued literary interests as well. He gave lectures on Universal History at the University of Edinburgh and among his students and admirers was Walter Scott.

Fraser Tytler and Scott shared an interest in Scottish ballads and songs and thus it cannot come as a surprise that Scott borrowed Fraser Tytler's ballads (Brown B) in 1795 (see date on the title page of N 3 at Abbotsford). Although his manuscript of Scottish Songs (N 3) is, with many sheets torn out, in a rather fragmented state today, it is still obvious from the remaining ones that Scott had copied most of Brown B (texts and tunes). Unlike Ritson's transcript, however, Scott's Scottish Songs is no accurate copy of the original manuscript; numerous changes, additions and corrections were made and Scott obviously did not take to Mrs Brown's ballads. After all, he was primarily interested in

Figure 7:
Alexander Fraser Tytler
(1747–1813)

historical ballads, especially from the Border region and her repertoire was from the north-east of Scotland and comprised mainly romantic and supernatural ballads, full of *Norlandisms* – as Scott writes in the introduction to his collection (Scottish Songs, p. 11):

> These Ballads [of Brown B] are all in the Northern dialect, but I recollect several of them as recited in the South of Scotland divested of their *Norlandisms*, & also varying considerably in other respects. In a few instances where my Memory served me I have adopted either additional verses or better readings than those in Mr Tytlers collection. Such variations can excite no reasonable surprise in any species of composition which owes its preservation to oral tradition only – The Music is copied as exactly as possible but as I do not know the value of a single note I am no judge of its merit, which however I suspect is not great.

Scott was continuing with his "raids into Liddesdale" in quest of Border ballads with his friend and guide Robert Shortreed (see Dobie; Robson; Wilson), and most likely would never have gone over Mrs Brown's ballad manuscript again, if it had not been for M. G. Lewis (1775–1818), better known as "Monk" Lewis, the author of the Gothic novel *The Monk* (1796).

In 1798 Scott was introduced to Lewis and immediately recognised a kindred spirit. While in Weimar in 1792–93, the centre of Enlightenment in the German-speaking provinces, Lewis had started to translate ballads from Herder, Bürger and Goethe and wanted Scott to do the same and contribute to his forthcoming collection of ballads and tales. Scott received this invitation as "a flattering compliment" (see Johnston 3) and sent him within weeks "Leonore" and "The Wild Huntsman", two ballads translated from the German (see Guthke, "Herder" and "Gruppenbild"). Lewis was pleased:

> I cannot delay expressing to you, how much I feel obliged to you for your permission to publish the Ballads, which I requested [...]. The Plan, which I propose to myself, is to collect all the *marvellous* Ballads, that I can lay my hands upon, and publish them under the title of "Tales of Terror". Antient as well as Modern, will be comprised in my design. (MS 3875, f. 47 at the NLS)

In this acknowledgement, Lewis outlined the plan for his collection: "marvellous Ballads" from tradition ("Antient") and ballad imitations ("Modern"). Scott was eager to contribute, but when the publication was delayed, he asked his friend John Ballantyne in 1799 instead to try his hand at publishing a small collection of ballads on his press in Kelso (see Johnston). Scott called this book *An Apology for the Tales of Terror* (1799) and it included the ballads he had intended for Lewis's publication of "the *marvellous* Ballads". "Monk" Lewis was not amused and asked Scott to stop "the intended publication of Ballads" immediately,[9] explaining the delay of *his* intended publication. He was "in terrible want" of more ballads: "Could not Mr. Tytler be persuaded to do something for me in this way?" (Letter to Walter Scott (31 December 1799); MS 3874, f. 51). It was this request to persuade "Mr Tytler" that led Scott to contact Alexander Fraser Tytler again in 1800.

In February 1800, Alexander Fraser Tytler wrote to Mrs Brown on behalf of Scott (and Lewis), remembering that her father had spoken of "a dozen more ballads" she might have. Thomas Gordon had died three years earlier and Anna had married and moved from Old Aberdeen to the Palace of Falkland in Fife. Although Fraser Tytler's letter is not to be found, Mrs Brown's reply has survived and is given here in full (NLS: Acc 3639, vol. 1, ff. 235–36). The letter is addressed to Alexander Fraser Tytler Esquire; Professor of Civil History; Edinburgh.

> [f. 235r] Falkland 17 March 1800
>
> Dear Sir
>
> I should long before this time have acknowledged yours of the 12 Feby. if I had not been prevented by bad health; immedietly upon the receit of your letter I set my memmory to work & soon found that I had still a good number of old Ballads. Much of the same class. with those which you have already in your possession. And I had wrote ~~several of~~ two or three of them down. when I was siezed with so severe a cold as made me suspend all my labours both mental and bodily! I am however now I thank God pretty well again & am. now once more set to work upon the old Ballads. I am much obliged to you for sending me the list of those you had already as without it I never should have been able to distinguish between. what I had formerly sent & what I had not sent, indeed it had intirily escaped my ~~memor~~ memmory that ever such a transaction had taken place. but your letter has brought back the recollection of [235v] of it with all its attendent circumstances.
>
> If. therefor your friend can have patience a little longer I hope in a few weeks to be able to send six or seven at least good long ones. with the music noted down for each has its own appropriate tune &

9 Only twelve copies are known to have been printed (see introduction to *An Apology* <*www.walterscott.lib.ed.ac.uk/works/poetry/apology/home.html*>)

some of them I think are pretty ennough tho all in the plaintive stile as indeed all the old scotch melodys are ~~which I ever heard~~ that I, ever heard! you need make no apologies Dear sir, for any trouble I may have in this transaction for I can assure you with the out most sincerity that there can be nothing more gratifying to my own feelings than to have it any how in my power to oblige ~~you~~ you or any Friend you value. I well remmember the Cordial & friendly intercourse that so long subsisted between our Fathers indeed the esteem I ever had for your Fathers Charecter is mixed with a veneration which increases with time. I recollect with pleasure the friendly visits which he & your Father & you Sir & your worthy ~~b~~ brother who is now no more used to make at Old Humanity Castle at the circuit times & the pleasure I took in listning to all [236r] that was said, as all was instructive, elegant, or amusing in short I meet with no such parties now & can only sigh for the days that are gone, you judge rightly in supposing that I should take pleasure in recalling those scenes of infancy & childhood which the recollection of these old Songs bring back to my mind. it is indeed what Ossian calls, the joy of Griefe. the memmory of joys that are past pleasent but mournful to the soul but ennough of this prattle; & now sir I hope [you] will take the trouble to let me know with y[our] convenience where the songs shall be sent when finished as they will come by the Carrier & as I do not know the street you lodge in he might not take the trouble of enquiring & all my labours might be lost. to prevent which you will be so good as write me a line to tell where they should be left

Dr Brown desires me to return you his respectful Compliments & I am Dear sir

your most obedient humb[le] serva[nt]
Anna Brown

Within a month, Mrs Brown had not only written out "six or seven at least good long ones" but nine texts. This is our manuscript C. Originally it was accompanied by the music, but the tunes were certainly not taken down on the same pages as the texts to which they belonged nor elsewhere in the notebook. They must have been on a separate sheet or sheets that went missing. Accordingly, we have no evidence to tell us who set down the music of these ballads. Manuscript C itself is in Anna Brown's hand. She intended to send the precious parcel by courier from Falkland in Fife across the Forth to Edinburgh, but in the end, it was personally delivered by her "young friend Mr Brown" as we learn from Fraser Tytler's letter.

For on 28 April 1800, Alexander Fraser Tytler acknowledged the receipt of the manuscript and of her letter of the 21 April,[10] saying how much he and his family are pleased with her ballads. His letter, addressed to "Mrs Brown at / The Revd Dr Brown s / Palace of / Falkland" is here given in full (MS 1809, ff. 244–45 at the NLS):

[f. 244r]

Woodhouselee 28th April 1800

My dear Madam

As I have been for these some weeks past in the Country with my Family at the foot of Pentland hills where I generally spend the vacations, I have not had the pleasure of seeing your young friend Mr Brown; but he has been so good as leave at my house in Town, *the Ballads*, which you have most obligingly written down for me, together with your very polite and excellent Letter of the 21t curt. As soon as I come to Town which will be in ten days hence, I shall find out Mr Brown and shew him, on your account, every attention in my power – With respect to the Ballads, I have been delighted with them – Some of them are highly beautiful, and all of them curious and interesting as specimens of our antient popular Poetry – The only one of which I had any previous acquaintance is *Love Gregor*, of which several Stanzas are printed in a Collection published at Edinh by one Mr Herd about 20 years ago – but your Edition is [244v] is much more complete – Those which please me most are *Fa'se Foutrage*, *the ~~little~~ Bonny Footboy* and *Bird Ellen*. They are indeed consummately beautiful, and I regard them as a high acquisition to the Stock of our old national Poetry – The Music is a valuable addition –

You say my dear Madam that you *may have fragments of others* – It is unconscionable in me to tax your politeness thus severely; but I own the desire I feel to rescue from Oblivion those precious morsels of Genius and Feeling, which are perhaps preserved in the memory of one or two of the present generation, who like yourself, have taste to cherish them, is a strong inducement with me to urge you to a new exertion of Your kindness in committing to Paper, for me, such even of those imperfect & detached fragments as Your happy Memory can recall – To assist you in this, I will send you *Mr Herd's Collection*, which I shall give to Your husband Dr Brown, when I have the pleasure, which I promise myself, of seeing him during the sitting of the Genl Assembly – Even though they were no more than different Editions of any of the Ballads there printed, it would be a pleasure to make those variations – Thus your Edition of [245r] of *Bird Ellen* is not the less valuable that it is in substance nearly the same with the

10 This letter seems to have been lost. A fragment of it is quoted in Anderson's letter to Percy (*Percy Letters* 9: 54, see below).

Child Waters of Dr Percy – Yours is in my opinion in some stanzas greatly superior to his, and the conclusion in particular is much more pleasing and satisfactory – Mrs Fraser Tytler and my Sister beg their kindest remembrance – they are equally delighted as I am with your *MS*. – With my best Compliments to Dr Brown I am my dear Madam with great Esteem

Your much obliged & most faithful
humble Servant
Alex. Fraser Tytler.

Although Fraser Tytler had asked Mrs Brown for more ballads on behalf of his friend Walter Scott, he was clearly at home with the Scottish ballad tradition himself, referring to the most important published ballad collections of the time (Percy's and Herd's). Note that he speaks, like his father, of Mrs Brown enhancing "the Stock of our old national Poetry". The ballads she wrote out are thus placed in a much wider cultural and national context. Fraser Tytler specifically mentions the music being "a valuable addition". When Robert Anderson inspected Brown C for Bishop Percy in August or September 1800 he specifically mentioned that the "Songs, in the MS, are accompanied with the music to which they are sung" (*Percy Letters* 9: 53).

Mrs Brown's choice of delivery through "young Mr Brown" is read by Fraser Tytler as a request to do something for him: "I shall find out Mr Brown and shew him, on your account, every attention in my power." Since her husband Andrew Brown is not known to have had a son, this is probably Robert Brown, the youngest son of his brother John. Five years later, he is specifically mentioned in the Rev. Andrew Brown's testament as being in need of support. Andrew Brown appoints his wife Anna to be his sole and only heir, but adds, "if she shall find that her situation and circumstances in life will permit or enable her to give a small allowance or donation to Robert Brown the youngest son of my eldest Brother John Brown deceased it will be considered & esteemed as a mark of her regard & respect for my memory" (RD4/277/766 at the NAS).

When Mrs Brown's third ballad manuscript (Brown C) arrived in Edinburgh at the end of April 1800, Lewis was in London and printing was about to commence of *Tales of Wonder*. Brown C would have come too late for him but he did have the use of Brown B through Richard Heber (1773–1833), as he acknowledges in a letter to Scott (see below; MS 3874, f. 47 at the NLS).

Almost at the end of his collection (pp. 445–57), as ballad numbers 56–58, Lewis gave three texts from Brown B: "LVI. Clerk Colvin" (Brown 21); "LVII. Willy's Lady" (Brown 15) and "LVIII. Courteous

King Jamie" (Brown 14) – interestingly all of them ballads of supernatural character. Thus, "Monk" Lewis came to be the first man to print Mrs Brown's ballads – but unfortunately not the last to do this without her knowledge and permission.[11] While "Clark Colven" and "Willie's Lady" were much changed but still recognisable, "King Henry" was published as "Courteous King Jamie" in a much altered state. As Lewis observed himself in 1800, "I have altered and added so much to this ballad, that I might almost claim it my own." (456).

The year 1800 was one of the most remarkable years in the history of Scottish balladry. If there had been only marginal interest in the "old Scotch songs", all of a sudden there was a great deal of rivalry among ballad enthusiasts and much of it was connected to Mrs Brown's repertoire. Walter Scott had borrowed Brown B in 1795, just after Ritson had had it in 1793–94, and again it was on loan to Scott in early 1800 (see the dated slip of 25 March 1800 in Scott's manuscript Scottish Songs). Before the end of May 1800, Scott had passed it on to M. G. Lewis and then Alexander Fraser Tytler presented it to Dr Robert Anderson, a surgeon in Edinburgh, who was well known for his devotion to literature. In 1792–95 he had published *A Complete Edition of the Poets of Great Britain* (14 vols) and he was also the editor of the *Edinburgh Magazine*; in this capacity, he had encouraged many young writers (see Brown, "Anderson"), including John Leyden (1775–1811) and Robert Jamieson (1772–1844).

Robert Anderson had the use of Brown B and C from August or September to December 1800 in order to give an account of them to Bishop Thomas Percy (see below). As he explained in his letter to Fraser Tytler upon their return (22 December 1800), he kept the Brown manuscripts until *Tales of Wonder* appeared (20 November 1800) for he knew, presumably through Walter Scott, that Lewis was intending to print some ballads from the Brown repertoire:

> I herewith return with my best thanks, your MS collection of old Scottish ballads, which you very obligingly put into my hands to enable me to give an account of it to Bishop Percy. I am unquestionably very much to blame for [...] detaining it a single day after I had an opportunity of perusing the "Tales of Wonder," I have no apology to make & must therefore, just ask your pardon.
>
> (Letter to AFT, Acc 3639, vol. 1, ff. 226–27)

[11] Mrs Brown's name was not mentioned; "Anon" is given instead as source.

Lewis's *Tales of Wonder*, however, received a very hostile reception. The reviewer in the *British Register* described Lewis's publication as "two thin octavo volumes, made up of shreds and scraps" (Anon. 605) and in the *British Critic* it fared even worse: "We do but express the feelings of the reading world in general, when we say that we consider this production as a very daring imposition on the public." (Anon. 681).

These reviews served as stark warnings to those who had in mind a ballad publication of ancient and modern compositions. As Anderson reports, Scott felt now ashamed of being associated with Lewis in that work and Robert Jamieson was about to give up on his intended ballad publication (Anderson's letter to Percy, 27 January 1801; *Percy Letters* 9: 48):

> Mr. Jamieson, of Macclesfield, is so much alarmed by the disapprobation expressed concerning the "Tales of Wonder," that he is more than half resolved to proceed no farther in his intended publication; but he is too easily dejected, and must be encouraged to proceed.

Despite his name being withheld, Jamieson can certainly be identified as the man who had, quite possibly through their common friend Richard Heber, met or contacted Lewis in London on 29 May 1800, asking for "Brown Adam" and "Gay Goss Hawk". These were ballads he already had in his manuscript Brown A, but he was very eager to find variants. Lewis mentioned the request to Scott,[12] but Scott was unwilling to let these ballad versions go to Jamieson, writing to Heber on 10 June 1800: "Take care however that the Gay Goss Hawk or Brown Adam do not slip into his collection as I have laid my clutches on both for the Minstrelsy of the Border" (*SL* 12: 163).

A year earlier, in March 1799, Jamieson had approached his teacher and friend the Rev. Dr Gilbert Gerard (1760–1815), Professor of Theology at King's College, Aberdeen, and received from him the

12 Lewis writes to Scott (29 May 1800): "Dear Scott, A Man who is going to publish a collection of old Ballads, is very anxious that I should give him Brown Adam and the Gay Goss Hawk. But as you mentioned an intention of publishing some Border Ballads, and I am not certain that these do not come under that description I have delayed granting his request, till I shall have your consent – I purpose setting out for Scotland on the 20th of June but shall visit the Lakes in my way – I am afraid, that our publication cannot appear till next season – only 17 Ballads are yet printed out of 60 – yours ever. M. G. L." (MS 3874, f. 47 at the NLS).

now lost source of manuscript A which had been written by Gerard's colleague Robert Eden Scott.[13]

With this treasure in hand, he began his quest for unpublished ballads "with spirit and confidence" (*PB* 1: v) and asked his friend Sir Frederick Morton Eden to introduce him to Bishop Thomas Percy, the most respected ballad editor at the time (see Nichols 8: 335–41; also Rieuwerts, "Percy"). He was thus introduced to Percy as "a gentleman who is engaged in making a collection of ancient ballads, and is anxious to avail himself of the folio MS. of the Bishop of Dromore" (Nichols 8: 335–36). This application for the use of his famous folio manuscript (which was ultimately turned down) prompted Percy to make inquiries about "a Mr Jamieson … who is preparing for the Press a Collection of Scottish Songs and Border Ballads, with some Translations from the Gaelic" and to consult Robert Anderson (*Percy Letters* 9: 36). His friend and correspondent in Edinburgh was able to give Percy an account of Jamieson, who had been introduced to him by Heber, saying: "Mr Jamieson is a native of one of the northern counties of Scotland, studied at Aberdeen, and has resided about eight years in England, is master of Macclesfield School, about 30 years of age" (*Percy Letters* 9: 44).

When asked about Jamieson, Anderson also took the opportunity to introduce to Percy Jamieson's rival in the ballad field, namely Walter Scott. In his letter of 21 June 1800, he speaks of his "ingenious friend" who is eager to send Percy for inspection "one or two of his compositions in the style of the ancient Scottish Ballad, in testimony of his high respect for your character and of his gratitude to the Editor of 'The Reliques', upon which he formed his taste for ballad thinking and expression" (*Percy Letters* 9: 29). Walter Scott is not only introduced as the translator of German poetry (mainly from Bürger and Goethe) but also described as the future editor of "a Collection of Border Ballads, to be entitled 'The Minstrelsy of The Border' in one volume, printing at Kelso, upon the plan of 'The Reliques'; which will be followed by two volumes of Illustrations of Border history, poetry, & popular antiquities" (*Percy Letters* 9: 29–30; see also Ruff).

Percy's interest was aroused by this sudden flurry of activity in ballad collecting and editing and in September 1800, with Brown B and C in hand, Anderson was eager to give Percy the context of the Brown manuscripts and a ballad text (*Percy Letters* 9: 42–43):

13 Jamieson probably first met Robert Eden Scott as a student in his Greek class when he entered King's College in 1790.

> I have to apoligize for troubling your Lordship with a packet containing so many scraps and notices. I thought it would be a little [amusement] to your Lordship to compare "Lord John and Bird Ellen" with "Child Waters" in "the Reliques," and I had it transcribed by a little girl at my elbow, in whose hands your volumes are very frequently, from a pretty large M.S collection of old Scottish Ballads communicated by Mrs Brown, wife of Dr Brown, minister of Falkland, in April last, to Professor Tytler, and lent by the Professor to me. The story seems to be [the] same with that of "Child Waters"; the one is apparently a Scottish, the other an English ballad; as to which is the oldest I pretend not to say. It is remarkable that Mrs Brown (a daughter of the la[te] Prof. Tho. Gordon of Aberdeen) never saw any of the ballads she has transmitted here, either in print or M.S. but learned them all when a child by hearing them sung by her mother and an old maid-servant who had been long in the family, and does not recollect to have heard any of them either sung or said by any one but herself since she was about ten years. She kept them as a little hoard of solitary entertainment, till, a few years ago, she wrote down as many as she could recollect, to oblige the late Mr W. Tytler, and again very late[ly] wrote down 9 ballads more to oblige his son the Professor.
>
> Mr Jamieson visited Mrs Brown, on his return[n] here from Aberdeen, and obtained from her recollection 5 or 6 ballads more and a fragment. If this treasure excite your Lordship's curiosity, I shall transmit to you the titles of the ballads, with the first stanza, and number of stanzas of each. The greater part of them is unknown to the oldest persons in this country. I accompanied Mr Jamieson to my friend Scott's house in the country, for the sake [of] bringing the collectors to a good understanding.

The text Anderson's daughter, "a little girl at my elbow", copied, is still extant among Anderson's papers at the NLS (see Adv.Ms.22.4.10 for the letter and MS 1001, ff. 79–81 for the text) and the additional information promised on Brown B and C (titles, number of verses, first stanzas, long extracts from letters and his own comments) was sent to Percy on 27 January 1801 (*Percy Letters* 9: 47–56).

Robert Anderson thus served as a mediator, being a friend to Percy, Scott and Jamieson. It was also Anderson who made Jamieson realise in the early summer of 1800 that Scott was engaged on a similar project. As Jamieson writes in the preface to *Popular Ballads*,

> I took a journey to the north of Scotland, and, stopping at Edinburgh in my way, was not a little mortified to find, that Mr Scott was engaged in an undertaking of the same kind, in which … the greater part of the materials collected for both works was the same. (*PB* 1: v)

Since Scott knew, possibly through Robert Anderson, that Jamieson was to pass through Edinburgh again in the late summer of 1800, he sent a letter to Anderson (13 August 1800), inviting both men to spend a day with him – "this week" or "the beginning of the next" – in his country cottage at Lasswade near Roslin Castle. Scott planned "to talk over the proposed publications & as far as possible prevent the possibility of interference" (*SL* 1: 100) and, when the meeting between the three men took place, he certainly succeeded in calming Jamieson's nerves.

As Anderson and Jamieson understood the situation, Scott intended to confine his publication with very few exceptions to the Border raid ballads, and to have one volume of ballads, followed by two volumes of Border history, poetry and antiquities (see MS 911, f. 73 and *PB* 1: vi; also: Dobie 70–76). This is Scott's own account of the decisive meeting in August 1800 (Scott's letter to Heber, 19 October 1800, in *SL* 12: 172–73):

> Jamieson spent a day with me when he was here – he had been at Mrs. Brown of Faulkland [sic] & got one or two good poems from her, but I think I had most of the rest of his collection. You will readily believe that far from wishing to hurt his collection I did all in my power to assist him – gave him several copies & even resigned some poems I had intended myself to publish. Indeed my heart being chiefly set upon the Border raid Ballads I was less anxious about those which are merely romantick & popular of which I believe an attentive Collector who would collect from recitation in the pastoral parts of the Country & not from Libraries in great towns might still recover a very great number indeed.

Jamieson had just collected the three ballads ("Willie's Lady", "King Henry" and "The Twa Sisters") that he said were seen by Scott in 1800 (see *PB* 2: 178; 2: 194; 1: 49); he possibly brought to the meeting his copy of Mrs Brown's ballads (Brown A) and showed it to Scott, not knowing that Scott was already familiar with the ballads in this manuscript through Heber. Scott may have had manuscript C or material copied from it available at the meeting. The two editors were certainly later able to discuss ballads from it that they both knew about. Brown 26 "Bonny Bee Ho'm" and Brown 27 "Cruel Brother Or The Bride's Testament" from manuscript C eventually found their way into Jamieson's publication *Popular Ballads* (1806).[14]

14 In his letter to Percy (11 November 1800) Jamieson gives a list of what he thinks is unique in his collection: "Among Mrs. Brown's Ballads, of which

While Scott was chiefly set on the Border raid ballads, Jamieson was primarily interested in ballads from the north-east of Scotland, so there should not have been too much rivalry, but Scott's intentions changed radically. However much Scott was trying to cover it up, he certainly did not hold to his end of the bargain (see Zug 400). It was probably through the influence of his collaborator John Leyden (see Maxwell; Zug 402) that he made more use of Mrs Brown's repertoire than he had originally intended (see Rieuwerts, "Scottish Muse" and *In the Footsteps of Herder*).

Jamieson was later "disheartened" when the second volume of Scott's *Minstrelsy* appeared in 1802 (Letter to Scott, 19 October 1804, MS 3875, ff. 20–21; Rieuwerts, *In the Footsteps*), but initially, following the meeting at Lasswade, he felt rather relieved about the most amicable arrangement he had made with Walter Scott, even calling him "one of the best friends of my little work", in his letter to Robert Eden Scott which is given here in full (MS 10998, ff. 184–85 at the NLS):

Macclesfield School, Cheshire, Decr 25th 1800.

Dear Sir

After the kind attentions with which you honoured me in Aberdeen, and the friendly politeness wt wc Mrs Scott offered to exert herself in procuring some ballads and fragments of ballads which she had in view for me; you may well have been surprised that I have not intruded myself and my hobby-horsical pursuits upon your leisure before now. But since I returned from Scotland, my mind has been taken up with concerns of a very interesting & painful kind, which alas! tho' very natural to a poet, have not been either poetical or pleasing. But you know, "*when things come to the worst, they must begin to mend*"; and mine, tho' at the worst, shewing no probability of amendment, I have at last pulled up resolution enough to endeavour to divert my thoughts into another channel, & so elude what I find myself unable to oppose. I have accordingly begun again to try to think of my friends & of myself, & have resumed my ballads & correspondence.

Your letter to Mrs Brown was of infinite service to me. Another Gentleman (who, as well as I, was disappointed in a seat in the mail)

no account has been sent to your Lordship, are, 'Hugh of Lincoln,' [...] 'Sweet Willie and May Margaret,' [...] 'Bonny Baby Livingston,' [...] 'Lady Jane,' [...] 'Burd Ellen and Lord John' [...] – 'The Bonny Birdy,' [...] – A complete copy of 'Lamkin' I shall have from Mrs. Brown" (Nichols 8: 337–41) and he could have added: "Young Bicham", "Allison Gross" and "The Birth of Robin Hood" – Scott did not have a copy of these three either.

and I, took a post-chaise from Arbroath thro' Fifeshire. At the New Inn I learned that Mrs Brown was at Dysart, whither Dr B. was to go to her next morning, so I sent him a note inclosing your letter, to Falkland; and had the pleasure of his company in the Morning to Dysart, where I spent two days and a half; and where I received every civility & attention from Mrs. & Dr Brown. I found Mrs B. all that I had expected, and all that I could have wished. We had much conversation, and I procured many valuable acquisitions to my collection. I have since been honoured with a long letter, & some valuable communications *from her*; and she has most obligingly promised me still more. I want words to express my gratitude to you and to her for the pleasure & advantage which I derive from such an acquaintance. Of all the many persons of respectability who have honoured me with their countenance & assistance in my undertaking, none has shewn so much kind interest & chearful & ready industry in my behalf as Mrs Brown. She and the Doctor spare no pains in making out and *transcribing*; and you know how tiresome a business that is.

I spent two very agreeable days with Mr (Walter) Scott at his house near Roslin Castle. We came to the most amicable adjustment, & he has turned out one of the best friends of my little work. He is indeed an admirable young fellow. I would send you two or three songs; but I am harassed with transcribing at present; and besides, I intend to send half a dozen to Mr Ross, to beg he will breathe somewhat of the Promethean fire of harmony (which I know he stole long ago, if not from Heaven, at least from the Genius of his Country) into them, and give me some hopes not only of their obtaining life, but long life, thro' his friendship. As I know Mr Ross only by Character, and he knows nothing of me; will you have the goodness to speak to him in my behalf, and say as much in my favour as your good nature can suggest, and your conscience will suffer. Please request from me the same favour of Dr Gerard, to whose friendly interference I have often been so much indebted.

Has Mrs Scott been as successful in recovering old ditties for me, as her kind politeness disposed her to hope she should be. If any thing has been procured, I hope you will take the trouble of having it transmitted by post (never mind expence) as soon as convenience will permit; as it is now Xmass vacation, & I am at leisure to work; & Mr Scott's Collection is in the Press.

I have had some very curious communications from Dr. Percy's Folio MS. which his Lordship has very obligingly made out for me, & promises more.

Please to remember me kindly & gratefully to Dr & Mrs Gerard when you see them. Begging my most respectful Complimmts to Mrs Scott, & wishing her & you a happy new *Century*,

I have the honr to be, Dear Sir,
Your much obliged Sert
R. Jamieson.

What is Mr McLachlane doing? Remember me kindly to him; and tell him that, notwithstanding he refused me the honour of his Correspondence, I'll take the liberty of writing to him the first time I have the opportunity of a *Frank*; as I wish to consult him about some Gaelic things. I must write to you again about your music for the ballads; but not till I have been favoured with another letter from Mrs Brown.

Have you ever discovered any traces of "Gil xxx *and Squire Ingram*?"[15]

This letter not only sheds light on the August meeting at Scott's cottage, but provides invaluable information about Jamieson recording ballads at Dysart from Mrs Brown, to whom he had been given a letter of introduction by her nephew, Robert Eden Scott.[16] Since he met her on his way back from the north to Edinburgh where he was expected to arrive about 13 August 1800, this meeting with Mrs and Dr Brown must have occurred just a couple of days earlier.[17] Jamieson had gone up from Macclesfield in the north of England to Scotland in the summer of 1800 in order "to do the utmost" to further his work on ballads, not only visiting his mother in Westfield near Elgin but also Robert Eden Scott and his wife in Aberdeen.

Jamieson had "a pretty large Manuscript" with him that was, as Mrs Brown understood it, "given him by professor Scott" (see her letter to AFT of 23 December 1800 below). It is highly unlikely that Jamieson had with him Robert Eden Scott's original manuscript, the now lost

15 The three xxx are in the source. The ballad mentioned is better known as "Lord Ingram and Child Wyet" (Child 66); see also "Lord Wa'Yates and Auld Ingram" in *PB* 2: 265–272, given "from Mr Herd's MS. transmitted by Mr Scott". Jamieson had asked for a conclusion of his version of the ballad in the *Scots Magazine* (see "To the Publisher").

16 Mrs Brown was in Dysart for health reasons (*PB* 1: viii) but what her illness was and whether it was connected to her earlier problems, is not known. In May 1794, her father Thomas Gordon gave this report to her sister Elizabeth in America: "Mrs Brown may be said to be perfectly recovered tho' she be still but weak, & the tender young skin that Nature hath kindly spread over her sore is so easily hurt & when this happens brings her such an aboundance of pain, that she is still an object of sympathy." (Peyton Papers at the VHS)

17 On his return journey from the north he had previously recorded ballads in Arbroath from Mrs Arrott, but no manuscript records have yet come to light.

source of A, considering that he had just come from Aberdeen and could have returned it if it had not already been returned by Heber who had spent some time in Scotland in the summer of 1799 (Cholmondeley 156; *SL* 12: 157n1).[18]

The manuscript "in his possession", as Mrs Brown put it, must have been Jamieson's own copy and not Robert Eden Scott's copy as Mrs Brown understood although it is surprising that she did not notice the difference in handwriting between Scott's original, now lost, manuscript, and the Jamieson copy, our manuscript A. If A was already interleaved, it is even more surprising that no more ballads seem to have been entered into it, unless he refrained from adding rough transcriptions because A was a fair copy and only later turned into a working copy.

By Robert Jamieson's own account, he spent two and a half days with Mrs Brown and her husband at Dysart and received "valuable acquisitions" to his collection. While he himself talks about writing down "from her unpremeditated repetition about a dozen pieces more" (see *PB* 1: viii), Anderson writes about Jamieson receiving in Dysart "from her recollection 5 or 6 ballads more and a fragment" in one letter to Percy (14 September 1800; *Percy Letters* 9: 43) and about "four or five more old Ballads or fragments" in another (29 December 1800; *Percy Letters* 9: 56). Since Anderson specifically mentions having seen these additional ballads from Mrs Brown's singing in Dysart, the new ballads Jamieson had taken from the recitation of Mrs Brown must have been recorded separately although no manuscript has been found.

It is still not possible to list the "dozen more" ballads Jamieson says he received. Most of them "will be found in this work" he added to the preface of *PB* (1: viii) but only five could clearly be identified (see Brown E). Apart from these, none of the texts Jamieson lists in his letter to Constable (7 October 1803), the Editor of the *Scots Magazine*, as having a fragmented or inferior form seem to be extant (see Jamieson, "To the Publisher"). Among Jamieson's papers in the Cowie manuscript are two ballads from Mrs Brown (see Neilson): No. 44 "Thomas the Rhymer" (Brown 22) and, beginning on the verso of the same sheet, No. 45 "Jellon Græm and Lillie Flower" (Brown 24),[19] but these look like

[18] It was also Richard Heber who had met John Leyden in August 1799 in Constable's bookshop and introduced him to Walter Scott (*SL* 12: 157n1).

[19] In his preface to *PB* (vi–vii) Jamieson lists the ballads he had shared with Scott in August 1800: "Of the pieces that were common property at the time of comparing notes in 1800, the following will be found in the second volume of the *Border Minstrelsy*: The Gay Goss Hawk, Brown Adam, Jellon Grame,

copies Jamieson had made from manuscript C rather than independent versions (see Notes).

Whatever he received at their meeting in Dysart, the tone in Mrs Brown's next letter – "For Mr Jamison [sic] / Macclesfield School / Cheshire / 16"– is very warm-hearted. It is given here in full from MS La.III.473 in the NLS. For the ballad enclosed, see Brown 29 D "Old Song – Bonny Baby Livingston".

> [f. 9r] Falkland palace Sept 15 1800
>
> Dear Sir
>
> Some days since I was agreably surprised at receiving by the carrier a most elegant copy of Wielands Oberon with Mr Jamisons Compliments As I entertain no doubts about who the Mr Jamison is to whom I am indebted I beg Sir you will accept of my grateful thanks, I have only to regret that you should have thought it necessary to put yourself to so unecessary an expence [on] my account. on the other page you will find the whole B[allad o]f [Bon]ny Baby Livingston. I found upon recollection that I had the w[hole] story in my memmory. & thought it better to write it out intire as what I repeated to you was I think more imperfect as to the fragment of Lamekin upon reading over the edition of it that is in herds Collection I find that mine differs from it very materially tho the story must have certainly been the same. if ~~I~~ you wish to have my way of it I shall send it. but Baby is ennough for one letter, so I ~~shall~~ request you will with your leisure write me a few Lines & let me know how Mr W Scott & you agreed about your joint labours I feel myself a good deal interested in the matter & shall be happy to contribute everything in my powe[r] to facilititate your scheme. Doctor Brown well joins with me in compliments & best wishes & I am Dear Sir
>
> Yours &ctra
>
> Anna Brown

This letter gives an indication that through his correspondence with Mrs Brown, Jamieson's repertoire was even further enlarged. In his letter to Percy (11 November 1800; in Nichols 8: 337–41), Jamieson tells the bishop of having received from Mrs Brown not only "Bonny Baby Livingston" but also "Hugh of Lincoln", which was later published in *PB* but for which no manuscript copy has survived. Interestingly he

Willie's Ladye, Rose the Red and White Lilly, Fause Foodrage, Kempion, Cospatrick, [...]." Brown 23 "Fa'se Footrage" and Brown 24 "Jellon Grame and Lillie Flower" were the only ballads not in manuscript A. No record of Jamieson's copy of Brown 23 has yet come to light.

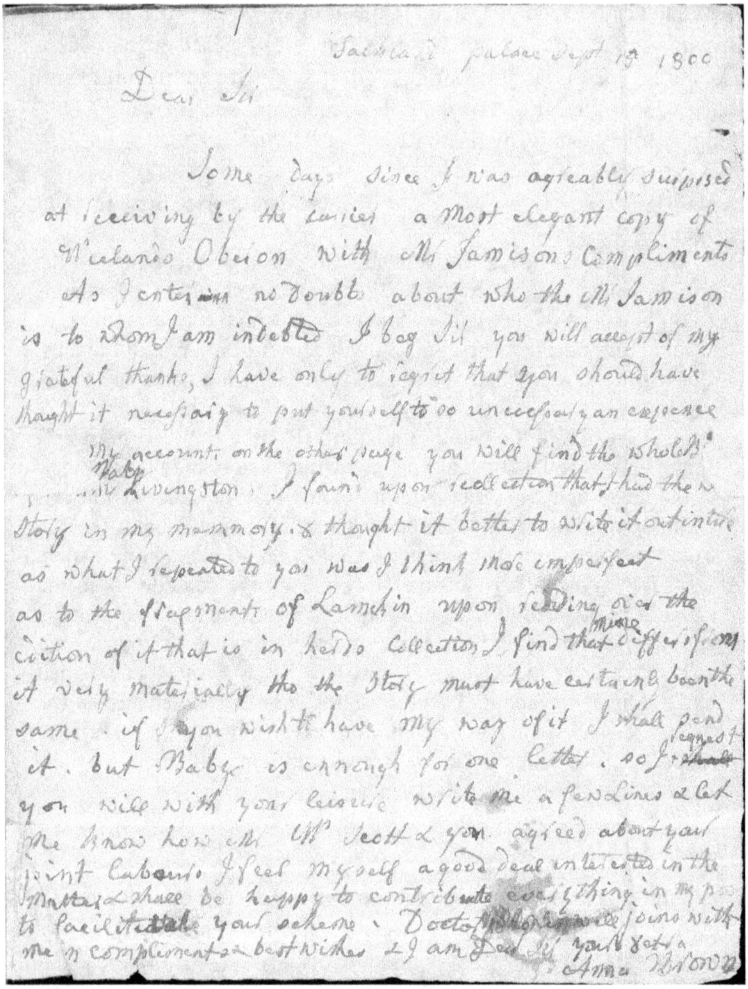

Figure 8:
Facsimile of folio 9r of D,
Anna Brown's letter to Robert Jamieson

adds: "A complete copy of 'Lamkin' I shall have from Mrs. Brown" (8: 339). Obviously he had either been recording an incomplete copy of "Lamkin" from Mrs Brown in the summer of 1800, or he had none at all. This ballad has not been found in manuscript but was published in *PB*.

While Mrs Brown was adding to Jamieson's ballad collection by sending him versions in letters, her other two ballad manuscripts (B and C) were in great demand and they were consulted by all the great ballad collectors and editors of the time, including David Herd and Archibald Constable (see La.IV.25.47, f. 121 at the EUL). Fortunately, she did not know this, for she would certainly not have approved of the enthusiasm that was being generated for her ballads. When she heard about the rivalry between Jamieson and Scott, she was upset first, and later relieved that they seemed to have come to an amicable agreement. She asked to be kept informed about their "joint labours". Her letter of December 1800 (Acc 3639, vol. 1, ff. 278–79), addressed to "Alexander Fraser Tytler Esqre, Professor of Civil History, Edinburgh", is an attempt to explain the situation. It is given here in full:

[1: 278v] Falkland December 23d 1800
Dear Sir

I dare say after so long an interval you will be surprized at being again addressed by me, upon the subject of Old Ballads. Indeed, after receiving & looking over the Book which you was so good as send me by Mr Brown, I did not for a considerable time think that I had any thing more worth communicating, but my recollecting faculties have been since aroused by an application, from another quarter, thro the medium of my Nephew Professor Scott. in behalf of a Mr Jamieson of Macclesfield who you doubtless have heard of in the course of the last summer he came here in the ~~Aut~~ end of summer with an introductery letter from my Nephew and at the same time shewd me a pretty large Manuscript which he had been in possession of I believe for some years & which had been given him by professor Scott. this Sir I think it necessary to explain to you. this manuscript of which Mr Jamieson is now in possession. was origanally made out with the intention of being sent to your Father but upon his additional request of having the tunes of the ballads noted down. my Father ordered Bob Scott then a very young Boy & a meer novice in musick. to try to do it & he & I set to work. but found the business so crabbed that in order to abridge our labours a little, we sellected what we thought the best of the Ballads. whose tunes being added in the best manner we could were sent to your Father the larger Manuscript which I thought had been destroyd. it seems Bob Scott had laid up

& has since given to Mr Jamieson [278v] this circumstance I did not recollect when Mr Jamieson was here & I was a good deal vexed to think of the odd appearence it might have in your eyes. that another should be in possession of what you had good reason to believe was yours exclusivly. . but I hope you will now be Convinced that it has all come about without any any sinister practices on any side I heard lately from Mr Jamieson. who informs me. that he had an interview with your Friend while in Scotland & that they had settld matters in the most amicable manner which I am very happy to hear indeed he writes in the highest terms of acknowledgement of the handsom & candid manner in which your Friend had conductd himself, Mr Jamieson likwise solicits me very earnestly for farther comunications. this Sir I shall defere giving him till I hear from you. who I still look upon as intitled to the first offer of whatever I can yet recollect. I have lately upon rummaging a bycorner of my ~~m~~ memmory, found out some Aberdeenshire Ballads, which totally escaped me before. they are of a different class from those I sent you not near so ancient but may be about a century ago. I cannot boast much of their poetical merits but the family incidents upon which they are founded & the local allusion which they contain may perhaps render them courious & not uninteresting to many people. they are as follows

1st the Baron of Braickly 2d the Lass of Philorth
3d the tryal of the Laird of Gycht
4th the death of the Countess of Aboyne
5th the Carrieng off of the Heiress of Kinady

[279r] all these I can recollect pretty exactly. I never saw any of them either in print or manuscript but have them intirely from hearing them sung when a child. I hope therefor you will write me with your convenience whether or not you wish to have them. Jamieson I see wishes much to have the Baron of Braichly, but he does not know that I have it as yet nor do I intend to write him till once I hear from you

~~Mr~~ Dr Brown who is in his usal health. requests to join with me in Compliments & best wishes to you & to Mrs Fraser, & Miss Tytlers, he & I are at present a good deal interested about the effects of a memorial of our worthy Friend Dr Gregories concerning the Royal Infirmary as we have never heard any thing of it since the time the Doctor was so good as send Mr Brown a copy of it May I sir take the liberty of requesting you when you favour me with an answer just to mention if it has yet or is likely to have any effects either upon the publick mind or upon the parties most concerned I hope you will pardon this freedom & believe me to be with sincere estem.

Yours. &ct &cra
Anna Brown

The ballads that Anna Brown said she could supply can be identified as Child 203 "The Baron of Brackley", Child 239 "Lord Saltoun and Auchanachie", Child 209 "Geordie", Child 234 "Charlie MacPherson" and Child 235 "The Earl of Aboyne". With her next letter to Jamieson, she sent her version of "The Baron of Brackley" as written down by her husband.

> [f. 7r] Falkland june 18 1801
> You see my good Sir that I have pay'd more regard to the request in your letter in the time I have taken to answer you. than to the example you set me. I am indeed very sorry to learn that your tranquillity is not before now perfectly restored according to my Ideas of these matters. a hopeless state which yours most certainly is ~~is~~ soon cures itself. but I see I have been wrong & I can only lament it. but would fain hope that time & refflection & your other avoc[a]tions would soon tranquilize your mind & make you more Master of its powers you will see that Mr Brown has coppied over the Baron of Braickly & the fragment of Allan O Maut. the Baron of Braickly is a simple Narritive of a true story which happned as I have been told about the latter end of the 17 century. John Gordon of Br[ai]ckly or as he was alwise call'd the Baron of Brackly w[as a fi]ne man universally esteem'd he was of the Family of Aboyne Farquharson of Inveray had a personal Ill will to him, & came with a train of Armed followers & drove off his Cattle the Baron went out to remonstrate with him & was instantle sorrounded & cut to pieces not many yards from his own gate. Inveray fled & was outlaw'd but was allow'd afterwards to return
>
> I have been at Braickly & seen the ruins of the Barrons Castle little of which now remain they show'd me the gate he rode out at about one half of which was then extant & a hollow way between two little knolls where the Farquharsons fell upon him ——
>
> I have given you all I remember of Allan O Maut. I do not know any thing of Rob Roy. Glen Kindy or rather Glen Skeeny I have heard & there is a Ballad in Percies collection that is very much the same he is there calld Glassgerrion but is the [f. 7v] same story in all. Lady Jane is a most respectable personage in the way you have pushet her up. I know ~~Robt~~ Bob Scotts indolence in letter writing too well to be surprised at any thing he may do, but you should write him again & put him in mind. I regret that you cannot spurr up your resoloution to the pitch of comeing to Scotland before you publish your Miscellany for I doubt not but in the course of conversation I might recollect something that might be new to you, tho I do not recollect any thing at present.
>
> Mr Brown desires to be remember'd to you & says he coppied the Ballads meerly to induce you to pull up your spirits. bothe he &

> I shall alwise be happy to hear of your wellfare & to see you when convenien[t] & in the meantime with best wishes I remain yours & ctra
>
> Anna Brown

Interestingly Mrs Brown sends Jamieson not another of her romantic or supernatural ballads but the "Baron of Braickly", a (semi-) historical ballad that is firmly placed in the north-east of Scotland and could not possibly have been of interest to the editor of the *Border Minstrelsy*. Because of his friendship with Tytler, Scott certainly had the advantage over Jamieson: "Whatever Mrs. Brown was able to dredge up from her fertile memory would come first to him" (Zug 401).

Despite the fact that Mrs Brown lived in Falkland in Fife and, from April 1802, even closer to Edinburgh in Tranent, Scott does not seem to have been known to her in person (see below, her letter to Jamieson, 2 December 1800). Unlike Jamieson, Scott obviously never collected ballads from her. He admits to Anderson and in his published work that he entertained some doubts about the genuineness of her ballads.[20] It was more important to Scott to have an aesthetic than an authentic version of a traditional ballad.[21] Thus, Mrs Brown's texts were not always given in the *Minstrelsy of the Scottish Border* in the way that Scott had received them in manuscripts B and C. Whether her ballads, if not "improved" by Scott, would have attracted less criticism will never be known, but in an anonymous review in 1803, Mrs Brown's "romantic ballads" were first described as having a "wild and pathetic complexion" and then dismissed as being "degraded recitations of old metrical romances" (in the *Monthly Review*).

20 See his introduction to "Fause Foodrage". The ballad, Scott claims, is "chiefly given from Mrs BROWN of Faulkland's MS. The expression / 'The boy stared wild like a gray goss hawk.' (Verse 31) / strongly resembles that in Hardyknute, / 'Norse e'en like gray goss hawk stared wild.' / a circumstance which led the editor to make the strictest enquiry into the authenticity of the song. But every doubt was removed by the evidence of a lady of high rank, who not only recollected the ballad, as having amused her infancy, but could repeat many of the verses; particularly those beautiful stanzas …" (*MSB* 2: 73).

21 In a letter to William Motherwell (3 May 1825) he called this a mistake: "I did wrong myself in endeavouring to make the best possible set of an ancient ballad out of several copies obtained from different quarters, and that in many respects if I improved the poetry I spoiled the simplicity of the old song" (*SL* 11: 101).

The effect of the publication of Scott's *Minstrelsy of the Scottish Border* (2 vols, 1802) on Jamieson was quite overwhelming. If he was irritated by Lewis's publication, he was stunned into silence, laying aside his papers for two years, when he saw Scott's two-volume edition in 1802.[22] Jamieson had not expected to see so many of Mrs Brown's ballads appear in print. Having to work for a living and being so far from Scotland, he saw no way to speed up the publication of his intended collection. In this situation another letter arrived from Mrs Brown – taken from La.III.374 and given here in full:

[f. 4r] Tranent December 2d 1802

Dear Sir

I have for a long time been in expectation of seeing your proposed publication of Ancient Ballads announced to the public, as in your last letter to me, which was in May was a year, you mention'd your intention of publishing them in the course of the ensuing winter – Circumstances however (sufficiently important I dare say) have hitherto prevented you, and I now avail myself of that delay, to make a request to you which I hope you will not fail to attend to. It is this – that when you do publish, if you think any of the ballads you got from me worth inserting. you will not give my name to the public. as I see Mr Scott has done in his Minstrelsy of the Border, which I have seen, & which I otherwise think a very curiose & very ingenious work & particularly the light which his notes & introduction casts upon that period of Border history gives him no small claim to literary merit.

But I am very much surprized indeed & not very well pleas'd to see A Gentleman so much prais'd by all his acquaintence for his politeness & aimiable qualities guilty of so great [f. 4v] an impsoprety as to publish any persons name to the world without ever asking directly or indiretly whether or not it would be agreable, & both Mr. Brown & I have been a good deal vexed at it. And it sugested to me the necessity of troubling you with this, to prevent you from falling into a simmilar

[22] Desperate for help in finding employment in Scotland, Jamieson eventually opened up the correspondence with Scott again on 19 October 1804: "My dear Sir, To enumerate half the circumstances which have occasioned my long silence, & the delay of my projected publication, would require a narrative far exceeding the bounds of a letter, and would but ill repay your trouble in perusing it. After reading the two first volumes of your excellent Work, I was so disheartened, (especially as you promised a third,) that for a considerable time I laid my papers aside altogether ..." (MS 3875, ff. 20–21 at the NLS).

mistake as indeed the seeing of Mr Scotts Book might very naturally make you think that the inserting my name in the manner he has done might be highly flatter ing to me. and I doubt not but he meant me a compliment but he should have known me better ~~better~~ & had my permission before he had given so public a testimony of his esteem. I make both you & him exceedinly welcome to all the share I had in the Ballads, and a privete acknowledgment was all I ever wish'd for or expected. That Sir you have already made, & from the short oppertunity I had of a personal acquaintence with you & subsequent correspondence which that brought on, I have formed so favourable an opinion of you that I shall be warmly interested in everything that concerns you – & if you should ever find it either convenient or agreable to take another jaunt to Scotland [f. 5v] I hope we shall have the pleasure of seeing you at Tranent which will not put you to the trouble of crossing the firth In the mean time I wish you all success in your litterary adventure & hope my application shall not be too late

Mr Brown joins with compliments & best wishes.

I am Dear Sir with sincere esteem yours &c

Anna Brown

That is the last letter from Mrs Brown to Robert Jamieson that has survived.[23] Jamieson fell into difficulties at Macclesfield and, not being able to find employment in Scotland, he left England eventually to take up a post in Riga in 1805. The following letter, sent by Robert Eden Scott on 9 June 1805 and addressed to "Mr R. Jamieson, / at Mrs Legh's / Kingston, Surry" (La.III.473) arrived just a few weeks before Jamieson set off. It included the ballad "Leezie Lindsay" (Child 226 A) and two songs. These were certainly not recorded from Mrs Brown but from an old maid-servant in the family and they are omitted in this edition. Only the letter is given in full:

[f. 2r] Dear Sir

Your favour of the 29th Ulto afforded me much pleasure by informing me that notwithstanding interruptions & untoward circumstances, the time approaches when your long expected ballads are to be given to the public –

You will find above, all I have been able to procure in order to replace the lost fragment of Lizie Lindsay – I believe it is not so correct or so complete as what was formerly sent – but there are

23 Besides the letters published in this edition there are other letters from Anna Brown extant; see those to her sister Elizabeth in Virginia in MSS 1 P4686 at the VHS.

materials enough to operate upon, & by forcing the memory of the recorder, more harm than good might have been done –

[f. 2v] I have found among my papers the scraps [Fragments No. 16 Ed. Mag] formerly alluded to as suggested by your advertisement in the Scots Magazine. They are not I presume very important but as likely to be more interesting to you than any thing I could write I shall here transcribe them. [...]

[f. 3r] I congratulate you on the prospect of an eligible [*sheet torn*] in so interesting a country as Russia – I hope y[ou will] [*sheet torn*] not forget your offer of being my correspondent from tha[t part] [*sheet torn*] of the world as I shall expect to be highly amused [*lost words, sheet torn*] by your letters from Livonia, & shall certainly think them cheap at an English postage –

I have seen Mrs Brown since the loss of our worthy friend the Doctor, & was happy to find her health & spirits as well as could reasonably be expected. She will be sufficiently comfortable in her circumstances, having no family to provide for. With respect to the assistance she has afforded to your ballads, I suspect she will be averse to having it publicly acknowledged, as I heard her express her displeasure at being mentioned in Mr Scotts publication, which was done entirely without her knowledge. You can however communicate with herself on the subject, & I am persuaded it will give her pleasure to hear from you. Her direction is Manse of *Tranent*.

I shall expect the pleasures of hearing from you before you leave England & hope to learn that the *Ballads* are at last fairly in the press.

Mrs Scott joins in good wishes
with Dear Sir
truly yours
Robt E. Scott.

King's College 9th June 1805

In August 1805 Jamieson left for Riga, not to return to the British Isles before 1809. He had prepared his *Popular Ballads* for publication, but it was Walter Scott who saw it through the press and had it published in 1806. And although Mrs Brown, and again her nephew Robert Eden Scott on her behalf, had specifically asked that her name should not to be mentioned, her wishes were ignored and her name was published once again (see Rieuwerts, "Scottish Muse"). All Mrs Brown ever wanted to give, were her ballads, not her identity.

The study of Mrs Brown and her repertoire leaves many questions open regarding her life and her ballads. The most important is the relationship between the various recordings of her repertoire. While the original source of manuscript A is no longer extant, very little is known of its character and thus its relationship with Brown B. Had it been sent to Tytler? And was it returned with the additional request for melodies? Or was it never sent and used as a working copy, perhaps with corrections made to the text that were later copied into B? According to Nygard ("Recollected Ballads" 79), "the circumstances support the view that Mrs. Brown sang the songs anew, not using the earlier copy as source or prompt". He argues that if her nephew had copied directly from the now lost source manuscript of A, surely the order of the ballads would be somehow similar but "not a single sequential pairing is retained from one MS to the other". Furthermore, Nygard points out that copying would have "prevented losses and additions of the few stanzas that are so involved, as well as transpositions of stanzas" and his third point is that "the many trivial literal changes (thirty-six for one ballad alone) would not have found their way into the Tytler MS [= Brown B]" if the now lost source of Brown A had served as copy source ("Recollected Ballads" 79). Despite all the evidence he provides, Nygard admits that the relationship between the two manuscripts cannot be established, especially since the source of A is lost and we can only assume but not prove that manuscript A was a faithful transcript. The similarities between Brown A and Brown B cannot fully be explained by assuming two independent recordings, nor the differences by accepting the idea of a verbatim transcript of the ballads they have in common.

The second manuscript of 1783 is certainly not a working copy but a fair copy of Mrs Brown's ballads with music being added later (see below). Mrs Brown speaks in her letter to AFT of 23 December 1800, quoted above, of finding the business of noting the ballads "so crabbed that in order to abridge our labours a little, we sellected what we thought the best of the Ballads". With the exception of Brown 21 "Clerk Colven", all ballads in B have parallels in A. Therefore it must be assumed that Mrs Brown and Robert Eden Scott had at least a list of A, if not the manuscript itself in hand while writing out B. If the latter was supposed to have been the case – writing out Brown B with the now lost source manuscript of A in hand – why was the music added later? Surely it would have been easier to record the music first. Thus, many questions remain and can perhaps only be answered satisfactorily by minute studies of her repertoire.

By printing parallel texts from A and B on facing pages, it is now possible for the first time to unravel the mystery of her variant texts. C is certainly in her hand and written out "near twenty years" later without having either A or B at hand. Alexander Fraser Tytler had merely sent her a list of ballad titles from Brown B to help her avoid duplicates. Thus, there is no overlap between B and C. Interestingly the only two ballads from Brown C that have parallels in Brown A have very different titles: Brown 10 is called "Burd Ellen" in manuscript A and "Lord John and Bird Ellen" in manuscript C; likewise Brown 12 is "Fair Anny" in Brown A and "Love Gregor" in Brown C. This raises the question of whether she had a list of the contents of Brown A as well and only did not recognise the two ballads because of the difference in name.

The songs in D are in Andrew Brown's hand and we can assume that he himself recorded them from his wife. No manuscripts have yet come to light for the additional ballads published by Robert Jamieson in his *Popular Ballads* in 1806 and, given that he was in a great hurry to finish his ballad collection before setting off for Riga at short notice, it is most likely that he did not copy her ballads out again but sent them to the printers in the way he had received them.

Since Mrs Brown's repertoire was taken down by various people at various times, we are fortunate enough to have her repertoire as "a thick corpus with organic variation" (see Honko).[24] It was Clifford Geertz who first insisted that culture can only be studied by doing a "thick description", a repeat collection and documentation of text and context (Geertz; see for ballad studies: Rieuwerts, "Same Story" and *Kulturnarratologie*). Variation is the life blood of oral tradition and a single recording is a "thin description" and would not capture the essence of the performance nor its life-setting, the so-called *Sitz-im-Leben* of a traditional ballad (see Rieuwerts, *Kulturnarratologie* 301–23). Thus "thick description" is necessary. While such multiplicity of data is common today, it is rare to find eighteenth- and nineteenth-century singers who were recorded more than once. Only the Harris repertoire of the mid to late nineteenth century, edited for the Scottish Text Society (by Lyle et al.), comes to mind. Mrs Brown of Falkland's repertoire is the earliest known thick corpus of Scottish ballads; seventeen of her ballads were recorded more than once and this is unique.

24 See Geertz for the original use of the concept and Honko and Rieuwerts for an adaptation to oral genres. I share Honko's notion that only "thick description" can help us understand variation in its individual, social and regional dimensions: "By producing 'thickness' of text and context through multiple documentation of expressions of folklore in their varying manifestations in performance within a 'biologically' definable tradition bearer, community or environment it has created a solid field of observation conducive to the understanding of prime 'causes' or sources of variation, i.e. the mental processes of oral textualisation and construction of meaning" (Honko 17).

The extent to which her repertoire exemplifies organic rather than artificial variation has been a matter of much debate. In her detailed study of oral traditions, Kekäläinen sums up Mrs Brown's ballads in the following way:

> Most of Mrs. Brown's ballads can be classified as love ballads. They often show connections with old romances or sagas and have a strong flavour of the supernatural. Her style is characterized as being both traditional and original, with a skilled use of the lingering techniques, incremental repetition, block composition with commonplace stanzas, and other features of the oral tradition, though her later versions become influenced by an increasing literary consciousness. The language of her versions is a mixture of Northern Scots, Mid Scots and English. Their study is further rendered difficult by the inconsistent orthography mixing the spellings and pronunciations of these variants. (Kekäläinen 7)

Her ballad versions have all the markers of orality, and yet, as Kekäläinen rightly points out, "an increasing literary consciousness" can be detected. What is the life-setting (*Sitz-im-Leben*) of her ballads or is it rather a book-setting (*Sitz-im-Buch*)? To what extent are her ballads informed by orality or literacy? Are her stories indeed "re-created by Mrs Brown at each singing", as David Buchan has suggested (see *Ballad and the Folk* 87)?

> The traditional singer does not learn individual songs as fixed texts, but learns instead both a method of composition and a number of stories. By this method he recomposes each individual story every time he performs. While, however, he recreates the story's narrative essence, he actually creates the individual lines and shapes the individual structure at the moment of performance: he composes the text as he re-composes the story. Each rendering of the story is, then, an "original text". (Buchan, *Ballad and Folk* 52)

Looking at the parallel versions in Mrs Brown's repertoire, it is difficult to believe that each text is a "re-composed" story. In most cases, the verbal similarities are so great that they cannot be explained by an oral-formulaic method of composition. On the other hand, in some parallel versions the differences are so great that they can almost be called different ballads. A good example is Brown 12 "The Lass of Roch Royal" (see Andersen and Pettitt; Pettitt; Fowler, "An Accused Queen"). According to Child (*ESPB* 2: 213–14), Mrs Brown was so steeped in oral tradition that she was just blending two independent versions of "The Lass of Roch Royal" and performed "Fair Anny" as well as "Love Gregor" (see also Bronson, "Mrs Brown").

On the other hand, it is argued, memory plays the most important role for "the process involved in her transmission [...] is the memorization of a fixed text" (Andersen and Pettitt 23; see also Friedman, "Oral-Formulaic"). Nygard points out the verbal similarity and indeed identity between corresponding items in her manuscripts and concludes: "Mrs. Brown's ballads are essentially repetitions of a text, not recreations of a story maintained in fluid solution subject to a free variation in successive singings" ("Recollected Ballads" 79).

Given the difficult plot structures of some of her versions (see Notes for details), both theories have their flaws and the controversy about "the theme of invariance versus change" (Donaldson) is far from over. Until now, as William Donaldson has pointed out, the evidence has been "ambiguous". With this edition in hand, however, the evidence is presented and it should now be possible to unravel the art of oral/written composition in Mrs Brown's repertoire.

Despite the fact that until now Mrs Brown's repertoire has only been available in a mediated, unreliable form, it has been the focal point for various scholarly disputes. The most prominent one is the question of authenticity. Mrs Brown's contemporaries had different views on this matter. Ritson admits the genuineness of her ballads but nevertheless rejects them on the grounds of their being too modern and too lyrical, Percy shows hardly any interest in them and Scott and Anderson are suspicious, as Anderson's letter to Percy reveals:

> I there took onus [on] me to hint my suspicion of modern manufacture in which Scott had secretly anticipated me. Mrs. B. is fond of ballad poetry, writes verses, and reads every thing in the marvellous way. Yet her character places her above the suspicion of literary imposture, but it is wonderful how she should happen to be the depository of so many curious and valuable ballads. (*Percy Letters* 9: 43)

Since neither Scott nor Anderson seems to have ever met Mrs Brown, the information that she is a poet in her own right must have come from the Tytler family, or, more likely, from Robert Jamieson who had only just met Mrs Brown and who was also present at the meeting in August 1800. There can be no doubt that Mrs Brown, the daughter of a professor and wife of a minister, was well educated for she quotes from Ossian and is expected to read Wieland's *Oberon*.[25]

25 Wieland's *Oberon* was translated from the German by William Sotheby and published in two volumes, often bound into one, by Cadell and Davies in 1798.

This leads a reviewer in the discussion of Mrs Brown's ballads in Jamieson's *Popular Ballads* (1806) to suggest that he should have collected his ballads

> fresh from their natural reporters, the country people; whose faithful memory is not exposed to disturbance in the discharge of its duty, from any intrusion of criticism or imagination.
>
> (Anon., "Art. III – *PB*" 22)

Men and women with her education and abilities cannot possibly be "faithful reporters of legendary tales. That which they cannot understand they are under a strong temptation to make intelligible by conjectural emendations, and fancy at times may supply the defects of recollection" (Anon., "Art. III – *PB*" 22). Jamieson did admit that Mrs Brown was an exception, commenting that there are only "very few persons of Mrs Brown's abilities and education, that repeat popular ballads from memory" (*PB* 1: ix). His authority should carry some weight. After all, with the exception of the Tytlers, Robert Jamieson is the only one familiar with Mrs Brown's thinking on ballads, having spent two and a half days with her and her husband. It is therefore worth quoting his discussion in *Popular Ballads* at length. Unlike Scott and Anderson, Jamieson entertains no doubt about the authenticity of Mrs Brown's ballads

> As to the *authenticity* of the pieces themselves, they are as authentic as traditionary poetry can be expected to be; and their being more entire than most other such pieces are found to be, may be easily accounted for, from the circumstance that there are very few persons of Mrs Brown's abilities and education, that repeat popular ballads from memory. She learnt most of them before she was twelve years old, from old women and maid-servants; what she once learnt, she never forgot; and such were her curiosity and industry, that she was not contented with merely knowing the story, according to one way of telling, but studied to acquire all the varieties of the same tale which she could meet with. In some instances, these different readings may have insensibly mixed with each other, and produced, from various disjointed fragments, a whole, such as reciters, whose memories and judgments are less perfect, can seldom produce. But this must be the case in all poetry, which depends for its authenticity upon oral tradition alone. (*PB* 1: ix–x)

Once she had learned them in her youth, Mrs Brown could later recite popular ballads from memory. In an authentic oral tradition there is more than one way of telling and thus through "curiosity and industry" Mrs

Brown had acquired "all the varieties of the same tale". Yet, Jamieson argued, this is still part and parcel of an authentic oral tradition, to tell a good tale in the best possible way. It is precisely the oral-formulaic character of Mrs Brown's ballads that gives rise to praise or condemnation. While Ritson saw tradition as a process that turns gold into lead (*Scotish Songs* 1: lxxxi, quoted in context above), Jamieson regarded it as the prerequisite for authenticity.

There can be no doubt that Mrs Brown of Falkland was deeply steeped in the Scottish ballad tradition, written and oral. She could clearly distinguish between different types of ballads, the ones that are "not near so ancient" and others that are "of a different sort" and she compared her texts, for example with the ones in Ramsay's *Tea-table Miscellany* (1723–37), Percy's *Reliques of Ancient English Poetry* (1765) and Herd's *Ancient and Modern Scottish Songs and Heroic Ballads* (2 vols, 1776). At times she even apologised for her own versions:

> I do not pretend to say that these Ballads are Correct in any way as they are written down entirely from recollection; for I never saw one of them in print or manuscript; but I learned them all when a child by hearing them sung by the lady you mentioned (Mrs Farquharson), by my own mother, and an old maid servant that had been long in the family – *I dare say I may have fragments of others*, but I could not so easily recollect them except the ballads they belonged to were mentioned. (Mrs Brown's Letter to A. F. Tytler (21 April 1800), quoted by Anderson in *Percy Letters* 9: 54)

The emphasis here is clearly on not having seen *her* version in a book, but she had indicated earlier that she had seen in some cases other versions of her repertoire in print.

Looking at her repertoire, it becomes immediately apparent that almost all her ballads are of a distinctly narrative character. Her stories are action-driven. As Mrs Brown points out herself, her repertoire consists of "ballads and tales" and although no tales in prose are on record, her ballads are certainly tales in rhyme. Her stories are set in earlier times, reflecting to a certain extent the repertoire of her aunt, Mrs Farquharson, which was described as consisting of "songs and tales of chivalry and love" (see Gordon's letter to Alexander Fraser Tytler, 13 January 1793, Brown C, f. 1).

Moreover, the life-setting of her ballad singing is mainly in the past. If she learned her ballads from old women and maid-servants before she was twelve years of age (see Jamieson, *PB* 1: ix), her repertoire reflects the singing in Upper Deeside before 1759 – but not only that, it seems.

Her mother's family, the Forbes of Disblair, were a highly musical family and her mother Lillias, her aunt Anne, better known as Mrs Farquharson, and "a maid-servant, long with the Forbes family at Disblair" are mentioned among the main sources of her repertoire.

Her ballads not only reflect this female line of tradition but they are "framed from an explicitly female, indeed even feminist, perspective" (Donaldson). Since Anna's maternal grandmother was English, her mother and aunt could not have had her as a source for old Scottish ballads, it is more likely that both sisters learned ballads "from their mother's domestic servants" (Johnson, "Musical Tradition" 92).

Despite the fact that their home in Disblair was no longer in the family by the time Anna Brown was born, her repertoire can nevertheless be located in that area in Aberdeenshire. It is the mysterious Old Lady's Collection, a contemporary ballad manuscript (watermarks date from 1805–07) that leads to the suggestion that Allanaquoich and Upper Deeside was not the only home of Mrs Brown's ballads. The manuscript was obtained by James Skene of Rubislaw in Aberdeenshire.[26] At least eight ballads[27] from the Brown repertoire were also known to the Old Lady, whose name, alas, has not been recorded (see Montgomerie, Part V).

Her mother's sister Anne also credits nurses and old women from Upper Deeside. The records for Allanaquoich, however, show that there were very few households in that remote area of the Upper Dee – for the 1750s only eight tenants were listed for Allanaquoich (see Ewen 326-29). Anne Farquharson, the Lady of Allanaquoich as she was called, left with her family Upper Deeside in the 1760s, moved first to the parish of Fintray and later closer to her two sisters in Old Aberdeen.

26 Anna's grandfather, William Forbes of Disblair, was heavily in debt to George Skene of Skene, but this seems to have been a different branch of the family (see MS 500 at the AUL).

27 These are Brown 5: "Young Beicham" (Child 53); Brown 10: "Fair Ellen" (Child 63); Brown 25 "Fair Mary of Wallington" (Child 91), Brown 34 "Lamkin" (Child 93); Brown 3 "Willie o Douglas Dale" (Child 101); Brown 30 "Baron Brackley" (Child 203); Brown 32 "The Mother's Malison, or, Clyde's Water" (Child 216) and Brown 27 "Kitchie Boy" (Child 252). Both women also knew "Lord Saltoun and Auchanie" (Child 239).

Wherever and however Mrs Brown acquired her repertoire, whether in Upper Deeside, Disblair, Old Aberdeen or elsewhere in the north-east of Scotland, all of her ballads[28] were canonised in Child's *English and Scottish Popular Ballads*, most of them given pride of place as A or B version: twenty-four were given the "A" status by Child, indicating that Mrs Brown's text represents the oldest, the best or the only variant of that ballad type. It is still mainly through *The English and Scottish Popular Ballads* (1882–98) that Mrs Brown's repertoire is known today. (See the table on pp. 64–65 below.)

When Francis J. Child started on his definitive collection he was particularly interested in the Herd and Brown manuscripts he had seen quoted in print: "Whether these are in existence, and, if so, where such inquiries as I have been able to make have not determined" (Child, "Appeal"). His Danish friend Grundtvig suggested contacting David Laing in Edinburgh, who was a learned bookseller before he became, from 1837 to 1878, the keeper of the library of the Writers to the Signet, Edinburgh. When Child wrote to him in August 1872, he was pleased to learn that Laing had indeed one copy, namely A. In 1855 Laing had bought Jamieson's manuscript of the Brown ballads as "a Memorial of an old friend" (La.IV.Chi.2 at EUL). Through the booksellers Trübner in London and Osgood in Boston (see La.IV.6.Chi.3 at EUL), Laing made the original manuscript available to Child. The receipt was acknowledged in April 1873 (see La.IV.6.Chi.4 at EUL) and, since Laing was in no particular hurry to have it returned, Child decided not to send it but to bring it to Scotland himself in the summer of 1874 after, as he said, having made a full copy for collation (MS Eng 1486.2 at Houghton; Letter to Laing, 25 April 1874; La.IV.6.Chi.14 at EUL).

While A and D were thus made available to Child, he still lacked other Brown material. Through a friend he was able to enrol the help of the Fraser Tytler family and a thorough search of their home at Aldourie Castle failed to locate B but eventually produced C and a number of letters connected to Mrs Brown's repertoire (all quoted above). Copies were made for Child of all the available material, but his knowledge of the Brown repertoire was still rather patchy (see Child's exchange of letters with the Tytler family: Acc 3639, vol. 2: 296–306 at the NLS; MS Am 1922, MS Am 2349 and MS Eng 1468 at Houghton). Although at

28 Only the fragment of "Allan O Maut" (Brown 31) has, because of its lyrical character, been classed as a song and is therefore not to be found in the edition of Child ballads.

least ten of her ballads were previously known through printed editions, Child always placed her versions above them. Her repertoire had the traditional touch and was not "bookish". To Child, who was looking for the genuine ballads of the people, Mrs Brown was one of the greatest singers of all time (see Rieuwerts, "Genuine" 19–21). With this edition in hand, her position in the history of ballad performance and study can now be fully assessed. As Bronson ("Mrs Brown" 72) points out, this will require "comparative study of other nearly contemporaneous records of her ballads as they came from different singers" but that, of course, is far beyond the remit of this work.

Child Ballad Numbers for Mrs Brown's Repertoire

The Child ballads in square brackets were known to Mrs Brown (see her letter to AFT of 23 December 1800 (Acc 3639, vol. 1, ff. 278–79), but no records are extant). The first column gives the Child ballad number in *ESPB*.

ESPB	Child Title	Brown	Child's Source
5 Aa	Gil Brenton	16 A	A
5 Ab		16 B	Anderson
6 a	Willie's Lady	15 B	Mary Fraser Tytler *MSB* 1802, 2: 27–32
6 b		15 A	A
10 Ba	The Twa Sisters	18 A	A
10 Bb		18 B	Anderson
10 Bc			Abbotsford MS
10 Bd			E
11 Aa	The Cruel Brother	28 C	C
11 Ab			E
32 a	King Henry	14 A	A
32 b		14 B	*MSB* 1802, 2: 132–37
34 Ba	Kemp Owyne	13A	A
34 Bb		13B	*MSB* 1802, 2: 93–97
35	Allison Gross	19A	A
37 A	Thomas Rymer	22 C	C and E
42 A	Clerk Colvill	21 B	Mary Fraser Tytler Abbotsford MS
53 A	Young Beichan	5 A	A
53 C		4 A	A and E
62 E	Fair Annie	9	A and E
63 Ba	Child Waters	10A	A
63 Bb		10C	C
65 A	Lady Maisry	11A	A and E

ESPB	Child Title	Brown	Child's Source
76 D	The Lass of Roch Royal	12 A	A and E
76 Ea		12 C	C
76 Eb			*MSB* 1802, 2: 49–59
82	The Bonny Birdy	20 A	A and E
89 A	Fause Foodrage	23 C	C
90 Aa	Jellon Grame	24 C	C
90 Ab			*MSB* 1802, 2: 20–26
91 C	Fair maid of Wallington	25 C	C
92 A	Bonny Bee Hom	26 C	C
93 A	Lamkin	34 E	E
96 A	The Gay Goshawk	6 A	A
97 Aa	Brown Robin	17 A	A
97 Ab		17 B	Abbotsford MS
98 A	Brown Adam	7 A	A
99 A	Johnie Scot	2 A	A and Abbotsford MS
101 A	Willie o Douglas Dale	3 A	A
102 A	Willie and Earl Richard's Daughter	35	E
103 A	Rose the Red and White Lily	1 A	A
155A	Sir Hugh, or, The Jew's Daughter	33 E	E
203 Ca	The Baron of Brackley	30 D	A and E
[209	Geordie]		
216 B	The Mother's Malison, or, Clyde's Water	32 E	E
222 Aa	Bonny Baby Livingston	29 D	A
222 Ab			E
[234	Charlie MacPherson]		
[235	The Earl of Aboyne]		
[239	Lord Saltoun and Auchanachie]		
247 a	Lady Elspat	8 A	A
247 b		8 B	Abbotsford MS
252 C	The Kitchie-Boy	27 C	C
——	Allan O Maut	31 D	

Mrs Brown is also said to have been the source of other ballads (see William Walker on the old Aberdeenshire Version of "Auld Lang Syne"), but these claims could not be substantiated and may have arisen from a patchy knowledge of her repertoire. Before Brown B and C were found, "Lord Woodhouselee's grand-daughter's manuscript: Scottish songs and ballads, probably before 1830" (copy, MS Eng 1486.3 at Houghton) in particular was thought to contain Mrs Brown of Falkland's repertoire.

The Music

Only one source, manuscript B, includes the music to Mrs Brown's ballads. At the time of recording, the texts of C also had accompanying music, but this is not now to be found. The fifteen tunes in B are each given in one line, set above the text, except in the case of the last ballad, "The cruel Sister" (p. 78), where the words of the first verse are matched to the tune. This, coupled with the fact that a fresh page was always used for a new ballad, makes it very likely that the words were written first, leaving space for one line of music above the text. This could explain why the music is sometimes rather crammed into one line, instead of being spread out over two lines (see Brown 3 "Willy o' Douglass-Dale" for example).

On the left-hand side of the stave, instructions are given as to tempo or singing style to be adopted. These instructions are in the hand of Robert Eden Scott and he was also the one who wrote out the tunes, according to the letters by his grandfather and aunt quoted above. That he was at that time about fourteen years of age and "a meer novice in musick" is reflected in his manner of recording. Sometimes notes are missing from a bar or the time signature is problematic. He generally tended to get the timing and rhythm wrong, as Bronson explains, "because it is much less likely that an amateur who can set down any notes at all, will get his notes wrong than that he will mistake the time values" ("Professor Child" 188). Bronson had the original manuscript available to him only for Child 247 "Lady Elspat" in his fourth and final volume of 1972, commenting in his notes to that ballad that it "was lately recovered at Aldourie Castle" (*TT* 4: 13). For the other ballads he was dependent on Ritson's and Scott's transcripts of B. He attempted to reconstruct, where possible, Mrs Brown's tunes by means of comparison with the texts and the tunes from other sources. These "conjectures" as to Mrs Brown's tunes are given in his *Traditional Tunes of the Child Ballads* along with the original records, sometimes transposed to a different key. Bronson's conjectures have been re-set by Katherine Campbell along with the words of the opening stanzas for this edition and appear in the Notes.

What Anne Dhu McLucas observed in the Harris repertoire is, albeit for different reasons, also true for the Brown repertoire: "even a musically literate ballad scholar might find the task of making sense of the tunes with their texts unnecessarily daunting" (see *Harris Repertoire*, ed. Lyle et al. xxxvii) and thus "singable" versions of Mrs Brown's ballads have been supplied, from Bronson in all cases, and in addition, in five cases (Nos 2, 8, 17, 18 and 21) also from Sophia Scott's Music Book. Ailie Munro has pointed out that these conjectures are far too stifled and scholarly and less singable than the versions sung by Walter Scott's daughter Sophia (Munro 215).

Given that only two of Mrs Brown's ballads have refrains, Bronson suspects Robert Eden Scott of not having recorded everything: "For a set of ballads taken down from actual singing, this is a very scanty proportion of refrains; and we may reasonably suspect that not everything was put into the record" (*TT* 1: 101).

Bronson discusses at length why "no great reliance" is to be placed upon their "representations" of Mrs Brown's actual singing (see "Professor Child" 186), and Gavin Greig in *Folk Song in Buchan* (52) even criticises the airs as "noted by a man of defective musicianship". Rhythm and mode seem to be the main problems. Brown 11 ("Lady Maisry") is a good example of these inconsistencies of scales and modes: is it Dorian (and Robert Eden Scott had simply "started on a new stave a note above the true one at the beginning of the fourth – or perhaps even the third – phrase, and kept it up consistently to the end" (*TT* 2: 50)), or Phrygian or Æolian? Whatever the answer, it will only be of interest to the scholar and is of little consequence to the traditional singer. In fact, classical standards of music do not apply to traditional singing and modal "inconsistencies", just like free rhythm, were the performance practice among traditional singers in eighteenth- and nineteenth-century Scotland.

Perhaps Robert Eden Scott captures more of his aunt's plaintive singing style than Bronson and Greig give him credit for. His tunes suggest a type of chanting, i.e. a monotonous, repetitive type of singing. It should also be borne in mind that the musical notation prefixed to the words was never intended to give William Tytler more than "some imperfect notion of the airs, or rather lilts, to which they were sung". Thus, "notwithstanding their incorrectness" (see Gordon's letter to Fraser Tytler, 13 January 1793), these melodies are the only ones documenting Mrs Brown's singing that have so far been discovered. The loss of the music for the ballads in C is very regrettable, especially in light of Mrs Brown's statement that "each [text] has its own appropriate tune & some of them I think are pretty ennough" (see her letter to Fraser Tytler, 17 March 1800). To Gordon and Tytler, these melodies were peculiar and unique. They had not come across them before, despite the fact that they were active themselves in music-making. They are "all in the plaintive stile as indeed all the old scotch melodys are ~~which I ever heard~~ that I, ever heard!" explains Mrs Brown in her letter to Tytler's son (17 March 1800).

We do not know whether Mrs Brown played a musical instrument herself; she certainly came from a musical family and the most likely instruments for her to play would have been guitar or spinet. Her sister Elizabeth in Virginia gave orders to buy such musical instruments in London and her sister Margaret spent a great deal of her time in the company of a musical family in Aberdeen who performed Handel's compositions (see MSS 1 P4686 at the VHS). Thomas Gordon must also have played an instrument, most likely one of the gentlemen's instruments such as the violin, the cello or the transverse flute (see Johnson, "Musical Traditions" 92), for this was a requirement for membership of the Musical Society of Aberdeen (see Walker Collection at the APL).

Robert Eden Scott is known to have played the transverse flute, an instrument that was made popular in Britain by the Hanoverian monarchs, hence known as the German flute. As Mrs Brown writes to her sister, Robert Eden Scott's mother, in Virginia when the boy was fifteen years old: "He inherits your musical talent & tho in a manner self taught can play anything that is not very difficult at sight upon the German flute" (21 October 1784; in Mss 1 P4686 at the VHS).

And this instrument might also be the clue to the musical setting of Mrs Brown's ballads by Robert Eden Scott. The music in B has certainly been added later (see above) and does not always go well together with the words. The settings in fact resemble instrumental settings. When ordered by his grandfather Thomas Gordon to set down the tunes from Mrs Brown's singing, Robert Eden Scott appears to have first tried to master it on his German flute and then set it down with his instrument in hand. This theory is supported by the fact that none of the melodies go beyond the lowest range of the German flute. Another interesting pointer in support of this theory can be found at the beginning of Brown 15, "Willie's Lady". It is a double parallel-angled stroke that signals a flourish or a decoration of some kind, most likely of the first note. In the seventeenth and early eighteenth centuries, this symbol was widely used for keyboard works and for the German flute. Thus, there can be no doubt that Mrs Brown's melodies were mediated by Robert Eden Scott's German flute. It is interesting to observe that this instrument was also played in the Tytler family, the original recipients of Brown B and Brown C. A manuscript with "Original Pieces and Arrangements for Violin or Flute" (Add. 35043 at BL) belonged to Alexander Fraser Tytler – his name and the year 1779 appear in his handwriting on the title page. This manuscript was obviously used for teaching since the music has been arranged as suites or lessons and detailed instructions are given on how to play the flute (see inside back cover).

However inaccurately Mrs Brown's tunes may have been taken down, it is clear that they may differ considerably from other tunes to the same ballad (see Brown 4, "Young Bekie", and Brown 18, "The twa Sisters"). Moreover, B is until now the only source for the tunes of "Clark Colven", "Kempion", "King Henry" and "Willie's Lady". It may indeed be that their "plaintive stile" (as Mrs Brown called it) was the hallmark of a vibrant oral tradition. Certainly, by being amongst the oldest and, in four cases, the only records of ballad tunes, they are invaluable to our understanding of an early Scottish ballad tradition.

Editorial Conventions

All the titles are given as in the sources, except that full stops have been omitted. For ease of reference, Child ballad numbers are added for this edition.

Part I presents all the ballads in manuscript A (1781–83). They are given in the original order with their parallel version from B (1783) or C (1800) set on facing pages. Part II presents the ballads in B (1783), C (1800), D (1800–01) and E (1806) that have no parallels in A.

The music in Brown B is reproduced in facsimile at the head of the B ballad text while the computer-set music notation is shown opposite at the head of the Brown A text in all cases except Brown 21 ("Clark Colven"), where there is no A text. In this case the computer-set music notation has been placed after the manuscript music.

The manuscript has been reproduced faithfully. In the manuscripts, quotation marks are used inconsistently. An opening quotation mark is not always closed nor a closed one opened, and nor is direct speech – even within one ballad text – consistently indicated by quotation marks. Furthermore, in Brown A double quotation marks are the rule, in Brown B single ones are used. For this edition, double quotation marks are adopted throughout and opening or closing quotation marks are completed. Missing quotation marks, however, are not added. Letters appearing in superscript are not elevated in this edition but are underlined. Each line of verse starts with a capital letter.

Specific to this first critical edition of Mrs Brown's ballad repertoire is the numbering of ballad stanzas. It is merely provided for better referencing and does not correspond to the witnesses, for in the manuscripts the numbering is either erratic (and sometimes fails to reflect the stanzaic structure) or absent altogether. Brown A is numbered throughout but, from the occasional omission of a stanza and the placing of numbers between lines, and not least from the difference in ink, it is evident that the numbers were added later by Robert Jamieson and formed no part of the original text. B has no numbering of stanzas and only the music indicates the length of a stanza for the lines are not separated by any spaces. Brown C, written by Mrs Brown herself, has no indication as to the length of a stanza, either by numbering or by blank lines.

The ballad texts are in quatrains with occasional six-line stanzas interspersed. In the case of the ballad stanza, i.e. a stanza with four-three-four-three beats and *abcb* rhyme scheme, the alternate lines are indented. As clearly indicated by the music, Brown 15 ("Willie's Lady") and Brown 16 ("Chil Brenton") consist of four-line verses in two couplets; Brown 30 ("Baron of Braikley") and Brown 31 ("Allan O Maut") are set in couplets.

In the Notes, a summary of the ballad is given first and this is followed by the textual notes. In cases where there is music, the direction for singing in Brown B is included. After this appears a reconstruction by Bronson (and sometimes also a reconstruction by Sophia Scott) and editorial comments on the tune.

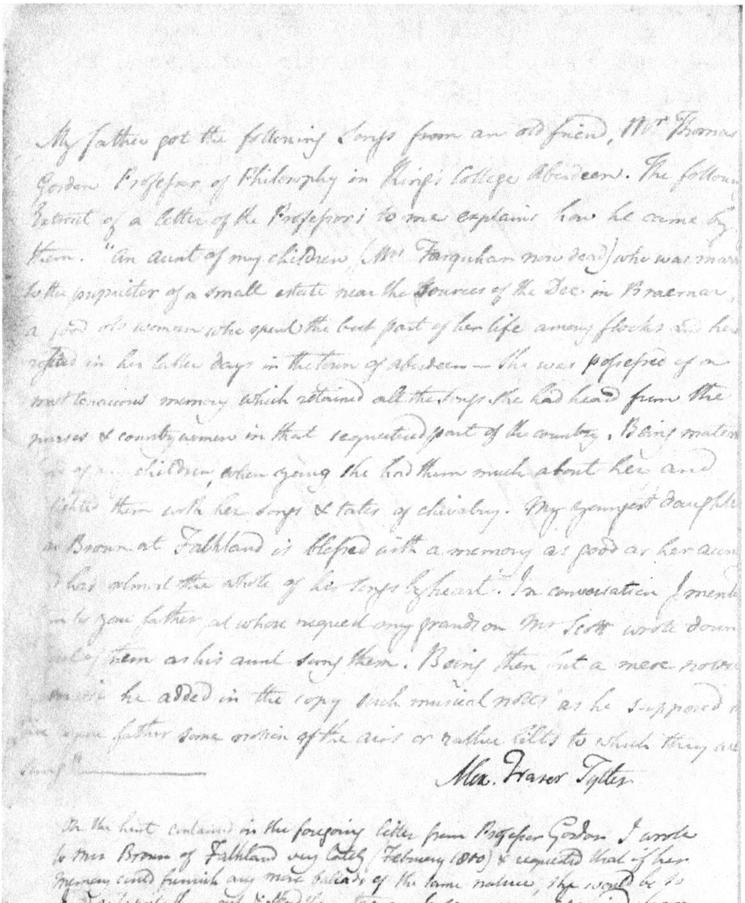

My father got the following Songs from an old friend, Mr Thomas Gordon Professor of Philosophy in King's College Aberdeen. The following Extract of a letter of the Professor's to me explains how he came by them. "An aunt of my children (Mrs Farquhar now dead) who was married to the proprietor of a small estate near the Sources of the Dee in Braemar, a good old woman who spent the best part of her life among flocks and herds, resided in her latter days in the town of Aberdeen — She was possessed of a most tenacious memory which retained all the songs she had heard from the nurses & countrywomen in that sequestered part of the country. Being maternally [illegible] of my children when young she had them much about her and delighted them with her songs & tales of chivalry. My youngest daughter Mrs Brown at Falkland is blessed with a memory as good as her aunt, and has almost the whole of her songs by heart. In conversation I mentioned this to your father at whose request my grandson Mr Scott wrote down [illegible] of them as his aunt sung them. Being then but a mere novice in music he added in the copy such musical notes as he supposed [illegible] give your father some notion of the airs or rather lilts to which they are sung."

Alex. Fraser Tytler

On the hint contained in the foregoing letter from Professor Gordon I wrote to Mrs Brown of Falkland very lately (February 1800) & requested that if her memory could furnish any more ballads of the same nature, she would be so kind as to write them out & send them to me. In consequence I received from her nine other ballads, some of them extremely curious & all of considerable antiquity, together with the music to which they are sung

Figure 9:
Facsimile of inside front cover of B
in Alexander Fraser Tytler's hand

The Ballad Titles

Part I:
Ballads in A with their Parallels from B and C

1.	A	Rose the red & White Lilly
	B	Rose the Red, & White Lilly (with tune)
2.	A	Jack the little Scot
	B	Jack the Little Scot (*with tune*)
3.	A	Willy o Douglass dale
	B	Willie o' Douglass-Dale (*with tune*)
4.	A	Young Bekie
	B	Young Bekie (*with tune*)
5.	A	Young Bicham
6.	A	The gay goss hawk
	B	The Gay Goss-Hawk (*with tune*)
7.	A	Brown Adam
	B	Brown Adam (*with tune*)
8.	A	Lady Elspat
	B	Lady Elzpat (*with tune*)
9.	A	Lady Jane
10.	A	Burd Ellen
	C	Lord John and Bird Ellen
11.	A	Lady Maisry
	B	Lady Maisery (*with tune*)
12.	A	Fair Anny
	C	Love Gregor
13.	A	Kempion
	B	Kempion (*with tune*)
14.	A	King Henry
	B	King Henry (*with tune*)
15.	A	Sweet Willy
	B	Willie's Lady (*with tune*)
16.	A	Gil Brenton
	B	Chil Brenton (*with tune*)
17.	A	Brown Robin
	B	Brown Robin (*with tune*)
18.	A	The twa Sisters
	B	The Cruel Sister (*with tune*)

19.	A	Allison Gross
20.	A	The bonny birdy

Part II:
Ballads in B, C, D and E without Parallels in A

21.	B	Clark Colven (*with tune*)
22.	C	Thomas Rymer, & Queen of Elfland
23.	C	Fa'se Footrage
24.	C	Jellon Grame and Lillie Flower
25.	C	The bonny Earl of Livingston
26.	C	Bonny Bee Ho'm
27.	C	Bonny Foot-Boy
28.	C	Cruel Brother Or The Bride's Testament
29.	D	Bonny Baby Livingston
	E	Bonny Baby Livingston
30.	D	The Baron of Braikly
31.	D	Allan O Maut
32.	E	Willie and May Margaret
33.	E	Hugh of Lincoln
34.	E	Lamkin
35.	E	The Birth of Robin Hood

Texts

Part I:

Ballads in A
with their Parallels
from B and C

A

1. Rose the red & White Lilly [Child 103]

p. 1

1. O Rose the red and White Lilly
   Their mother dear was dead
   And their father married an ill woman
   Wish'd them twa little guede
2. Yet she had twa as fu' fair Sons
   As eer brake manis bread
   And the tane of them loed her White Lilly
   An' the tither lood Rose the Red
3. O Biggit ha they a bigly bow'r
   And strawn it oer wi San'
   And there was mair mirth i' the Ladies bowr.
   Than in a their fathers lan
4. But out it spake their Step-mother,
   Wha stood a little foreby
   "I hope to live and play the prank
   Sal gar your loud sang ly."
5. She's call'd upon her eldest son
   "Come here my son to me
   It fears me sair my eldest son;
   That ye maun sail the Sea."
6. "Gin it fear you sair my Mither dear,
   Your bidding I maun dee
   But be never war to Rose the Red
   Than ye ha' been to me."
7. "O had your tongue my eldest son
   For sma sal be her part
   You'll nae get a kiss o' her comely mouth
   Gin your very fair heart should break"
8. She s call'd upon her younges son
   "Come here my son to me
   It fears me sair my youngest Son
   That ye maun sail the sea."

1. Rose the Red, & White Lilly [Child 103]

1. O Rose the red & White Lilly p. 37
Their mother dear was dead
An' their father married an ill woman,
Wist them twa little gueed.
2. But she had twa as fu' fair sons
As e'er brak' manis bread,
An' the teen o' them loo'd her white Lilly,
An' the tither, Rose the Red.
3. O bigged ha' they a bigly bow'r,
An' strawn it o'er wi' sand,
An' there was mair mirth i' the Ladies' bow'r,
Nor in a' their father's land.
4. But out it spake their step-mother,
Who stood a little foreby,
"I hope to live & play the prank,
Shall gar your loud sang lie."
5. She's call'd upon her eldest son,
"Come here my son to me,
It fears me sair my eldest son
That you man sail the sea."
6. "An' 't fear you sair my mother dear, p. 38
Your bidding I man dee,
But be never war to Rose the red,
Than ye have been to me."
7. "O had your tongue my eldest son,
For sma' shall be her part,
Ye's nae get ae kiss o' her comely mouth,
An' your very fair heart shou'd break."
8. She's call'd upon her youngest son,
"Come here my son to me
It fears me sair my youngest son,
That ye man sail the sea."

9. "Gin it fear you sair my mither dear
Your bidding I maun dee
But be never war to White Lilly
Than ye ha been to me."

10. "O haud your tongue my youngest son
For sma sall be her part
You'll nee'r get a kiss o her comely mouth.
Tho your very fair heart should break"

11. When Rose the Red and White Lilly
Saw their twa loves were gane
Then stopped ha they their loud loud sang
And tane up the still mournin
And their Step mother stood listnin by
To hear the Ladies mean.

12. Then out it spake her White Lilly.
My sister we'll be gane
Why should we stay in Barnsdale
To waste our youth in pain?

13. Then cutted ha they their Green cloathing
A little below their knee
An' sae ha' they they there Yallow hair
A little aboon there bree
An' they've doen them to haely chapel
Was christened by our Lady

p. 2 14. There ha' they chang'd their ain twa names
Sae far frae ony town
An' the tane o' them Hight Sweet Willy
An the tither o' them Roge the roun

15. Between this twa a vow was made
An they sware it to fulfil
That at three blasts o' a bugle horn
She'd come her sister till

16. Now sweet Willy's gane to the kingis court
Her true love for to see
An' Roge the roun' to good green wood
Brown Robins man to be

17. As it fell out upon a day
They a' did put the Stane
Full seven foot ayont them a'
She gar'd the puttin stane gang.

9. "An' 't fear you sair my mother dear,
Your bidding I man dee,
But be never war to White Lilly,
Nor ye have been to me."
10. "O had your tongue my youngest son,
For sma shall be her part,
You'se nae get ae kiss o' her comely mouth
Tho' your very fair heart shou'd break."
11. When Rose the red & white Lilly,
Saw their twa loves was gane,
Soon did they drop the loud, loud sang,
Took up the still mourning.
An' their step mother stood a little foreby, p. 39
To hear the Ladies' moan.
12. An' out it spake her white Lilly,
"My sister we'll be gane,
Why shou'd we stay in Barnsdale,
To mourn our bow'r within."
13. O cutted ha' they their green cloathing
A little abeen their knee,
An' sae ha' they their yallow hair,
A little abeen their bree;
An' theyve ta'en them to a haely chapel
Was christen'd by our Lady.
14. O they ha' changed their twa names,
Sae far frae ony town,
An' the teen o' them hight Sweet Willy,
An' the tither Roge the round.
15. Between this twa a promise is,
An' they swear it to fulfil,
Whene'er th' ane blew a bugle horn,
She'd come her sister 'till.
16. Sweet Willy's gane to the king's court,
Her true love for to see,
An' Roge the round to good green wood,
Brown Robin's man to be.
17. O it fell once upon a day, p. 40
That they did put the stane,
An' seven feet ayont them a'
She's gar't the putting stane gang.

18. She lean'd her back against an oak
And gae a loud Ohone!
Then out it spake him brown Robin
"But thats a Womans moan."

19. "O ken ye by my red rose lip?
Or by my Yallow hair?
Or ken ye by my milk white breast,
For ye never saw it bare."

20. I ken no by your red rose lip
Nor by your Yallow hair
Nor ken I by your milk white breast
For I never saw it bare
But come to your bowr whaever sae likes
Will find a lady there

21. "O gin ye come to my bow'r within,
Thro' fraud deceit or guile
Wi this same bran thats in my han'
I sear I will the kill"

22. "But I will come thy bowr within
An' spear nae leave" quoth he
"An' this same bran thats i' my han'
I sall ware back on the"

23. About the tenth hour of the night
The Ladies bower door was broken
An' eer the first howr of the day
The bonny knave bairn was gotten

24. When days were gane & months were run
The lady took travailing
An sair she cry'd for a bowr woman
For to wait her upon

25. Then out it spake him brown Robin
Now what needs a this din
For what cou'd any woman do
But I cou'd do the same

26. "Twas never my mithers fashion" she says
"Nor sall it ever be mine
p. 3 That belted k[n]ights shou'd ee'r remain
Where ladies dreeid their pine.

18. She lean'd her back against an oak
    An' gae a cauld ohon!
An' out it speaks him brown Robin,
    "But that's a woman's moan."
19. "O kent ye by my red rose lips,
    Or by my yallow hair,
Or kent ye by my milke white breast
    For ye never saw it bare."
20. "I kent nae by your red rose lips,
    Nor by your yallow hair,
But come to your bo'wr wha ever sae likes,
    They'll find a Lady there."

21. "O gin you come my bow'r within
    Thro' fraud deceit or guile,
Wi' this same brand thats i' my hand,
    I vow I will thee kill;"
22. "O I will come your bow'r within
    An' ask nae leave," quoth he,
"An' this same brand that's i' my hand
    I'll ware it back on thee."
23. About the tenth hour i' the night p. 41
    The Lady's bow'r door was broken,
An' or the first hour o' the day,
    The bonny knave bairn was gotten.
24. Whan days was gane, & months was come,
    The Lady took travelling,
An' ay she cried for a bow'r woman,
    For to wait her upon.
25. O out it speaks him Brown Robin,
    Says, "what means a' this din?
For what can ony woman dee?
    But I can dee the same?"
26. "'Twas never my mother's fashion," she says,
    "Nor shall it e'er be mine,
That belted knights shou'd e'er remain
    White Ladys dried their pine.

27. "But ye take up that bugle horn
An blaw a blast for me
I ha' a brother i the kingis court
Will come me quickly ti'."

28. O gin ye ha' a brither on earth,
That ye love better nor me
Ye blaw the horn yoursel' he says
For ae blast I winna gie

29. She's set the horn till her mouth
And she's blawn three blasts sae shrill
Sweet Willy heard i' the kingis court
And came her quckly till

30. Then up it started Brown Robin
An an angry man was he
There comes nae man this bow'r within
But first must fight wi me

31. O they hae fought that bowr within
Till the sun was gaing down
Till drops o blude frae rose the Red,
Came hailing to the groun

32. She lean'd her back against the wa.
Says Robin let a be
For it is a lady born and bred,
Thats foughten sae well wi thee

33. O seven foot he lap a back
Says alas and wae is me
I never wisht in a my life
A womans blude to see
An a for the sake of ae fair maid
Whose name was White lilly.

34. Then out it spake her White Lilly
An a hearty laugh leugh she
She's lived wi you this year an mair
Tho ye kentna it was she." –

35. Now word has gane thro a the lan
Before a month was done
That brown Robins man in good green wood
Had born a bonny young son

27. "But up you tak that bugle horn,
An blaw a blast for me,
I have a brother i' the king's court,
Will come me quickly ti'."
28. "O gin you ha' a brother on earth,
That ye prefer to me,
Ye blaw the horn yoursel'" he says,
"For a blast I winna gie."
29. She's ta'en the horn until her hand, p. 42
An' she's blawn a blast sae shrill,
That her sister heard it in the king's court,
An' came her quickly 'till.
30. O up it starts him Brown Robin
An' swears by our Lady,
"Nae man shall come this bow'r within
But first man fight wi' me."
31. O they ha' fought that bow'r within,
'Till the sun was going down,
'Till draps o' bleed frae Rose the Red
Came haling to the ground.
32. She leant her back against the wa',
Says "Robin lat a be,
For 'tis a Lady bred & born,
That's fought so well wi' thee."
33. O seven foot he started back,
Says "alas! & woe is me!
For I wish'd never in a' my life,
A woman's blood to see;
An' a' for the sake o' ae fair maid
Whose name was white Lilly."
34. O out it spake her white Lilly,
And leugh right heartily,
"She's been wi' you this year & mair, p. 43
Tho' ye kent nae it was she." –
35. Now word has spred thro' a' the land,
Before a month was gone,
That Brown Robin's man in good green-wood,
Had born a bonny young son.

36. The word has gane to the kingis court
    An to the king himsel
Now by my fay the king could say
    The like was never heard tell
37. Then out it spake him bold Arthur
    An a hearty laugh leugh he
I trow some may has play'd the loun
    And fled her ain country
38. Bring me my steed then cry'd the king
    My bow and arrows keen
I'l ride mysel to good green wood
    An see whats to be seen
p. 4 39. An't please your Grace said bold Arthur
    My liege I ll gang you wi
An' try to fin a little foot page
    Thats stray'd awa frae me
40. O they've hunted i the good green wood
    The buck but an the rae
An' they drew near Brown Robins bow'r
    About the close of day
41. Then out it spake the king in hast
    Say's Arthur look an see
Gin that be no your little foot page
    That leans against yon tree
42. Then Arthur took his bugle horn
    An blew a blast sae shrill
Sweet Willy started at the sound
    An ran him quckly till
43. "O wanted ye your meat Willy
    Or wanted ye your fee
Or gat ye ever an angry word
    That ye ran awa frae me"
44. I wanted nought my master dear
    To me ye ay was good
I came but to see my ae brother
    That wons in this green wood
45. Then out it spake the king again
    Says "bonny boy tell to me
Wha lives into yon bigly bowr
    Stands by yon green oak tree"

36. The word gi'd to the king his court,
    And to the king himsell,
"Now by my fay" the king did say,
    "The like was never heard tell."
37. Then out it spake him bold Arthur,
    An' a hearty laugh leugh he,
"I true some May has play'd the loon,
    An' fled her ain country."
38. "Bring me my steed the king then cried,
    My bow, & arrows keen,
I'll go & hunt in good green-wood,
    And see what's to be seen."
39. "An't please your grace said bold Arthur,
    My liege I'll gang you wi'
An' see gin I meet wi' a bonny foot page,
    That's stray'd awa' frae me."
40. They've hunted up, & they've hunted down,
    The buck, but & the rae,
An they drew near Brown Robin's bow'r, p. 44
    About the close o' day.
41. Then out it spake the king himsel'
    Says "Arthur look & see,
Gin that be not your bonny foot page,
    That leans against yon tree."
42. O Arthur's tae'n a bugle horn,
    An' blawn a blast sae shrill,
Sweet Willie started at the sound,
    And ran him quickly 'till.
43. "O wanted ye your meat Willie,
    Or wanted ye your fee,
Or got you e'er an angry word
    That you ran awa' frae me."
44. "I wanted nought my master dear,
    To me ye ay was gude,
I came to see my ae brother,
    Who wons in this green wood."
45. Then out it spake the king again,
    "My boy tell to me,
Who lives into that bigly bow'r
    Stands by yon green oak-tree."

46. O pardon me says sweet Willy
    "My liege I dare no tell
An' I pray you go no near that bow'r
    For fear they do you fell"
47. O haud your tongue my bonny boy
    For I winna be said nay
But I will gang that bow'r within.
    Betide me well or wae
48. They've lighted off their milk white steeds
    An saftly enter'd in
An' there they saw her White Lilly
    Nursing her bonny yong son
49. "Now by the rood" the the king cou'd say
    This is a comely sight
I trow instead of a Forresters man
    This is a Lady bright
50. Then out it spake her Rose the red
    An fell low down on her knee
O pardon us my gracious liege
    An our story I'll tell thee.
51. "Our father was a wealthy lord
    That won'd in Barnsdale
But we had a wicked step-mother
    That wrought us meickle bale
p. 5 52. "Yet she had twa as fu fair sons
    As ever the sun did see
An' the tane o them lood my sister dear
    An the tither say'd he lood me"
53. Then out it speke him bold Arthur
    As by the king he stood
Now by the faith o my body
    This shou'd be Rose the red.

54. Then in it came him Brown Robin
    Frae hunting o the deer
But whan he saw the king was there
    He started back for fear

46. "O pardon me" said Sweet Willy,
    "My liege I darna' tell,
I pray you gang nae near that bow'r,
    For fear they shou'd you fell."
47. "O had your tongue my bonny boy, p. 45
    For I winna' be said nae,
But I will gang that bow'r within,
    Betide me well or wae."
48. They've lighted off their milke-white steeds,
    An' saftly enter'd in,
An there they saw her White Lilly,
    Nursing her bonny young son.
49. "Now by the mass," the king then said,
    "This is a comely sight,
I true instead of a forrester's man,
    This is a Lady bright."
50. Then out it spake her Rose the red,
    An' fell low down on her knee,
"O pardon us my gracious liege,
    An' our story I'll tell thee.
51. "Our father is a wealthy Lord
    Lives into Barnsdale,
But we had a wicked step mother,
    That wrought us meickle bale:
52. "Yet she had twa as fu' fair sons
    As e'er the sun did see,
And the tane o' them lov'd my sister dear,
    And the tither said he lov'd me."
53. Then out it cried him bold Arthur, p. 46
    As by the king he steed,
"Now by the faith o' my body,
    This shou'd be Rose the red."
54. The king has sent for robes o' green,
    And girdles o' shining gold,
And soon the Ladies' dress'd themsels
    Most glorious to behold.
55. Then in it came him Brown Robin,
    Frae hunting o' the Deer,
But whan he saw the king himsel'
    He started back for fear.

55. The king has taen him by the hand
An bade him naething dread
Says ye maun leave the good green wood.
Come to the court wi speed
56. Then up he took White Lilly s son
An set him on his knee
Says gin ye live to wield a bran
My bowman ye sall bee
57. The king he sent for robes of green
An girdles o shinning gold
He gart the ladies be array'd
Most comely to behold
58. They've done them unto Mary kirk
An' there gat fair wedding
An fan the news spread oer the lan
For joy the bells did ring
59. Then out it spake her Rose the red
An a hearty laugh leugh she
I wonder what would our step dame say
Gin she this sight did see

56. The king has ta'en him by the han',
    An' bade him nothing dread,
But said he, "leave the good green wood,
    And come to the court wi' speed."
57. Then up has he ta'en white Lilly's son,
    An' set him on his knee,
Says "gin ye live to wield a bran'
    My bowman ye shall be."

58. They've done them to the haely chapel,
    An' there got fair wedding,
An' whan they came to the king'is court,
    For joy the bells did ring. –

A

2. Jack the little Scot [Child 99]

p. 5 1. O Johney was as brave a knight
As ever saild the sea
An he's done him to the English court
To serve for meat and fee

2. He had nae been in fair England
But yet a little while
Untill the kingis ae daughter
To Johney proves wi chil'.

3. O word's come to the king himsel
In his chair where he sat
That his ae daughter was wi bairn
To Jack the little Scott

4. Gin this be true that I do hear
As I trust well it be
Ye pit her into prison strong
An' starve her till she die

p. 6 5. O Johneys on to fair Scotland
Awot he went wi speed
An he has left the kingis court
Awot good was his need

6. O it fell once upon a day
That Johney he thought lang
An he's gane to the good green wood
As fast as he cou'd gang

7. "O whare will I get a bonny boy
To rin my errand soon?
That will rin into fair England
An haste him back again"

8. O up it starts a bonny boy
Gold yallow was his hair
I wist his mither meickle joy
His bonny love mieckle mair

2. Jack the Little Scot [Child 99]

1. Johny was as brave a knight p. 11
As ever sail'd the sea,
And he is to the English court
To serve for meat & fee.
2. He had nae been in fair England
But yet a little while,
Until the king his ae daughter
To Johny grows wi' chil'.
3. O word's come to the king himsel'
In his chair where he sat,
That his ae daughter was wi' bairn
To Jack the little Scot.
4. "Gin this be true 'at I do hear,
As I trust well it be,
Ye put her into prison strong
And starve her 'till she dee."
5. O Johny's on to fair Scotland,
I wot he went wi' speed,
And he has left the king his court
I wot good was his need.
6. O it fell once upon a day, p. 12
That Johny he thought lang,
An' he's doen him to the good green wood
As fast as he cou'd gang.
7. "O whare'll I get a bonny boy,
To run my errand seen,
That will gang unto fair England,
An' haste him back again."
8. O up it starts a bonny boy
Gold yallow was his hair,
I wish his mother meickle joy,
His bonny love meickle mair.

9. O here am I a bonny boy
Will rin your errand soon
I will gang into fair England
An come right soon again

10. O whan he came to broken briggs
He bent his bow and swam
An whan he came to the green grass growan
He slackèd his shoone & ran

11. Whan he came to yon high castil
He ran it roun' about.
An there he saw the kings daughter
At the window looking out.

12. O heres a sark o' silk Lady.
Your ain han' sew'd the sleeve
Your bidden come to fair Scotlan,
Speer nane o' your parents leave

13. Ha take this sark o silk Lady
Your ain han sew'd the gare
Your'e bidden come to good green wood
Love Johney waits you there

14. She's turn'd her right and roun about
The tear was in her ee
How can I come to my true love
Except I had wings to flee?

15. Here am I kept wi bars and bolts
Most grievous to behold
My breast plates o' the sturdy steel
Instead of the beaten gold

16. But tak this purse my bonny boy
Ye well deserve a fee
An bear this letter to my love
An tell him what you see

17. Then quickly ran the bonny boy
Again to Scotlan fair
An soon he reach'd Pitnachtons tow'rs
An soon found Johney there

p. 7 18. He pat the letter in his han'
An tau'l him what he sa
But e'er he half the letter read
He loote the tears doun fa'.

9. "O here am I a bonny boy
   Will run your errand soon,
I will gang unto fair England,
   An' come right soon again."
10. O whan he came to broken brigs
   He bent his bow & swam,
And whan he came to the green grass grow'n
   He slack'd his sheen & ran.
11. Whan he came to yon high castle, p. 13
   He ran it round about,
And there he saw the king's daughter
   At the window looking out.
12. "O here's a sark o' silk, Lady
   Your ain hand sew'd the sleeve
Your bidden come to fair Scotland,
   Speer nane o' your parents' leave.
13. "Ha' tak' this sark o' silk, Lady,
   Your ain hand sew'd the gare,
Your bidden come to good green wood
   Love Johny waits you there."
14. She's turn'd her right, & round about,
   The tear was in her ee,
"How can I come to my true love
   Except I had wings to flee.
15. "Here am I kept wi' bars & bolts,
   Most grievous to behold,
My breast-plate's o' the sturdy steel,
   Instead o' the beaten gold.
16. But tak' this purse, my bonny boy, p. 14
   Ye well deserve a fee,
An' bear this letter to my love,
   And tell him what you see."
17. Then quickly ran the bonny boy,
   Again to Scotland fair,
An' soon he reach'd Pitnachton's tow'rs
   And soon found Johny there.
18. He pat the letter in his hand,
   An' taul' him what he saw,
But e'er he half the letter read,
   He leet the tears down fa'.

19. O I will gae back to fair Englan
    Tho death shou'd me betide
    An I will relieve the damesel
    That lay last by my side.
20. Then out it spake his father dear
    My son you are to blame
    An gin your catch'd on English groun
    I fear you'll nee'r win hame
21. Then out it spake a valiant knight
    Johnys best friend was he
    I can commaun five hunder men
    An I'll his surety be
22. The firstin town that they came 'till
    They gar'd the bells be rung
    An the nextin town that they came 'till
    They gar'd the mess be sung
23. The thirdin town that they came 'till
    They gar'd the drums beat roun
    The king but an his nobles a
    Was startld at the soun
24. Whan they came to the kings palace
    They rade it roun about
    An there they saw the king himsel
    At the window looking out
25. Is this the duke o Albany
    Or James the Scottish king
    Or are ye some great foreign lord
    Thats come a visiting
26. Im nae the duke of Albany
    Nor James the Scottish king
    But I'm a valiant Scottish knight
    Pitnachton is my name
27. O if Pitnachton be your name
    As I trust well it be
    The morn or I tast meat or drink
    You shall be hanged hi
28. Then out it spake the valiant knight
    That came brave Johney wi
    Behold five hunder bowmen bold
    Will die to set him free

19. "O I'll gae back to fair England,
    Tho' death shou'd me betide,
An' I'll relieve the Damesel,
    That lay last by my side."
20. Then out it spake his father dear,
    "My son you are to blame,
An' gin you're catch'd in English ground,
    I fear you'll ne'er win hame."
21. Then out it spake a valiant knight,
    Johny's best friend was he,
"I can command five hundred men,
    An' his surety I will be."
22. The firstin town that they came 'till p. 15
    They gar'd the bells be rung,
The nextin town that they came 'till
    They gar'd the mess be sung:
23. The thirdin town that they came 'till
    They gar'd the drums beat round,
The king but & his nobles a'
    Was startled at the sound.
24. Whan they came 'till the king's palace,
    They rode it round about,
An' there they saw the king himsel'
    At the window looking out.
25. "Is this the Duke of Albany,
    Or James the Scottish king,
Or are you some great foreign Lord
    That's come a visiting."
26. "I'm no the Duke of Albany
    Nor yet the Scottish king,
But I'm a valiant Scottish knight
    Pitnachton is my name."
27. "O if Pitnachton be your name,
    As I trust well it be,
The morn e'er I taste meat or drink,
    You shall be hanged hi'."
28. Then out it spake the valiant knight p. 16
    That came brave Johny wi',
"Behold five hundred bowmen bold,
    Will die or set him free."

29. Then out it spake the king again
An a scornfu' laugh leugh he
I have an Italion i my house
Will fight you three by three

30. O grant me a boon brave Johney cried
Bring your Italian here
Then if he fall beneath my sword
I've won your daughter dear

p. 8 31. Then out it came that Italian
An a gurious ghost was he
Upo' the point o' Johneys sword
This Italian did die

32. Out has he draw'n his lang lang bran
Struck it across the plain
Is there any more o' your English dogs
That you want to be slain?

33. A clark a clark the king then cried
To write her tocher free.
A priest a priest says love Johney
To marry my love & me.

34. I'm seeking nane o your gold he says
Nor of your silver clear
I only seek your daughter fair
Whose love has cost her deear

29. Then out it spake the king again,
    An' a scornfu' laugh leugh he,
"I have an Italian i' my house,
    Will fight you three by three."
30. "O grant me a boon" brave Johny cried,
    "Bring out your Italian here,
Then if he falls beneath my sword,
    I've won your daughter dear."
31. Then out it came this Italian,
    An' a gurious ghost was he,
Upo' the point o' Johny's sword,
    This Italian did dee.
32. Out has he drawn his lang lang bran
    Struck it across the plain,
"Is there any more o' your English dogs,
    That you want for to be slain."
33. "A Clark, a Clark" then cried the king,
    "To write her tocher free:"
"A priest, a priest says love Johny,
    To marry my love, & me."

A

3. Willy o Douglass dale [Child 101]

p. 8

1. O Willy was as brave a lord
   As ever saild the sea
   And he has gane to the English court
   To serve for meat and fee
2. He had nae been at the kingis court
   A twelvemonth and a day
   Till he long'd for a sight o' the kings daughter
   But ane he cou'd never see
3. O it fell ance upon a day
   To the green wood she has gane
   An Willy he has follow'd her
   With the clear light o' the moon
4. He looted him low. By her did go
   Wi his hat intill his hand
   O whats your will wi me Sir Knight
   I pray keep your hat on
5. O I am not a knight Madam
   Nor never thinks to be
   For I am Willy o Douglass dale
   An I serve for meat and fee
6. "O I'll gang to my Bow'r" she says
   "An sigh baith even & morn
   That ever I saw your face Willy
   Or that ever ye was born"
7. O I'll gang to my bow'r she says
   An I'll pray baith night & day
   To keep me frae your tempting looks
   An frae your great beauty
8. O in a little after that
   He keepit Dame Oliphants bow'r
   An the Love that pass'd between this twa
   It was like paramour.

3. Willie o' Douglass-Dale [Child 101]

1. Willie was as brave a Lord p. 51
   As ever sail'd the sea,
   An' he's gone to the English court,
   To serve for meat & fee.
2. He had nae been at the kingis court
   A twelvemonth & a day,
   'Till he long'd for a sight o' the king's daughter
   But her he cou'd never see.
3. O it fell once upon a day,
   To the green-wood she has gane,
   An' Willie he has follow'd her
   Wi' the clear light o' the meen.
4. He looted him low, by her did go,
   Wi' his hat in his han',
   "O what's your will wi' me Sir knight
   I pray keep your hat on."
5. "O I am not a knight he says,
   Nor never thinks to be,
   For I am Willie o' Douglass' Dale,
   An' I serve for meat & fee."
6. "O I'll gang to my bow'r" she says, p. 52
   "An' sigh baith even & morn,
   That ever I saw your face Willy,
   Or that ever ye was born."
7. "O I'll gang to my bow'r" he says
   "An' I'll pray baith night & day,
   To keep me frae your tempting looks,
   An' frae your great beauty."
8. O in a little after that
   He keeped dame Olliphant's bow'r,
   An' the love that pass'd this twa' between,
   It was like paramour.

p. 9

9. O narrow narrow's my gown Willy
   That wont to be sae wide
An' short short is my coats Willy
   That wont to be sae side
An gane is a' my fair colour
   An low laid is my pride

10. But an' my father get word of this
   He'll never drink again
An gin my mother get word of this
   In her ain bow'r shell go brain
An gin my bold brothers get word o this
   I fear Willy you'll be slain

11. O will you leave your fathers court
   An go along wi me
I'll carry you unto fair Scotland
   And mak' you a lady free

12. She pat her han' in her pocket
   An gae him five hunder poun'
An take you that now Squire Willy
   Till awa that we do won

13. Whan day was gane and night was come
   She lap the castle wa
But Willy kepit his gay lady
   He was laith to lat her fa

14. Whan night was gane & day come in
   An lions gaed to their dens
An ay the lady follow'd him
   An the tears came hailing down

15. O want ye ribbons to your hair
   Or roses to your shoone?
Or want ye as meickle dear bought love
   As your ain heart can contain

16. I want nae ribbons to my hair
   Nor roses till my shoone
An Ohone alas! for dear bought love
   I have mair nor I can contain

17. O he's pu'd the oak in good green wood
   An he's made to her a fire
He cover'd it o'er wi withred leaves
   An gar'd it burn thro ire

9. "O narrow, narrow's my gowns Willy,
That wont to be sae wide,
An' short, short are my petticoats,
That wont to be sae side,
An' gane is a' my fair collour,
An' low laid is my pride.

10. "But an' my father gets word o' this
He'll never drink again,
An' gin my mother gets word o' this,
In her ain bow'r she'll go brain,
An' gin my bold brothers get word o' this, p. 53
I fear Willy, you'll be slain."

11. "O will you leave your father's court,
An' go along wi' me,
I'll carry you unto fair Scotland,
An' make you a Lady free."

12. She pat her hand in her pocket
An' gae him five hundred pound,
"And tak' ye that now Squire Willy,
'Till awa' that we can win."

13. Whan day was gane, & night was come,
She lap the castle wa',
But Willie kaped his gay Lady,
He was laith to lat her fa'.

14. Whan night was gone, & day came on,
An' lions gi'd to their dens,
An' ay the Lady follow'd him,
And the tears came haling down.

15. "O want you ribbons to your hair?
Or roses to your sheen?
Or want you as meickle dear bought love, p. 54
As your ain heart can contain?"

16. "I want nae ribbons to my hair,
Nor roses to my sheen,
An' ohon! alas! for dear bought love,
I've mair nor I can contain."

17. O he's pu'd the oak in good-green-wood,
An' he's made to her a fire,
He cover'd it o'er wi' wither'd leaves,
And gar'd it burn thro' ire.

18. He made a bed i the good green wood
An he's laid his lady down
An he's cover'd her oer wi fig tree leaves
But an his ain night gown

19. "O had I a bunch o yon red roddins
That grows in yonder wood
But an a drink o' water clear
I think it wou'd do me good."

20. He's pu'd her a bunch o' yon red roddins
That grew beside yon thorn
But an a drink o water clear
Intill his hunting horn.

p. 10 21. He's bent his bow and shot the deer
An thro' the green wood gane
An ere that he came back again
His lady took travailing

22. O up ye tak that horn she says
An ye blaw a blast for me
Gin my father be in good green wood
Sae seens he'll come me tie

23. O gin there be a man on earth
That ye loo better nor me
Ye blaw the horn yoursel' he says
For its never be blawn by me

24. O he's bent the bow & shot the deer
An thro the green wood has he gone
An lang or he came back again
His lady bare him a son.

25. O up has he tane his bonny young son
An wash'n him wi the milk
An up has he tane his gay lady
An row'd her i the silk.

26. He's bent his bow and shot the deer
An thro the green wood has he gone
Till he met wi a well fard May
Her fathers flock feeding

27. Ye leave your fathers flock feeding
An go along wi me
I'll carry you to a lady fair
Will gi you both meat and fee

18. He made a bed i' the good green-wood,
An' he's laid his Lady down,
An' he's cover'd her o'er wi' fig tree-leaves,
But an' his ae night gown.
19. "O & I had a bunch o' yon' red roddins,
That grows in yonder wood,
But an' a drink o' water clear,
I think it wou'd do me good."
20. He's pu'd her a branch o' yon' red roddins,
That grows in yonder wood,
But & a drink o' water clear,
An' awot it did her good.
21. He's bent his bow & shot the deer, p. 55
An' thro' the green wood gane,
An' lang e're he came back again
His Lady took traveling.
22. "O up ye tak' that horn" she says,
"An' ye blaw a blast for me,
Gin my father be in good green-wood
Sae seen's he'll come me ti'."
23. "O gin there be a man on earth,
That ye lee better than me,
Ye blaw the horn yoursel'" he says,
"For it's never be blawn by me."
24. O he's bent his bow, & shot the deer,
An' thro' the green wood gone,
An' lang or he came back again,
His Lady bare him a son.
25. O up has he ta'en his bonny young son,
An' washen him wi' the milke,
An' up has he ta'en his gay Lady,
And row'd her i' the silk.
26. He's bent his bow, & he's shot the deer, p. 56
An' thro' the green-wood gane,
'Till he met wi' a well far'd May,
Her father's flocks feeding.
27. "Ye leave your father's flocks," he says,
"An' come along wi' me,
I'll carry you 'till a Lady fair,
Will gie you both meat & fee."

28. O whan she came the lady before
    She's fa'n down on her knee
O whats your will wi me my dame
    An a dame you seem to be
29. O I'm dame Oliphant the kings daughter
    Nae doubt but yeve heard o me
Will you leave your fathers flock feeding
    An go to Scotlan wi me
30. An ye sal get a nouriship
    Intill an Earldome
An I will gar provide for the
    To marry some brave Scotsman
31. The May she keepit the bonny boy
    An Willy led his lady
Untill they took their fair shippin
    Then quikly hame came they
32. The win was fair an the sea was clear
    An they a wan safe to lan
He's haild her lady of Douglass dale
    Himsel the lord within.

28. O whan she came the Lady before,
She's fa'n down on her knee,
"O what's your will wi' me my Dame
(An' a dame you seem to be)."

29. "O I'm dame Olliphant the king's daughter;
Nae doubt yo've hear'd o' me,
Will you leave your father's flocks feeding?
An' go to fair Scotland wi' me?

30. "An' ye shall get a nourisship,
Intil an earldome,
An' I will gar provide for thee,
To marry some brave Scotchman."

31. The May she keeped the bonny boy, p. 57
An' Willie led his Lady,
Until that they took fair shipping,
Then quickly hame came they.

32. The win' was fair, the sea was clear,
An' they a' got safe to land,
He's hail'd her Lady o' Douglass'-dale,
Himself the Lord within.

A

4. Young Bekie [Child 53]

p. 11

1. Young Bekie was as brave a knight
   As ever sail'd the sea
An he's doen him to the court of France
   To serve for meat and fee
2. He had nae been i the court of France
   A twelve month nor sae long
Til he fell in love with the kings daughter
   An was thrown in prison strong
3. The king he had but ae daughter
   Burd Isbel was her name
An she has to the prison house gane
   To hear the prisoners mane
4. "O gin a lady would borrow me
   At her stirrup foot I wou'd rin
Or gin a widow wou'ld borrow me
   I wou'd swear to be her son
5. "Or gin a virgin wou'd borrow me
   I wou'd wed her wi a ring
I'd gi her ha's I'd gie her bowers
   The bonny tow'rs o' Linne."
6. O bare foot barefoot gaed she but
   An barefoot came she ben
It was no for want o' hose an Shoone
   Nor time to put them on
7. But a for fear that her father dear
   Had heard her making din
She's stow'n the keys o' the prison house dor
   An latten the prisoner gang
8. O whan she saw him young Bekie
   Her heart was wondrous sair
For the mice but an the bold rottons
   Had eaten his yallow hair

4. Young Bekie [Child 53]

1. Young Bekie was as brave a knight p. 30
As ever sailed the sea,
An' he's ta'en him to the court of France
To serve for meat & fee;
2. He had nae been in the French court
A twelvemonth nor sae long
'Till he fell in love wi' the king's daughter
An' was thrown in prison strong.
3. The king he had but ae daughter,
Burd Is'bel was her name,
An' she has to the prison house gane
To hear the prisoners moan.
4. "O gin a Lady wou'd borrow me,
At her stirrup-foot I wou'd run,
Or gin a widow wou'd borrow me
I'd swear to be her son –
5. "Or gin a virgin wou'd borrow me p. 31
I'd wed her wi' a ring,
I'd gi' her ha's I'd gi' her tow'rs
The bonny tow'r o' Lin."
6. O barefoot, barefoot gi'd she but
An' barefoot came she ben,
It was nae for want o' hose & sheen
Nor time to put them on,
7. But a' for fear, her father dear,
Had hear'd her making din.
She's stown the keys o' the prison-house' door
An' latten the prisoner gang.
8. O whan she saw him young Bekie
Her heart was wond'rous sair,
For the mice but & the bold Rottens
Had cutted his yallow hair.

9. She's gien him a shaver for his beard
   A comber till his hair
Five hunder pound in his pocket
   To spen an nae to spair
10. She's gien him a steed was good in need
   An a saddle o royal bone
A leash o hounds o ae litter
   An hector called one
11. Atween this twa a vow was made
   T'was made full solemnly
That or three years was come an gane
   Well married they shou'd be
12. He had nae been in's ain country
   A twelve month till an end.
Till hes forc'd to marry a dukes daughter
   Or than lose a his land
13. "Ohon alas!" says young Beekie
   "I know not what to dee
For I canno win to Burd Isbel
   An she kensnae to come to me"
p. 12 14. O it fell once upon a day
   Burd Isbel fell asleep
An up it starts the Belly Blin'
   An stood at her bed feet
15. O waken waken Burd Isbel
   How y   you sleep so soun
Whan this is Bekies wedding day
   An the marriage gain on
16. Ye do ye to your mithers bow'r
   Think neither sin nor shame
An ye tak twa o your mithers mary's
   To keep ye frae thinking lang
17. Ye dress yoursel in the red scarlet
   An your mary's in dainty green
An ye pit girdles about your middles
   Wou'd buy an Earldome

9. She's gi'n him a shaver for his beard,
A comber for his hair,
Five hundred pound in his pocket
To spend & nae to spare.

10. She's gi'n him a steed was good in need,
An' a sadle o' royal bone,
A leash o' hounds of ae litter p. 32
An' Hector called one.

11. Atween this twa, a vow was made,
'Twas made full solemnly
That e'er three years was come & gone
Well married they should be.

12. He had nae been in's ain country
A twelvemonth 'till an end
'Till he's forc'd to marry a Duke's daughter,
Or than lose a' his land.

13. "Ohon! alas!" says young Bekie,
"I know no what to dee
For I canno' win to burd Is'bel
An' she kens nae to come to me."

14. It fell once upon a day,
Burd Is'bel fell asleep,
An' up it starts the Belly-blind,
An' stood at her bed feet.

15. "O waken, waken burd Is'bel
How can you sleep sae soun'
Whan this is Bekie's marriage day,
An the marriage going on.

16. "Ye doe ye to your mither's bow'r p. 33
Think neither sin nor shame
An' tak' ye twa o' your mither's Marys
To keep you frae thinking lang.

17. "Ye dress yoursel' i' the scarlet red
Your Marys in dainty green,
An' ye put girdles about your middles
Would buy an earldome.

18. "Ye put nae money in your pocket
But barely guineas three
And that to gie to the proud porter
To bid him speak you wi.

18. O ye gang down by yon sea side
An down by yon sea stran
Sae bonny will the Hollans boats
Come rowin till your han
19. Ye set your milk white foot abord
Cry "hail ye Domine"!
An I shal be the Steerer ot
To row you oer the Sea
20. She's tane her till her mithers bow'r
Thought neither sin nor shame
An she took twa o her mithers marys
To keep her frae thinking lang
21. She dress'd hersel i the red scarlet
Her marys in dainty green
An they pat girdles about their middles
Wou'd buy an earldome
22. An they gid down by yon sea side
An down by yon sea stran
Sae bonny did the Hollan boats
Come rowin to their han
23. She set her milk white foot on board
Cried "hail ye Domine."
An the Belly Blin was the steerer ot
To row her oer the Sea
24. Whan she came to young Bekies gate
She heard the music play
Sae well she kent frae a she heard
It was his wedding day
25. She's pitten her han in her pocket
Gin the porter guineas three
Hae tak ye that ye proud porter
Bid the bride groom speake to me
26. O whan that he came up the stair
He fell low down on his knee
He haild the king an he haild the queen.
An he haild him young Bekie
p. 13 27. O I've been porter at your yates
This thirty years an three
But there's three ladies at them now
Their like I never did see

19. "O ye gang down to yon sea-side,
An' down by yon sea-strand
Sae bonny will the Holland boats
Come rowing 'till your hand.

20. "Ye set your milke white foot on board
Cry hail ye dominee!
And I shall be the steerer o't
To row you o'er the sea."

21. She's ta'en her to her mither's bow'r
Thought neither sin nor shame,
An' she took twa' o' her mither's Marys
To keep her frae thinking lang.

22. She dress'd hersel' i' the red scarlet
Her Marys in dainty green
An' they pat girdles about their middles
Would buy an earldome.

23. An' they gi'd down to yon sea-side p. 34
An' down by yon' sea-strand,
Sae bonny did the Holland boats
Come rowing to their hand.

24. She set her milke white foot on board,
Cried hail ye Dominee!
And the Belly blind was the steerer o't
To row her o'er the sea.

25. Whan she came to young Bekie's yate,
She hear'd the musick play,
Sae well she kent frae a' she heard
It was his wedding day.

26. She's pitten her hand in her pocket,
Gi'n the porter guineas three,
Tak' ye that ye proud Porter,
Bid the bride-groom speak to me.

27. O whan that he came up the stair,
He fell low down on's knee,
He hail'd the king & he hail'd the queen
An' he hail'd him young Bekie.

28. "O I've been porter at your yates
This thirty years & three
But there's three Ladys at them now,
Their like I ne'er did see:

28. Theres ane o them dressd in red scarlet
An twa in dainty green
An they hae girdles about their middles
Wou'd buy an earldome

29. Then out it spake the bierly bride
Was a goud to the chin
Gin she be braw without she says
We's be as braw within

30. Then up it starts him young Bekie
An the tears was in his ee
I'll lay my life its Burd Isbel
Come oer the sea to me

31. O quikly ran he down the stair
An whan he saw 'twas shee
He kindly took her in his arms
And kissd her tenderly

32. O hae ye forgotten young Bekie
The vow ye made to me
Whan I took you out o the prison strong
Whan ye was condemnd to die

33. I gae you a steed was good in need
An a sadle o royal bone
A leash o hounds o ae litter
An hector called one

34. It was well kent what the lady said
That it was nae a lee
For at ilka word the Lady spake
The hound fell at her knee

35. Tak hame tak hame your daughter dear
A blessing gae her wi
For I maun marry my Burd Isbel
That's come oer the sea to me

36. Is this the custom o your house
Or the fashion o your lan
To marry a maid in a may mornin
An send her back at even

29. "There's ane of them dress'd in red scarlet, p. 35
An' twa in dainty green,
An' they ha' girdles about their middles
Wou'd buy an earldome."

30. Then out it spake the bierly bride
Was a' gou'd to the chin,
"Gin they be braw without she says
We's be as braw within."

31. "It's nae to anger the king," he says,
"Nor yet to vex your grace,
But the blackest bit o' the sole o' her fit
Is whiter nor your face."

32. Then up it starts him young Bekie,
An' the tears was in his eye,
"I'll lay my life its Burd Is'bel
Come oe'r the sea to me."

33. O quickly ran he down the stair,
An' whan he saw 'twas she,
He kindly took her in his arms,
An' kiss'd her tenderly.

34. "O ha' you forgotten, young Bekie?
The vow you made to me?
Whan I took you out o' prison strong?
Whan you was condemn'd to dee?

35. "I ga' you a steed was good in need p. 36
An' a sadle o' royal bone,
A leash o' hounds of ae litter
And Hector called one."

36. It was well kent what the Lady said,
That it was no a lee,
For at ilka word 'at the Lady spake
The hound fell at her knee.

37. "Take hame, take hame your daughter,
A blessing gae her wi',
For I man marry my Burd Is'bel
That's come o'er the sea to me."

38. "Is this the custom o' your house?
Or the fashion o' your lan'?
To marry a maid in a May morning?
An' send her hame at even?"

A

5. Young Bicham [Child 53]

p. 13 1. In London city was Bicham born
He long'd strange countries for to see
But he was taen by a savage moor
Who handld him right cruely

2. For thro' his shoulder he pit a bore
An thro the bore has pitten a tree
An hes gard him draw the carts o wine
Where horse & oxen had wont to be

p. 14 3. Hes castin in a dungeon deep
Where he cou'd neither hear nor see
He s shut him up in a prison strong
An he's handld him right cruely

4. O this this moor he had but ae daughter
I wot her name was Shusy Pye
Shes doen her to the prison house
An shes calld young Bicham one word by

5. O hae ye ony lands or rents
Or citys in your ain country?
Cou'd free you out of prison strong
An cou'd mantain a lady free

6. O London city is my own
An other citys twa or three
Coud loose me out o prison strong
An cou'd mantain a lady free

7. O she has bribed her fathers men
Wi meikle goud & white money
She's gotten the key o the prison doors
An she has set young Bicham fre[e]

8. She's gi'n him a loaf o good white bread
But an a flask o spanish wine
An she bad him mind on the ladies love
That sae kindly freed him out o pi[ne]

9. Go set your foot on good ship board
An haste you back to your ain country
An before that seven years has an end
Come back again love & marry me

[No parallel text]

10. It was long or seven years had an end
    She long'd fu sair her love to see
She's set her foot on good ship board
    An turn'd her back on her ain country
11. She's saild up so has she doun
    Till she came to the other side
She's landed at young Bichams yates
    An I hop this day she sal be his brid[e]
12. Is this young Bichams yates? says she
    Or is that noble prince within
He's up the stairs wi his bonny bride
    An monny a lord & lady wi him
13. O has he taen a bonny bride
    An has he clean forgotten me
An sighing said that gay lady
    I wish I were i my ain country
14. But she's pitten her han in her pocket
    An gin the porter guineas three
Says take ye that ye proud porter
    An bid the bridegroom speak to me
15. O whan the porter came up the stair
    He's fan low down upon his knee
Won up Won up ye proud porter
    An what makes a this courtesy
p. 15 16. O Ive been porter at your yates
    This mair nor seven years & three
But there is a lady at them now
    The like of whom I never did see
17. For on every finger she has a ring
    An on the mid finger she has three
An theres as meikle goud aboon her brow
    As wou'd buy an earldome o lan to me
18. Then up it started young Bicham
    An sware so loud by our lady
It can be nane but Shusy Pye
    That has come oer the sea to me
19. O quickly ran he down the stair
    O fifteen steps he has made but three
He's tane his bonny love in his arms
    An a wot he kissd her tenderly

[No parallel text]

20. O hae you tane a bonny bride?
    An hae you quite forsaken me
An hae ye quite forgotten her
    That gae you life an liberty?
21. Shes lookit oer her left shoulder
    To hide the tears stood in her ee
Now fare the well young Bicham she says
    I'll strive to think nae mair on thee
22. Take back your daughter Madam he says
    An a double dow'ry I'll gi her wi
For I maun marry my first true love
    Thats done & suffered so much for me
23. Hes take his bonny love by the han
    And led her to yon fountain Stane
Hes changd her name frae Shusy Pye
    And hes cald her his bonny love lady Jane

[No parallel text]

A

6. The gay goss hawk [Child 96]

p. 15 1. O wells me o my gay goss hawk
That he can speak and flee
Hell carry a letter to my love
Bring back another to me

2. O how can I your true love ken
Or how can I her know
Whan frae her mouth I never heard couth
Nor wi my eyes her saw

3. O well sal ye my true love ken
As soon as you her see
For of a the flowrs in fair Englan
The fairest flowr is she

4. At even at my loves bow'r door
There grows a bowing birk
An sit ye down and sing thereon
As she gangs to the kirk

p. 16 5. An four and twenty Ladies fair
Will wash & go to kirk
But well shall ye my true love ken
For she wears goud on her skirt

6. An four and twenty gay ladies
Will to the mass repair
But well sal ye my true love ken
For she wears goud on her hair

7. O even at that ladys bow'r door
There grows a bowin birk
An she set down & sang thereon
As she ged to the kirk

6. The Gay Goss-Hawk [Child 96]

1. “O well’s me o’ my gay goss-hawk, p. 24
   That he can speak & flee,
He’ll carry a letter to my love
   Bring another back to me.”
2. “O how can I your true love ken?
   Or how can I her know?
When frae her mouth I ne’er heard couth,
   Nor wi’ my eyes her saw?”
3. “O well shall ye my true-love ken,
   As soon as you her see,
For of a’ the flow’rs in fair England,
   The fairest flow’r is she:
4. “An’ even at my love’s bow’r door,
   There grows a bowing birk
An’ sit ye down & sing thereon,
   As she gaes to the kirk.
5. “And four & twenty Ladies fair,
   Will wash & go to kirk,
But well shall ye my true-love ken p. 25
   For she wears gold on her skirt.
6. “An’ four & twenty gay Ladies
   Will to the mass repair,
But well shall ye my true love ken
   For she wears gold on her hair.”
7. O even at that Lady’s bow’r door,
   There grew a bowing birk,
An’ he sat down & sang thereon,
   As she gi’d to the kirk:
8. An’ even at that Lady’s window,
   There was a silver pin,
An’ ay he sat & sang thereon,
   As she gi’d out & in.

8. O eet & drink my Marys a
 The wine flows you amon'
Till I gang to my shot window
 An hear yon bonny birds song
9. Sing on sing on my bonny bird
 The song ye sang the streen
For I ken by your sweet singin
 Your frae my true love sen
10. O first he sung a merry song
 And then he sang a grave
An then he peck'd his feathers gray
 To her the letter gave
11. Ha theres a letter frae your love
 He says he sent you three
He canna wait your love langer
 But for your sake hell die
12. He bids you write a letter to him
 He says he's sent you five
He canna wait your love langer
 Tho youre the fairest woman aliv[e]
13. Ye bid him bake his bridal bread
 And brew his bridal ale
An I'll meet him in fair Scotlan
 Lang lang or it be stale
14. Shes doen her to her father dear
 Fa'n low down on her knee
A boon a boon my father dear
 I pray you grant it me
15. Ask on ask on my daughter
 An granted it sal be
Except ae squire in fair Scotlan
 An him you sall never see
16. The only boon my father dear
 That I do crave of the
Is gin I die in southin lands
 In scotland to bury me
17. An the firstin kirk that ye come till
 Ye gar the Bells be rung
An the nextin kirk that ye come till
 ye gar the mess be sung

9. "O eat & drink my Marys a'
The wine flows you among,
'Till I gang to my shot window
An' hear yon bonny bird's song.

10. "Sing on, Sing on, my bonny bird,
The song you sang the streen,
For I ken by your sweet singing,
You're frae my true-love sen'."

11. O first he sang a merry song, p. 26
An' then he sang a grave,
And then he peck'd his feathers gray,
To her the letter gave.

12. "Ha' there's a letter frae your love,
He says he's sent you three,
He canno' wait your love langer
But for your sake he'll dee."

13. "Ye bid him bake his bridal bread,
An' brew his bridal ale,
And I'll meet him in fair Scotland,
Lang, lang, or it be stale."

14. She's doen her to her father dear,
Fa'n low down on her knee;
"A boon, a boon my father dear,
I pray you grant it me."

15. "Ask on, ask on, my daughter dear,
An' granted it shall be,
Except ae Squire in fair Scotland,
An' him you'se never see."

16. "The only boon, my father dear,
Which I do crave o' thee,
Is, gin I dee in Southing lands p. 27
In Scotland to bury me:

17. "An' the firstin kirk that ye come till
Ye gar the bells be rung,
An' the nextin kirk 'at ye come till
Ye gar the mess be sung:

p. 17

18. An the thirdin kirk that ye come till
You deal gold for my sake
An the fourthin kirk that ye come till
You tarry there till night
19. Shes doen her to her bigly bow'r
As fast as she coud fare
An she has tane a sleepy draught
That she had mix'd wi care
20. Shes laid her down upon her bed
An soon shes fa'n asleep
And soon oer every tender limb
Cauld death began to creep
21. Whan night was flown & day was come
Nae ane that did her see
But thought she was as surely dead
As ony lady cou'd be
22. Her father & her brothers dear
Gard make to her a bier
The tae half was o guide red gold
The tither o silver clear
23. Her mither & her sisters fair
Gard work for her a sark
The tae half was o cambrick fine
The tither o needle wark
24. The firstin kirk that they came till
They gard the bells be rung
And the nextin kirk that they came till
They gard the mess be sung
25. The thirdin kirk that they came till
They dealt gold for her sake
An the fourthin kirk that they came till
Lo! there they met her make
26. Lay down lay down the bigly bier
Lat me the dead look on
Wi cherry cheeks & ruby lips
She lay an smil'd on him
27. O ae sheave o your bread true love
An ae glass o your wine
For I hae fasted for your sake
These fully days is nine

18. "An' the thirdin kirk 'at ye come 'till
Ye deal gold for my sake;
An' the fourthin kirk 'at ye come 'till
Ye tarry there till night."
19. She's ta'en her 'till her bigly bow'r
As fast as she cou'd fare,
An' she has drunken a sleepy draught
That she had mix'd wi' care.
20. She's laid her down upon her bed,
An' soon she's fa'n asleep,
An' soon o'er every tender limb
Cauld death began to creep.
21. Whan night was flow'n, & day was come,
Nae ane that did her see,
But thought she was as surely dead,
As ony ane cou'd be.
22. Her father & her brother dear,
Gar'd make for her a bier
The tae half was o' good red gou'd, p. 28
The tither o' silver clear.
23. Her mither & her sister fair,
Gar'd work for her a sark,
The tae half was o' cambrick fine,
The tither o' needle wark.
24. The firstin kirk that they came 'till
They gar'd the bells be rung,
The nextin kirk 'at they came 'till
They gar'd the mass be sung:
25. The thirdin kirk at they came till
They dealt gold for her sake,
An' the fourthin kirk 'at they came till
Lo! there they met her make.
26. Lay down, lay down the bigly bier,
Lat me the dead look on,
Wi' cherry Cheeks & ruby lips
She lay & leugh on him.
27. "O ae sheave o' your bread true love,
An' ae glass o' your wine,
For I have fasted for your sake p. 29
These fully dayes nine.

28. Gang hame gang hame my seven bold brothers
    Gang hame & sound your horn
An ye may boast in Southin lands
    Your sisters play'd you scorn

28. "Gae hame, gae hame my seven bold brothers,
    Gae hame & sound your horn,
An' ye may boast in Southing land,
    Your sister's play'd you the scorn."

A

7. Brown Adam [Child 98]

p. 17 1. O wha woud wish the win' to blaw
Or the green leaves fa therewith
Or wha wad wish a leeler love
Than brown Adam the smith

p. 18 2. His hammers o the beaten gold
His studys o the steel
His fingers white are my delite
He blows his bellows well

3. But they ha banish'd him brown Adam
Frae father & frae mothe[r]
An they ha banish'd him brown Adam
Frae sister & frae brither

4. And they ha banishd brown Adam
Frae the flowr o' a his kin
An hes bigget a bowr i the good greenwood
Betwen his lady & him

5. O it fell once upon a day
Brown Adam he thought lang
An he wou'd to the green wood gang
To hunt some venison

6. Hes taen his his bow his arm oer
His bran intill his han
And he is to the good green wood
As fast as he coud gang

7. O hes shot up an hes shot down
The bird upo the briar
An hes sent it hame to his lady
Bade her be of good cheer

8. O hes shot up an hes shot down
The bird upo the thorn
And sent it hame to his lady
And hee'd be hame the morn

7. Brown Adam [Child 98]

1. O wha wou'd wish the wind to blaw? p. 8
Or the green leaves fa' therewith?
Or wha wou'ld wish a Leeler Love?
Than brown Adam the Smith?

2. His hammer's o' the beaten gold,
His study's o' the steel,
His fingers white, are my delight,
He blows his bellows well.

3. But they ha' banish'd him brown Adam,
Frae father, & frae Mother,
And they ha' banish'd him brown Adam,
Frae Sister, & frae Brother.

4. An' they ha' banish'd him brown Adam,
The flow'r o' a' his kin;
And he's bigged a bow'r in good Green wood,
Atween his Lady & him.

5. O it fell once upon a day,
Brown Adam he thought Lang,
An' he wou'd to the green wood gang, p. 9
To hunt some venison.

6. He's ta'en his bow his arm o'er,
His bran' intil his hand,
And he is to the good green wood,
As fast as he cou'd gang.

7. O he's shot up, & he's shot down,
The bird upon the briar,
And he's sent it hame to his Lady,
Bade her be of good cheer.

8. O he's shot up, & he's shot down,
The bird upo' the thorn,
An' sent it unto his Lady,
Said he'd be hame the morn.

9. Whan he came till his ladys bow'r door
H[e] stood a little foreby
And there he heard a fu fa'se knight
Temptin his gay lady

10. O hes taen out a gay gold ring
Had cost him mony a poun
O grant me love for love lady
An this sal be your own

11. I loo brown Adam well she says
I wot sae does he me
An I wou'd na gi brown Adams love
For nae fa'se knight I see

12. Out has he taen a purse of gold
Was a fu to the string
Grant me but love for love lady
An a this sal be thine

13. I loo brown Adam well she says
An I ken sae does he me
An I wou'dna be your light leman
For mair nor ye cou'd gie

14. Then out has he drawn his lang lang bran
An hes flashd it in her een
Now grant me love for love lady
Or thro you this sal gang

p. 19 15. O sighing said that gay lady
Brown Adam tarrys long
Then up it starts brown Adam
Says I'm just at your han'

16. Hes gard him leave his bow his bow
Hes gard him leave his bran
Hes gard him leave a better pledge
Four fingers o his right han

9. Whan he came 'til his Lady's bow'r door
He stood a little forebye,
An' there he heard a foul fa'se knight,
Tempting his gay Lady.
10. O he's taen out a gay gold ring,
Had cost him mony a pound,
"O grant me love for love Lady
An' this shall be your own."
11. "I loo, Brown Adam well," she says, p. 10
"I wot so does he me,
An' I wou'd nae gie Brown Adam's love,
For nae fa'se knight I see."
12. Out has he taen a purse o' goud,
Was a' fu' to the string,
"Grant me but love for love Lady,
An' a' this shall be thine."
13. "I loo brown Adam well," she says,
"And I ken sae does he me,
An' I wou'd nae be your light Lemman,
For mair nor ye could gie."
14. Then out has he drawn his lang lang bran'
An' he flash'd it in her een,
"Now grant me love for love Lady,
Or thro' you this shall gang."
15. O sighing says that fair Lady,
"Brown Adam tarrys lang;"
Then up it starts him brown Adam,
Says, "I'm just at your han'."
16. He's gar'd him leave his bow, his bow;
He's gar'd him leave his bran',
He's gar'd him leave a better pledge,
Four fingers o' his right hand.

A

8. Lady Elspat [Child 247]

p. 19 1. How brents your brow my lady Elspat
How golden yallow is your hair
Of all the maids of fair Scotland
Theres nane like lady Elspat fair

2. Perform your vows sweet William she says
The vows which ye ha' made to me
An at the back o my mothers castle
This night I'll surely meet wi thee

3. But wae be to our brothers page
Who heard the words this twa did say
Hes told them to her lady mother
Who wrought sweet William mieckle wae

4. For she has taen him sweet William
An shes gard bind him wi his bow string
Till the red bluide o his fair body
Frae ilka nail o his hand did spring

5. O it fell once upon a time
That the lord Justice came to town
Out has he taen him sweet William
Brought him before lord Justice boun

6. An what is the crime now madame he says
Has been committed by this young man
O he has broken my bonny caltel
That was well biggit wi lime & stane

7. An he has broken my bonny coffers
That was well banded wi aiken ban
An he has stoln my rich jewels
I wot he has them every one

8. Then out it spake her lady Elspat
As she sat by lord Justice knee
Now ye hae taul your tale mother
I pray lord Justice youl now hear me

8. Lady Elzpat [Child 247]

1. "How brent is your brow my Lady Elspat, p. 63
   How golden yallow is your hair,
   Of all the maids in fair Scotland,
   There's nane like Lady Elspat fair."
2. "Perform your vows sweet William" she says
   "The vows which ye have made to me,
   And at the back o' my mither's castle,
   This night I'll surely meet wi' thee."
3. But wae be to her brither's foot page,
   Who heerd the words this two did say,
   He's told them to her Lady mother,
   Who wrought sweet Willliam meickle wae.
4. For she has taen him Sweet William,
   And she's gar'd bind him wi' his bow-string,
   'Till the red blude o' his body,
   Frae ilka nail o's hand did spring.
5. O it fell once upon a time, p. 64
   That the Lord justice came to town,
   Out has she taen him sweet William,
   Brought him before lord justice bound.
6. "An' what is the crime now Madam?" he says
   "Has been committed by this young man?"
   "O he has broken my bonny castle,
   That was well bigged wi' lime & stane,
7. "An' he has broken my bonny coffers,
   That was well banded wi' aiken beam;
   An' he has stolen my rich jewels,
   I wat he has them every one."
8. Then out it spake her Lady Elspat,
   As she sat by Lord justice' knee,
   "Now ye have tauld your tale mother
   I pray Lord justice hear you me.

9. He has na broken her bonny castel
   That was well biggit wi lime & stane
Nor has he stoln her rich jewels
   For I wot she has them every one

10. But tho he was my first true love
   An tho I had sworn to be his bride
Cause he had not a great estate
   She would this way our loves divide

p. 20 11. An out it spake the lord Justice
   I wot the tear was in his ee
I see nae fault in this young man
   Sae loose his ban's & set him free

12. Take back your love now lady Elspat
   An my best blessing you baith upon
For gin he be your first true love
   He is my eldest sisters son

13. There is a steed in my stable
   Cost me baith gold and white money
Ye's get as mieckle o my free lan
   As hell ride about in a summers day

9. "He has not broken her bonny castle
That was well bigget wi' lime & stane,
Nor has he stol'n her rich jewels p. 65
For I wot she has them ev'ry one.

10. "But tho' he was my first fair love,
And tho' I'd sworn to be his bride,
Cause he had not a great estate,
She wou'd this way our loves divide."

11. Then out it spake the good lord justice,
I wot the tear was in his ee,
"I see nae fault in this young man,
So loose his bands & set him free:

12. "Take back your love now lady Elspat,
An' my best blessing you baith upon,
For gin he be your first fair love
He is my eldest sister's son."

A

9. Lady Jane [Child 62]

p. 20

1. O Wha will bake my bridal bread
   And brew my bridal ale
   Wha will welcome my bright bride
   That I bring oer the dale
2. O I will bake your bridal bread
   An brew your bridal ale
   An I will welcome your bright bride
   That you bring oer the dale
3. O she that welcomes my bright bride
   Maun gang like maiden fair
   She maun lace her in her green cloathin
   An braid her yallow hair
4. O how can I gang maiden like
   Whan maiden I am nane
   Whan I ha born you seven sons
   An am wi bairn again?
5. The lady stood in her bow'r door
   An lookit oe'r the lan'
   An there she saw her ain good lord
   Leadin his bride by the han'
6. She's dress'd her sons i the scarlet red
   Hersel i the dainty green
   An' tho her cheek look'd pale and wan
   She well might ha' been a queen
7. She calld upon her eldest son
   Look yonder what you see
   For yonder comes your father dear
   Your step mother him wi
8. O your welcome home my ain good lord
   To your ha's but an your bowrs
   Your welcome hame my ain good lord
   To youre castles & your tow'rs
   Sae is your bright bride you beside
   She's fairer nor the flowers

[No parallel text]

9. O what'n a ladys that she says
That welcoms you an me
If Im lang lady about this place
Some good I will her dee
p. 21 She looks sae like my sister Jane
Was stoln ithe bowr frae me
10. O she has serv'd the lang tables
Wi the white bread an the wine
But ay she drank the wan water
To keep her colour fine
11. An she gi'd by the first table
An leugh amo them a
But ere she reach'd the second table
She let the tears down fa
12. She's taen a napkin lang an white
An hung't upon a pin
It was to dry her wat'ry eyes
As she went out and in.
13. Whan bells were rung & mass was sung
An a man boun to bed
The bride but an the bonny bridegroom
In ae chamber was laid
14. She's taen her harp intill her han'
To harp this twa asleep
An ay as she harp'd and she sang
Full sorely did she weep
15. O seven fu fair sons I have born
To the good lord o this place
An I wish that they were seven hares
To run the castle race
An I mysel a good gray houn
An I wou'd gi them chase
16. O seven fu fair sons I have born
To the good lord o' this ha
I wish that they were seven rottons
To rin the castle wa
An I mysell a good gray cat
I wot I woud worry them a

[No parallel text]

17. The earle o Richmond was my father
    An the lady was my mother
An a the bairns bisides mysel
    Was a sister an a brother
18. Sing on sing on ye gay lady
    I wot ye hae sung in time
Gin the Earle o Richmond was your father
    I wot sae was he mine
19. Rise up rise up my beirly bride
    I think my beds but caul
I wou'd na hear my lady lament
    For your tocher ten times taul
20. O seven ships did bring you hame
    An an sal tak you hame
The leve I'll keep to your sister Jane
    For tocher she gat nane

[No parallel text]

A

10. Burd Ellen [Child 63]

p. 22

1. I warn ye all ye gay ladies
   That wear scarlet an brown
That ye dinna leave your fathers house
   To follow young men frae town

2. O! here am I a lady gay
   That wears scarlet & brown
Yet I will leave my father s house
   An follow lord John frae the town

3. Lord John stood in his stable door
   Said he was bound to ride
Burd Ellen stood in her bow'r door
   Said she'd rin by his side

4. He's pitten on his cork heel'd shoone
   An fast awa rade he
She's clade hersel in page array
   An after him ran she

5. Till they came till a wan water
   An folks do ca it Clyde
Then he's lookit oer his left shoulder
   Says lady can ye ride

6. O! I learn't it i my father house
   And I learnt it for my weal
Wheneer I came to a wan water
   To swim like ony eel

7. But the firstin stap the lady the lady stappit
   The water came til her knee
Ohon alas! Said the lady
   This waters o'er deep for me

8. The nextin stap the lady stappit
   The water came till her middle
An sighin says that gay lady
   I've wat my gouden girdle

9. The nextin stap the lady stappit
   The water came till her pap
An the bairn that was in her twa sides
   For caul begane to quake

C

10. Lord John and Bird Ellen [Child 63]

1. I forbid you a ye gay Ladies p. 39
   That wear scarlet and brown
   To leave your fathers families
   And follow young men frae the town
2. O! here am I a gay Ladie
   That wear scarlet and brown
   Yet I will leave my father s castle
   And follow Lord John frae the town
3. Lord John stands in his stable door
   Says I am boon to ride
   Bird Ellen stands in her bower door
   Says I'll run by your side
4. He has mounted on his Berry brown steed
   And fast awa rode he
   She's clad her in a pages weed
   And ay as fast ran shee
5. Till they came to a wan water
   The folks do call it Clyde
   He's look'd oer his left shoulder
   Says Ellen will ye ride
6. O! I learn'd it when I was a bairn p. 40
   And I learn'd it for my weel
   When ere I came to a wan water
   To swim like any Eel
7. But the firsten step that Ladie steppit
   It was aboon her knee
   Ohon alas says bird Ellen
   This water's o'er deep for me
8. The niesten step that Ladie steppit
   It was up till her middle
   Ohon alas says bird Ellen
   I have wat my gowden girdle
9. The thirden step that Ladie steppit
   The water touch'd her pap
   The bairn between her sides twa
   For cauld begood to quake

10. Lye still lye still my ain dear babe
  Ye work your mither wae
Your father rides on high horse back
  Cares little for us twae
11. O about the midst o Clyden water
  There was a yeard fast stane
He lightly turn'd his horse about
  An took her on him behin
12. O tell me this now good lord John
  An a word ye dinna lee
How far it is to your lodgin
  Whare we this night maun be
13. O see you nae yon castle Ellen
  That shines sae fair to see
There is a lady in it Ellen
  Will sunder you & me
p. 23 14. There is a lady in that castle
  Will sunder you and I
Betide me well betide me wae
  I sal go there & try
15. O my dogs sal eat the good white bread
  An ye sal eat the bran
Then will ye sigh an say alas
  That ever I was a man
16. O I sal eat the good white bread
  An your dogs sal eat the bran
An I hope to live an bless the day
  That ever ye was a man
17. O my horse sal eat the good white meal
  An ye sal eat the corn
Then will ye curse the heavy hour
  That ever your love was born
18. O I sal eat the good white meal
  An your horse sal eat the corn
An I ay sall bless the happy hour
  That ever my love was born
19. O four & twenty gay ladies
  Welcom'd lord John to the ha'
But a fairer lady than them a
  Led his horse to the stable sta'

10. Ly still ly still my ain dear babe
You gie your mother pain
Your father rides ofn hie horse back
And care's little for us twain

11. About the midst of Clydes water p. 41
There stands a yerdfast stane
He has turn'd about his berry brown steed
And taen her up him behind

12. O! tell me this now good Lord John
And a word ye dinna lie
How far is it to your lodging
Where this night you mean to be

13. Do not ye see yon castle Ellen
That shines so far and hie
There is a Ladie there he say s
Will sunder you and me

14. Altho there be a Ladie there
Should sunder you and me
Betide my life betide my death
I will go thither and see

15. O! my dogs shall eat the good white bread
And you shall eat the brann
Then you will sigh & cry alas
That ever you loo'd a man

16. O! tis I shall eat the good white bread p. 42
And your dogs shall eat the brann
But I ne'er shall live to cry alas
That ever I loo'd a man

17. My horse shall eat the baken meat
And you shall eat the corn
You then will curse the heavy hour
That ever your Love was born

18. O! I shall eat the baken meat
And your horse shall eat the corn
And I still shall bless the happy hour
That ever my Love was born

19. O four & twenty gay Ladies
Welcom'd Lord John to the ha'
But a fairer Ladie than them a'
Led his horse to the stable sta'

20. An four & twenty gay ladies
    Welcom'd lord John to the green
But a fairer lady than them a
    At the manger stood alane
21. Whan bells were rung & mass was sung
    An a man boun to meat
Burd Ellen at a bye table
    Amo' the footmen was set
22. O eat & drink my bonny boy
    The white bread & the beer
The never a bit can I eat or drink
    My hearts sae full of fear
23. O eat an drink my bonny boy
    The white bread an the wine
O I canna eat nor drink master
    My hearts sae full of pine
24. But out it spake lord Johns mother
    An a wise woman was she
Whare met ye wi that bonny boy
    That looks sae sad on thee?
25. Sometimes his cheek is rosy red
    An sometimes deadly wan
He's liker a woman big wi bairn
    Than a young lords serving man
26. O it makes me laugh my mother dear
    Sic words to hear frae thee
He is a squires ae dearest son
    That for love has follow'd me
p. 24 27. Rise up rise up my bonny boy
    Gi my horse corn an hay
O that I will my master dear
    As quickly as I may
28. She's taen the hay under her arm
    The corn intill her han'
An she's gane to the great stable
    As fast as e'er she can
29. O room ye roun my bonny broun steeds
    O room ye near the wa
For the pain that strikes me thro my sides
    Full soon will gar me fa

20. And four and twenty gay Ladies
    Welcomed Lord John to the green
But a fairer Lady than them a
    At the manger stood her lane
21. When bells were rung and mass was sung p. 43
    And a' were boon to meat
Bird Ellen at a by table
    Amang the foot men was set
22. O! eat and drink my bonny boy
    The white bread and the wine
O I can neither eat nor drink
    My heart's sae full of pine
23. O eat and drink my bonny boy
    The white bread and the beer
O I can neither eat nor drink
    My heart sae full of fear
24. Then out it spake Lord Johns mother
    And a wise woman was she
My son where gat ye that foot page
    You have brought hame to me
25. Some times his cheeks look rosey red
    And some times pale and wan
He looks mair like a Ladie wi bairn
    Than a young Lords serving man
26. He has look'd oer his left shoulder p. 44
    And a loud laugh laughed he
Says he's a squires ae dear son
    I got in the north countrie
27. Win up win up my bonny boy
    Gie my horse corn and hay
And so I will my mas'ter dear
    As fast as ever I may.
28. She has ta'en the hay under her arm
    And the corn in her right hand
And she's hied her to the stable door
    As fast as she could gang
29. O! room ye round my bonny brown steeds
    Stand nearer to the wa
For the pain that strikes between my sides
    Full soon will gar me fa

30. She's lean'd her back against the wa
    Strong traivail seiz'd her on
An even amo the great horse feet
    Burd Ellen brought forth her son
31. Lord John mither intill her bow'r
    Was sitting all alone
Whan ithe silence o the night
    She heard fair Ellens moan
32. Won up won up my son she says
    Go se how a does fare
For I think I hear a womans groans
    An a bairn greeting sair
33. O hastily he gat him up
    Stay'd neither for hose nor shoone
An he's doen him to the stable door
    Wi the clear light o the moon

34. He strack the door hard wi his foot
    An sae has he wi his knee
An iron locks an iron bars
    Into the floor flung he
Be not afraid Burd Ellen he says
    Thers nane come in but me

35. Up he has taen his bonny young son
    An gard wash him wi the milk
An up has he taen his fair lady
    Gard row her i the silk
36. Cheer up your heart Burd Ellen he says
    Look nae mair sad nor wae
For your marriage & your kirkin too
    Sal baith be in ae day

30. She has leand to the manger side
    And gien a grieveous groan
And even amang the great horse feet
    Bird Ellen brought hame a son
31. Then out it spake Lord Johns mother p. 45
    As she stood on the stair
I think I hear a womans groan
    And a bairn greeting sair.

32. O! quickly quickly raise he up
    Stay'd neither for hose nor shoone
But hied him to the stable door
    Wi the clear light o' the moon
33. Now open the door Bird Ellen he says
    O open and let me in
Or baith the door and the door cheeks
    Into the floor I'll fling
34. He's struck the door wi has right foot
    And push'd it wi his knee
Till Iron bolts and Iron bars
    In flinders he has gar'd flee
Be not afraid Bird Ellen he says
    For there s nane win in but me
35. The never a word spake that Ladie
    As on the floor she lay
But hush'd her young son in her arms p. 46
    And turn'd her face away
36. Now up ye take my bonny young son
    And wash him wi the milk
And up ye take my fair Ladie
    And row her i the silk
37. And smile on me now bird Ellen
    And cast awa your care
For I'll make you Ladie of a my Lands
    And your son shall be my heir

A

10. Burd Ellen

38. Bless'd be the day say'd bird Ellen
    That I followd you frae the town
For I'd rather far be your foot page
    Than the queen that wears the crown

A

11. Lady Maisry [Child 65]

p. 24 1. The young lords o the north country
Have all awooing gone
To win the love of lady Maisry
But o them she wou'd hae none

2. O they hae courted lady Maisry
Wi a kin kind o things
An they hae sought her lady Maisry
Wi brotches an wi rings

p. 25 3. An they ha sought her lady Maisry
Frae father an frae mother
An they ha sought her lady Maisry
Frae sister an frae brother

4. An they ha followd her lady Maisry
Thro chamber an thro ha'
But a that they cou'd say to her
Her answer still was na

5. O had your tongues young men she says
An think nae mair o me
For I've gien my love to an english lord
An think nae mair o me

6. Her fathers kitchy boy heard that
An ill death may he dee
An he is on to her brother
As fast as gang cou'd hee

7. O is my father an my mother well
But an my brothers three
Gin my sister lady Maisry be well
Theres naething can ail me

8. Your father an your mother is well
But an your brothers three
Your sister lady Maisry's well
So big wi bairn gangs she

11. Lady Maisery [Child 65]

1. The young Lords o' the North country, p. 71
    Have all a-wooing gane,
To win the love o' Lady Maisery,
    But of them she wou'd ha' nane.
2. O they have courted lady Maisery,
    Wi' broaches & wi' rings,
An' they ha' courted her lady Maisery,
    Wi' a' kin' kind o' things.
3. An' they ha' sought her lady Maisery,
    Frae father, & frae mother,
An' they have sought her lady Maisery,
    Frae sister, & frae brother.
4. And they ha' follow'd her lady Maisery,
    Thro' cha'mer & thro' ha',
But a' that they cou'd say to her,
    Her answer still was na'.
5. "O had your tongues young men," she says, p. 72
    "An' think nae mair o' me,
For I've gi'n my love to an English lord,
    An' I have nae mair to gi'."
6. Her father's kitchy boy hard that,
    Ane ill dead may he dee,
An' he has on to her brother;
    As fast as gang cou'd he.
7. "O is my father & mother well,
    But & my brother's three,
Gin my sister lady Mais'ry be well,
    There's naething can ail me."
8. "Your father, & your mother is well,
    Likewise your brothers three,
Your sister lady Maisery is well,
    So big wi' bairn gangs she."

9. Gin this be true you tell to me
   My mailison light on thee
But gin it be a lie you tell
   You sal be hangit hie
10. He's done him to his sisters bow'r
   Wi meikle doole an care
An there he saw her lady Maisry
   Kembing her yallow hair
11. O wha is aught that bairn she says
   That ye sae big are wi?
An gin ye winna own the truth
   This moment ye sal dee
12. She turn'd her right an roun about
   An the kem fell frae her han
A trembling seiz'd her fair body
   An her rosy cheek grew wan
13. O pardon me my brother dear
   An the truth I'll tell to thee
My bairn it is to lord William
   An he is betroth'd to me
14. O cou'd na ye gotten dukes or lords
   In till your ain country
That ye draw up wi an english dog
   To bring this shame on me
15. But ye maun gi up the english lord
   Whan youre young babe is born
For gin you keep by him an hour langer
   Your life sall be forlorn
p. 26 16. I will gi up this English blood,
   Till my young babe be born,
But the never a day nor hour langer
   Tho my life should be forlorn
17. O whare is a my merry young men
   Whom I gi meat and fee
To pu' the thistle and the thorn
   To burn this wile whore wi?
18. O whare will I get a bonny boy
   To help me in my need?
To rin wi hast to Lord William
   And bid him come wi speed

9. "Gin this be true you tell to me,
    My melison light on thee,
But gin it be a lie you tell,
    You shall be hanged hi'."
10. He's done him to his sister's bow'r p. 73
    Wi' meickle deil & care,
An' there he saw her lady Maisery,
    Keming her yallow hair.
11. "O wha is aught that bairn?" he says,
    "That ye sae big are wi'?
An' gin you winna' own the truth,
    This moment you shall die."
12. She turn'd her right, & round about,
    An' the kem fell frae her hand,
A trembling seiz'd her fair body,
    An' her rosy cheek grew wan.
13. "O pardon me my brother dear,
    An' the truth I'll own to thee,
My Bairn it is to Lord William,
    And now he is betrothed to me."
14. "O cou'd na ye gotten Dukes or Lords
    Into your own country,
That ye drew up wi' an English dog,
    To bring this shame on me.
15. "But ye man gie up the English blood, p. 74
    The moment your babe is born,
For gin you keep by'm an hour longer,
    Your life shall be forborn."
16. "I will gie up this English blood,
    'Till my young babe be born,
But the never a day nor hour langer,
    'Tho' my life shou'd be forborn."
17. "O whare is a' my merry young men?
    Whom I gie meat & fee?
To pu' the thistle & the thorn?
    To burn this vile whore wi'?"
18. "O whare will I get a bonny boy?
    To help me in my need?
To run with haste to Lord William?
    An' bid him come wi' speed?"

19. O out it spake a bonny boy
    Stood by her brothers side
"O I would rin your errand Lady
    O'er a the world wide
20. "Aft have I run your errands Lady
    Whan blawn baith win' & weet
But now I'll rin your errand Lady
    Wi sa't tears on my cheek"
21. O whan he came to broken briggs
    He bent his bow and swam
An whan the came to the green grass growin
    He slack'd his shoone & ran
22. O whan he came to Lord Williams yates
    He baed na' to chap or ca
But set his bent bow till his breast,
    An lightly lap the wa',
An or the porter was at the yate
    The boy was i the ha',
23. O is my biggins broken boy,
    Or is my towers won?
Or is my Lady lighter yet
    Of a dear daughter or son?
24. Your biggin is na broken Sir
    Nor is your towers won
But the fairest Lady in a the lan
    For you this day maun burn
25. O saddle me the black the black
    Or saddle me the brown
O saddle me the swiftest steed
    That ever rade frae a town
26. Or he was near a mile awa
    She heard his wild horse sneeze
Mend up the fire my false brother
    Its na come to my knees
27. O whan he lighted at the yate
    She heard his bridle ring
Mend up the fire my false brother
    Its far yet frae my chin

19. O out it spake a bonny boy,
    Stood by her brother's side,
"O I wou'd run your errand Lady,
    O'er all the world wide:
20. "Aft have I run your errands Lady, p. 75
    Wi' sa't tears on my cheek;
Aft have I run your errands Lady,
    Whan blawn baith win' & weet."
21. O whan he came to broken briggs,
    He bent his bow & swam,
An' whan he came to green grass growing
    He took off his sheen, & ran.
22. And he came to lord William's yates,
    He bade na to chap or ca',
But set his bent bow till his breast,
    An lightly lap the wa'.
And or the porter was at the gate,
    The boy was in the ha'.
23. "O is my biggins broken boy?
    Or is my towers wone?
Or is my Lady lighter yet?
    Of a dear daughter, or son?"
24. "Your biggins is no brunt my Lord,
    Nor is your towers wone,
But the fairest Lady in a' the land, p. 76
    For you this day man burn."
25. "O saddle to me the black, the black,
    Or saddle to me the brown,
O saddle to me the swiftest steed,
    That ere rode frae a town."
26. Or he was near a mile awa',
    She hear'd his wild horse sneeze,
"Mend up the fire my false brother,
    It's nae come to my knees;"
27. And whan he lighted at the yate,
    She hard his bridle ring,
"Mend up the fire my false brother,
    It's far yet frae my chin."

p. 27

28. Mend up the fire to me brother
    Mend up the fire to me
For I see him comin' hard an fast
    Will soon men't up to thee
29. O gin my hands had been loose Willy
    Sae hard as they are boun'
I would have turnd me frae the gleed
    An casten out your young son
30. O I'll gar burn for you Maisry
    Your father an your mother
An I'll gar burn for you Maisry
    Your sister an your brother
31. An I'll gar burn for you Maisry
    The cheif of a' your kin
An the last bonfire that I come to
    Mysel' I will cast in

28. "Mend up the fire to me" she says,
 "Mend up the fire to me,
For I see him coming hard & fast,
 Will soon men't up to thee.
29. "O gin my hands had been loose Willie,
 So hard as they are bound,
I wou'd have turn'd me frae the gleed, p. 77
 An' casten out your young son."
30. "O I'll gar burn for the Mais'ry
 Your sister & your brother,
An' I'll gar burn for thee Mais'ry
 Your father & your mother.
31. "And I'll gar burn for thee Mais'ry,
 The chief of all your kin,
An' the last bonfire that I come to,
 My sel' I will cast in –"

A

12. Fair Anny [Child 76]

p. 27 1. O wha will shoe my fu fair foot
An wha will glove my han?
An wha will lace my middle gimp
Wi the new made london ban?

2. Or wha will kemb my yallow hair
Wi the new made silver kemb
Or wha'll be father to my young bairn
Till love Gregor come hame

3. Her father shoe'd her fu fair foot
Her mother glov'd her han
Her sister lac'd her middle gimp
Wi the new made linnen ban

4. Her brother kemb'd her yallow hair
Wi the new made silver kemb
But the king o' heaven maun father her bairn
Till love Gregor come hame

5. O gin I had a bony ship
An men to sail wi me
It's I would gang to my true love
Since he winna come to me

6. Her fathers gien her a bonny ship
An sent her to the stran
She's tane her young son in her arms
An turn'd her back to the lan

7. She had na been o' the sea salllin
About a month or more
Till landed has she her bonny ship
Near her true loves door

8. The night was dark & the win' blew caul
An her love was fast asleep
An the bairn that was in her twa arms
Fu sair began to weep

p. 28 9. Lang stood she at her true loves door
An lang tirl'd at the pin
At length up gat his fa'se mither
Says wha's that wou'd be in

C

12. Love Gregor [Child 76]

1. O wha will shoe my fu fair foot p. 5
   And wha will glove my hand
   And wha will lace my middle jimp
   Wi the new made london band
2. And wha will kaim my yellow hair
   Wi the new made silver kaim
   And wha will father my young son
   Till Love Gregor come hame
3. Your father will shoe your fu fair foot
   Your mother will glove your hand
   Your sister will lace your middle jimp
   Wi the new made london band
4. Your brother will kaim your yellow hair
   Wi the new made silver kaim
   And the King of heaven will father your bairn
   Till Love Gregor come hame
5. But I will get a bonny boat
   And I will sail the sea
   Far I maun gang to Love Gregor
   Since he canno come hame to me
6. O she has gotten a bonny boat p. 6
   And saill'd the sa't sea fame
   She langd to see her ain true love
   Since he could no come hame
7. O row your boat my mariners
   And bring me to the land
   For yonder I see my Loves castle
   Closs by the sa't sea strand
8. She has ta'en her young son in her arms
   And to the door she s gone
   And lang she s knocked & sair she s ca'd
   But answer got she nane
9. O open the door Love Gregor she says
   O open and let me in
   For the wind blaws thro my yellow hair
   And the rain draps oer my chin

10. “O it is Anny of Roch-royal
Your love come o’er the sea
But an your young son in her arms
So open the door to me”
11. Awa’ Awa you ill woman
You’re na’ come here for gude
You’re but a witch or wile warlock
Or mermaid o the flude
12. “I’m na a witch or wile warlock
Nor mermaiden” said she
“I’m but fair Anny o’ Roch-royal
O open the door to me”
13. O gin ye be Anny o Roch-royal
As trust not ye be
What taiken can ye gie that ever
I kept your company?
14. O dinna ye mind love Gregor she says
Whan we sat at the wine?
How we changèd the napkins frae our necks
Its na sae lang sin syne
15. An yours was good & good enough
But nae sae good as mine
For yours was o the cambrick clear
But mine was silk sae fine
16. An dinna ye mind love Gregor? she says
As we twa sat at dine
How we changed the rings frae our fingers
But ay the best was mine
17. For yours was good & good enough
Yet nae sae good as mine
For yours was of the good red gold
But mine o the diamonds fine
18. Sae open the door now love Gregor
An open it wi speed
Or your young son that is in my arms
For cauld will soon be dead
19. Awa awa you ill woman
Gae frae my door for shame
For I hae gotten another fair love
Sae ye may hye you hame

10. Awa awa ye Ill woman
    Your nae come here for good
You'r but some witch or wile warlock
    Or mer maid of the flood
11. I am neither a witch nor a wile warlock p. 7
    Nor mer maid of the sea
I am fair Annie of rough royal
    O! open the door to me
12. Gin ye be Annie of rough royal
    And I trust ye are not she
Now tell me some o the love tokens
    That past between you and me
13. O dinna you mind now love Gregor
    When we sat at the wine
How we changed the rings frae our fingers
    And I can shaw thee thine

14. O yours was good and good enneugh
    But ay the best was mine
For yours was o the good red gou'd
    But mine o the dimonds fine
15. But open the door now Love Gregor
    O open the door I pray
For your young son that is in my arms
    Will be dead ere it be day
16. Awa awa ye ill woman p. 8
    For here ye shanno win in
Gae drown ye in the raging sea
    Or hang on the gallows pin

20. O hae you gotten another fair love
    For a the oaths you sware?
Then fair you well now fas'e Gregor
    For me you's never see mare
21. O heely heely gid she back
    As the day began to peep
She set her foot on good ship board
    An sair sair did she weep
p. 29 22. Love Gregor started frae his sleep
    An to his mither did say
I dream'd a dreem this night mither
    That mak's my heart right wae
23. I dream'd that Anny of Roch-royal
    The flowr o a her kin
Was standin mournin' at my door
    But nane would lat her in
24. O there was a woman stood at the door
    Wi a bairn intill her arms
But I wou'd na lat her within the bow'r
    For fear she had done you harm

25. O quickly quickly raise he up
    An fast ran to the stran
An there he saw her fair Anny
    Was sailin frae the lan
26. An heigh Anny! & hou' Anny!
    O Anny speak to me!
But ay the louder that he cried Anny
    The louder roar'd the sea
27. An heigh Anny! & hou! Anny
    O Anny winna you bide
But ay the langer that he cried Anny
    The higher roar'd the tide
28. The win grew loud & the sea grew rough
    An the ship was rent in twain
An soon he saw her fair Anny
    Come floating 'oer the main

17. When the cock had craw'n & day did dawn
And the sun began to peep
Then it raise him Love Gregor
And sair sair did he weep

18. O I dream'd a dream my mother dear
The thoughts o' it gars me greet
That fair Annie of Rough Royal
Lay cauld dead at my feet

19. Gin it be for Annie of Rough Royal
That ye make a this din
She stood a last night at this door
But I trow she wan no in

20. O wae betide ye Ill woman
An Ill dead may ye die
That ye wou'dno open the door to her
Nor yet wou'd waken me

21. O! he has gane down to yond shore side p. 9
As fast as he could fare
He saw fair Annie in her boat
But the wind it toss'd her sair

22. And hey Annie and how Annie
O! Annie winna ye bide
But ay the mair that he cried Annie
The braider grew the tide

23. And hey Annie and how Annie
Dear Annie speak to me
But ay the louder he cried Annie
The louder roar'd the sea

24. The wind blew loud the sea grew rough
And dash'd the boat on shore
Fair Annie floats on the raging sea
But her young son raise no more

29. He saw his young son in her arms
    Baith toss'd aboon the tide
He wrang his hands then fast he ran
    An plung'd i' the sea sae wide
30. He catch'd her by the yallow hair
    An drew her to the strand
But cauld & stiff was every limb
    Before he reach'd the land
31. O first he kissd her cherry cheek
    An than he kiss'd her chin
An sair he kissd her ruby lips
    But there was nae breath within
32. O he has mourn'd oer fair Anny
    Till the sun was gaing down
Then wi a sigh his heart it brast
    An his soul to heaven has flow'n

25. Love Gregor tare his yellow hair
And made a heavy moan
Fair Annies corpse lay at his feet
But her bonny young son was gone
26. O! cherry cherry was her cheek p. 10
And gowden was her hair
But clay cold were her rosey lips
Nae spark of life was there
27. And first he's kiss'd her cherry cheek
And niest he s kiss'd her chin
And saftly press'd her rosey lips
But there was nae breath within
28. O! wae betide my cruel mother
And an ill dead may she die
For she turn'd my true Love frae my door
When she came sae far to me

A

13. Kempion [Child 34]

p. 29 1. Come here come here you freely feed
An lay your head low on my knee
The hardest weird I will you read
That ee'r was read to a lady

p. 30 2. O meikle dollour sall you dree
An ay the sat seas or ye swim
An far mair dollour sall ye dree
On east-muir craigs or ye them clim

3. I wot ye's be a weary wight
An releived sall ye never be
Till Kempion the kingis son
Come to the craig & thrice kiss thee

4. O meickle dollour did she dree
An ay the sat seas or she swam
An far mair dollour did she dree
On eastmuir craigs or them she clam
An ay she cried for Kempion
Gin he would come till her han

5. Now word has gane to Kempion
That sich a beast was in his lan
An a be sure she would gae mad
Gin she gat nae help frae his han

6. Now by my sooth says Kempion
This fiery beast I gang to see
An by my sooth says Segramour
My ae brother I'll gang you wi

7. O biggit ha they a bonny boat
An they hae set her to the sea
An' Kempion an Segramour
The fiery beast ha gane to see
A mile afore they reach'd the shore
I wot she gar'd the red fire flee

13. Kempion [Child 34]

1. "Come here, come here, ye freely feed, p. 58
   An' lay your head low on my knee,
The heaviest wierd I will you read,
   That ever was read 'till a Lady;
2. "O meickle dolor shall you dree;
   An' ay the sa't seas o'er ye swim,
An far mair dolor shall you dree,
   On East-muir craigs e're ye them clim'.
3. "I wot ye's be a weary wight,
   An' relieved shall you never be,
'Till Kempion the kingis son,
   Come to the craig & thrice kiss thee."
4. O meickle dolor did she dree,
   An' ay the sa't seas o'er she swam,
An' far mair dolor did she dree,
   On East-Muir craigs e're she them clam'.
An' ay she cri'd for Kempion p. 59
   Gin he wou'd But come 'till her hand.
5. Now word has gane to Kempion,
   That sic a beast was in his land,
An' a be sure she wou'd gae mad,
   Gin' she got nae helping frae his hand.
6. "Now by my sooth," says Kempion,
   "This fiery beast I'll gang & see;"
"And by my sooth," says Segramour,
   "My ae brother I'll gang you wi'."
7. O bigget ha' they a bonny boat,
   An' they ha' set her to the sea,
An' Kempion & Segramour,
   The fiery beast ha' gane to see,
A mile afore they reach'd the shore,
   She gar'd the red fire flee.

8. O Segramour keep my boat afloat
An lat her no the lan so near
For the wicked beast she'll sure gae mad
An set fire to the landy mair

9. O out o my stye I winna rise
An it is na for the fear o thee
Till Kempion the kingis son
Come to the craig & thrice kiss me

10. He's louted him oe'r the east-muir craig
An he has gien her kisses ane
Awa she gid & again she came
The fieryest beast that ever was seen

11. O out o my stye I winna rise
An it is na for fear o thee
Till Kempion the kingis son
Come to the craig & twice kiss me

12. He louted him oe'r the east-muir craig
An he has gien her kisses twa
Awa she gid & again she came
The fieryest beast that ever you saw

13. O out o my stye I winna rise
An it is na for fear o ye
Till Kempion the kingis son
Come to the craig & thrice kiss me

p. 31 14. He's louted him oer the eastmuir craig
An he has gie'n her kisses three
Awa she gid an again she came
The fairest lady that ever cou'd be

15. An by my sooth say Kempion
My ain true love for this is she
O was it wolf into the wood
Or was it fish intill the sea
Or was it man or wile woman
My true love that mis-shapit thee

16. It was na wolf into the wood
Nor was it fish into the sea
But it was my wicked step mother
An wae an weary mot she be

8. "O Segramour keep my boat afloat,
An' lat her nae the land sae near,
For the wicked beast shall sure gae mad,
An' set fire to a' my land & mair."
9. "O out o' my stye I winna' rise, p. 60
And it is not for the awe o' thee,
'Till Kempion the kingis son,
Come to the craig, & thrice kiss me."
10. He's looted him oe'r the East muir craig,
An' he has gane her kisses ane,
Awa' she gi'd, & again she came,
The fieryest beast that ever was seen.
11. "O out o' my stye I winna' rise,
An' it is not for the awe o' thee,
Till Kempion the kingis son
Come to the craig, & twice kiss me."
12. He's looted him o'er the East muir craig,
An' he has gien her kisses twa,
Awa' she gi'd & again she came,
The fieryest beast that ever you saw.
13. "O out o' my stye I wina' rise,
An' it is not for the awe o' thee,
Till Kempion the kingis son,
Come to the craig & thrice kiss me."
14. He's looted him o'er the East muir craigs, p. 61
And he has gi'n her kisses three;
Awa' she gi'd & again she came,
The bonniest Lady that ever cou'd be.
15. "An' by my sooth," says Kempion,
"My ain true love (for this is she)
O was it wolf into the wood?
Or was it fish into the sea?
Or was it man, or vile woman?
My ain true love, that mis-shap'd thee?"
16. "It was not wolf into the wood,
Nor was it fish into the sea,
But it was my wicked step-mother,
An' wae & weary may she be.

17. O a heavier weird light her upon
    Than ever fell on wile woman
Her hairs grow rough an her teeths grow lang
    An on her four feet sal she gang
Nane sall tack pity her upon
    But in wormies wood she sall ay won
18. An relieved sall she never be
    Till St Mungo come oer the sea

17. "O a heavier wierd light her upon,
    Than ever fell on wile woman,
Her hair's grow rough, & her teeth's grow lang,
    And on her four feet shall she gang;
Nane shall take pity her upon,
    But in worme's wood she shall ay wone.
18. "An' relieved shall she never be, p. 62
    'Till St. Mungo come o'er the sea."
An' sighing said that weary wight,
    "I fear that day I'll never sea – "

A

14. King Henry [Child 32]

p. 31 1. Lat never a man a wooing wend
That lacketh thingis three
A routh o gold an open heart
Ay fu o Charity
2. As this I speak of King Henry
For he lay burd alone
An he's doen him to a jelly hunts ha
Was seven miles frae a town
3. He chas'd the deer now him before
An the roe down by the den
Till the fattest buck in a the flock
King Henry he has slain
4. O he has doen him to his ha
To make him beerly cheer
An in it came a griesly ghost
Steed stappin ithe fleer
5. Her head hat the reef tree o the house
Her middle ye mot well span
He's thrown to her his gay mantle
Says lady hap your lingcan.
6. Her teeth was a like teather stakes
Her nose like club or mell
An I ken naething she 'peard to be
But the fiend that wons in hell
7. Some meat some meat ye King Henry
Some meat ye gie to me?
An what meats in this house lady
An what ha I to gie?
p. 32 O ye do kill your berry brown steed
An you bring him here to me

14. King Henry [Child 32]

1. Lat never a man a wooing wend p. 66
   That lacketh thingis three,
   A routh o' gold, & open heart,
   An' fu' o' Charity!
2. As this I speak o' king Henry,
   (For he lay burd alone)
   And he's taen until a jelly hunt's ha',
   Was seven miles frae a town.
3. He chas'd the deer now him before,
   An' the roe down by the den,
   'Till the fattest buck in a' the flock,
   King Henry he has slain.
4. O he has ta'en him 'till his ha',
   To make him beerly cheer,
   An' in it came a griesly ghost,
   Stood stapping in the fleer.
5. Her head hat the reef-tree o' the house, p. 67
   An' her middle ye ma't well span,
   He's thrown to her his gay mantle,
   Says "Lady hap your Lingcan."
6. Her teeth was a' like taether stakes,
   Her nose like club or mell,
   An' I ken nae thing she peer'd to be,
   But the fiend that wiends in hell.
7. "Some meat, some meat ye king Henry,
   Some meat ye gie to me;"
   "An' what meat's i' this house Lady?
   An' fat have I to gie?"
   "O ye dee slay your berry brown steed,
   An' you bring him here to me;"

8. O whan he slew his berry brown steed
   Wow but his heart was sair,
   She eat him a up skin an bane
   Left naething but hide an hair.
9. Mair meat mair meat ye king Henry
   Mair meat ye gi to me!
   An what meats in this house Lady
   An what ha I to gi?
   O ye do kill your good gray hounds
   An ye bring them a to me.
10. O whan he Slew his good gray hounds
   Wow but his heart was sair
   She eat them a up skin an bane
   Left naething but hide an hair
11. Mair meat mair meat ye king Henry
   Mair meat ye gi to me
   An what meats i this house lady
   An what ha I to gi
   O ye do kill your gay gos hawks
   An ye bring them here to me
12. O whan he slew his gay gos-hawks
   Wow but his heart was sair
   She eat them a up skin an bane,
   Left naething but feathers bare
13. Some drink some drink now king Henry
   Some drink ye bring to me
   O what drinks i this house lady
   That youre nae welcome ti?
   O ye shew up your horses hide
   An bring in a drink to me
14. A bed a bed now king Henry
   A bed you mak' to me
   For ye maun pu the heather green
   An mak' a bed to me

15. O pu'd has he the heather green
   An made to her a bed
   An up has he taen his gay mantle
   An oe'r it has he spread

8. O whan he slew his berry brown steed
Wow but his heart was sair,
She eat him a’ up skin & been
Left naething but hide & hair.

9. “Mair meat, mair meat ye king Henry,
Mair meat ye gie to me;”
“An’ fat meat’s i’ this house Lady, p. 68
An’ what have I to gie.”
“O ye do kill your good gray hounds,
An’ bring them a’ to me.”

10. O whan he slew his good grey hounds
Wow but his heart was sair,
She eat them a’ up skin & bane,
Left naething but hide & hair.

11. “Mair meat, mair meat ye king Henry,
Mair meat ye bring to me;”
“An’ what meat’s i’ this house Lady
That yee’r nae welcome ti!”
“O ye do fell your gay goss-hawks,
An’ you bring them a’ to me.”

12. O whan he fell’d his gay Goss-hawks,
Wow but his heart was sair,
She eat them a’ up bane by bane,
Left naething but feathers bare.

13. “Some drink, some drink ye king Henry p. 69
Some drink ye bring to me;”
“O what drinks i’ this house Lady,
That you’re nae welcome ti!”
“O ye sew up your horse’s hide,
An’ bring in a drink to me.”

14. “A bed, a bed now king Henry,
An’ a bed you mak’ to me;”
“O what bed’s i’ this house Lady,
That you’re nae welcome ti!”
“O ye man pu’ the green heather,
An’ mak’ a bed to me.”

15. O pu’d has he the heather green
An’ made to her a bed,
An’ up has he ta’en his gay mantle,
And o’er it has he spread.

16. Tak' aff your claiths now king Henry
An lye down by my side
O God forbid says king Henry
That ever the like betide
p. 33 That ever the fiend that wons in hell
Shou'd streak down by my side
17. Whan night was gane & day was come
An the sun shone throw the ha
The fairest lady that ever was seen
Lay atween him an the wa
18. O well is me says King Henry
How lang'll this last wi me
Then out it spake that fair lady
"Even till the day you dee
19. "For I've met wi mony a gentle knight
Thats gi'en me sick a fill
But never before wi a courteous knight
That ga me a my will"

16. "Tak' aff your claiths now king Henry,
An' lye down me beside;"
"O God forbid" said, king Henry, p. 70
"That ever the like betide,
That ever the fiend that wons in hell,
Shou'd streak down by my side."

17. Whan night was gane & day was come,
An' the sun shone thro' the ha',
The fairest Lady that ever was seen,
Lay atween him & the wa'.

18. "O well is me" said king Henry,
"How lang will this last wi' me;"
An' out it spake that fair Lady,
"Even 'till the day you dee.

19. "For I've met wi' mony a gentle knight,
That's gi'n me sick a fill,
But never before wi' a Courteous knight,
That gae me a' my will"

A

15. Sweet Willy [Child 6]

p. 33

1. Sweet Willy's taen him oer the fame
He's wood a wife and brought her hame
He's woo'd her for her yallow hair
But's mither wrought her mieckle care
2. And mieckle dollour gar'd her dree
For lighter she can never be
But in her bow'r she sits wi pain
An' Willy mourns o'er her in vain
3. Now to his mither he has gane
That wile rank witch o' vilest kin
He say "my lady has a girdle
Its a red gold unto the middle"
4. "An ay at ilka silver hem
Hings fifty silver bells an ten
That goodly gift sall be your ain
An lat her be lighter o' her young bairn"
5. O her young bairn she's never be lighter
Nor in her bow'r to shine the brighter
But she sal die an turn to clay
An you sal wed another May
6. Another May I'll never wed
Another May I'll never bring hame
But sighing says that weary Wight
I wish my life was at an en'
7. He did him till his mither again
That wile rank witch o wilest kin
An said, "My lady has a steed
The like o' him's na i the lands o Leed
8. "For he is golden shod before
An he is Golden shod behin'
An at ilka tate o that horse mane
Theres a golden chess & a bell ringin'
This goodly gift sal be your ain
An lat her be lighter o' her young bairn"

B

15. Willie's Lady [Child 6]

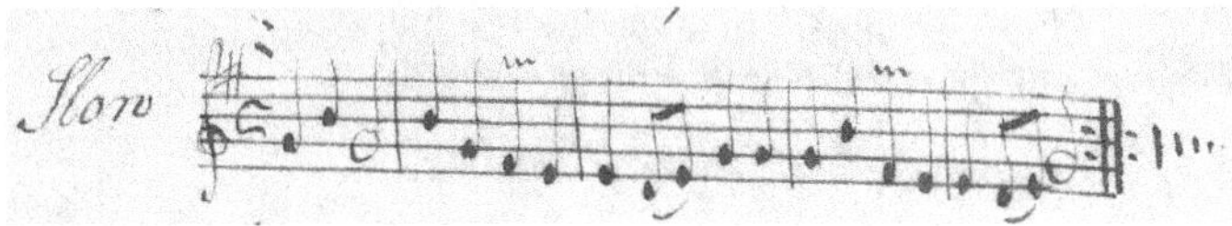

1. Willie's taen him o'er the fame, p. 1
He's woo'd a wife, & brought her hame;
He's wood her for her yallow hair,
But's Mother wrought her meickle care;
2. And meickle Dolor gar'd her dree
For lighter she can never bee;
But in her bow'r she sits wi' pain
And Willie mourns o'er her in vain.
3. And to his mither he has gane,
That vile rank witch o' vilest kind,
He says, "my Lady has a cup,
Wi' gold & silver set about;
4. This goodly gift shall be your ain
And lat her be lighter o' her young bairn."
"Of her young bairn she's never be lighter,
Nor in her bow'r to shine the brighter,
5. But she shall die & turn to clay
And you shall wed another May."
"Another May I'll never wed p. 2
Another May I'll never bring hame:"
6. But sighing says that weary wight,
"I wish my life were at an end – "
"Ye dae unto your mother again,
That vile rank witch of viler kind,
7. "And say your Lady has a steed,
The like o'm's nae i' the Lands of Leed;
For he is golden shod before,
And he is golden shod behind,
8. "An' at ilka Tet of that horse' main
There's a golden chess, & a bell ringing:
This goodly gift shall be her ain,
And lat me be lighter of my young bairn."

9. O her young bairn she's never be lighter
No in her bow'r to shine the brighter
But she sal die an go to clay
An you sal wed another May

10. Another May I'll never wed
Another May I'll never bring hame
But sighin' says that weary wight
I wish my life were at an en'

p. 34 11. Then out it spake the belly blin
She spake ay in a good time
"Ye do ye to the market place
An there ye buy a loaf o' wax

12. "Ye shape it bairn an bairnly like
An in twa glazen een ye pit
An do you to your mither then
An bid her come to your boys christnen

13. "For dear's the boy he's been to you
Then notice well what she shall do
An do you stan a little forbye
An listen well what she shall say"

14. He did him to the market place
An there he bought a loaf o' wax
He shap'd it bairn an bairnly like
An in't twa glazen een he pat

9. "Of her young bairn she's never be lighter,
Nor in her bow'r to shine the brighter,
But she shall die, & turn to clay,
And you shall wed another May."
10. "Another May I'll never wed,
Another May I'll never bring hame"
But sighing says that weary wight, p. 3
"I wish my life were at an end."
11. "Ye doe you to your mother again,
That vile rank witch o' viler kind,
An' say your Lady has a girdle
'Its a' red goud unto the middle,
12. "And ay at ilka silver hem
Hings fifty silver bells, & ten;
That goodly gift shall be her ain,
An' lat me be lighter o' my young bairn."
13. "Of her young bairn she's never be lighter,
Nor in her bow'r to shine the brighter,
But she shall die, & go to clay,
And you shall wed another May. –"
14. "Another; &.c.

15. Then out it spake the Belly-blind
(He spake ay in a good time)
"Ye doe ye to the market place,
And there ye buy a loaf o' wax,
16. "You shape it, bairn & bairnly like,
And in twa glasen een you pit;
An' bid her come to your boy's christ'ning:
Then notice well what she shall do;
And do you stand a little forbye,
And listen well what she will say;"

15. He did him till his mither then
An bade to his boys christnen
An he did stan a little forebye
An notic'd well what she did say

16. O wha has loos'd the nine witch knots
That was amo' that lady's locks
An wha's taen out the kaimbs o' care
That hang amo' that ladys hair

17. "An wha has kill'd the master kid
That ran aneath that ladys bed
An wha has loos'd her left foot shee
An latten that lady lighter b[e]

18. "O Willy's loosd the nine witch knots
That hang amo' his ladys locks
An Willy s taen out the kemb o' care
That hang amo' his ladys hair

19. An Willy's killd the master kid
That ran aneath his ladys bed
An Willy's loosd her left foot shee
An latten his lady lighter be

17. "O, wha has loos'd the nine witch knots
That was amo' that Lady's locks;
An' wha's ta'en out the kaims o' Care,
That hang amo' that Lady's hair;

18. An' wha's taen down the bush o' wood-bine
That hang a'tween her bower & mine;
And wha has kill'd the master kid
That ran beneath that Lady's bed;
19. An' wha has loos'd her left foot shee,
An' latten that Lady lighter be."
O! Willy's loos'd the nine witch knots,
That was amo' his Lady's locks;
20. And Willy's &.c.

21.

And now hes gotten a bonny young son,
And meickle grace be him upon –

A

16. Gil Brenton [Child 5]

p. 34 1. Gil Brenton has sent o'er the fame
He's woo'd a wife & brought her ham[e]
Full sevn score o' ships came her wi
The lady by the green wood tree
2. There was twal' & twal wi beer & wine
An twal & twal wi muskadine
An twall & twall wi bouted flowr
An twall & twall wi paramour
3. An twall & twall wi baken bread
An twall & twall wi the goud sae red
Sweet Willy was a widows son
An at her stirrup foot he did run
p. 35 4. An she was dress'd i the finest pa
But ay she loot the tears down fa
An she was deck'd wi the fairest flowrs
But ay she loot the tears down powr
5. O is there water i your shee
Or does the win' blaw i your glee
Or are you mourning i your meed
That ee'r you left your mither gueede
6. Or are ye mourning i your tide
That ever ye was Gil Brentons bride
The is nae water i my shee
Nor does the win' blaw i my glee
7. Nor am I mourning i my tide
That ee'r I was Gil Brentons bride
But I am mourning i my meed
That ever I left my mither gueede
8. But bonny boy tell to me,
What is the customs o your country
The customs o't my dame he says
Will ill a gentle lady please

16. Chil Brenton [Child 5]

1. Chil' Brenton has sent o'er the fame p. 17
Chil' Brenton's brought his Lady hame,
An' seven score o' ships came her wi'
The Lady by the greenwood tree.
2. There was twal' & twal' wi' bear & wine
And twal' & twal' wi' muskadine
An' twal' & twal' wi' bouted flow'r,
And twal', & twal wi' the paramour:
3. And twal & twal wi' baken bread
And twal & twal wi' the gou'd sae red.
Sweet Willy was a widow's son
And at her stirrup foot he did run;
4. An' she was dress'd i' the finest pa',
But ay she loot the tears down fa';
And she was dress'd wi' the finest flow'rs
But ay' she loot the tears down pour.
5. "O is there water i' your shee,
Or does the wind blaw i' your glee;
Or are you mourning in your meed
That e'er you left your mither gueed;
6. "Or are you mourning i' your tide, p. 18
That e're you was Chil' Brenton's bride."
"There is nae water i' my shee,
Nor does the wind blaw i' my glee;
7. "Nor am I mourning i' my tide
That e're I was Chil' Brenton's bride;
But I am mourning i' my meed
That e're I left my mither gueed.
8. "But bonny boy tell to me,
What is the customes o' your country."
"The customes o' it my dame," he says,
"Will ill a gentle Lady please:"

9. Seven kings daughter has our king wedded
An seven kings daughter has our king bedded
But he's cutted the paps frae their breast bane
An sent them mourning hame again
10. But whan you come to the palace yate
His mither a golden chair will set
An be you maid or be you nane
O sit you there till the day be dane
11. An gin youre sure that you are a maid
Ye may gang safely to his bed
But gin o that you be na sure
Then hire some woman o youre bow'r
12. O whan she came to the palace yate
His mither a golden chair did set
An was she maid or was she nane
She sat in it till the day was dane
13. An she's call'd on her bow'r woman
That waiting was her bowr within
Five hundred pound maid I'll gi to the
An sleep this night wi the king for me
14. Whan bells was rung & mass was sung
An a man unto bed was gone
Gil Brenton & the bonny maid
Intill ae chamber they were laid
15. O speak to me blankets & speak to me sheets
An speak to me cods that under me sleeps
Is this a maid that I ha wedded
Is this a maid that I ha bedded
16. It's nae a maid that you ha wedded
But its a maid that you ha bedded
Your lady's in her bigly bowr
An for you she drees mony sharp show'r
17. O he has taen him thro the ha
p. 36 An on his mither he did ca
I am the most unhappy man
That ever was in christen'd lan
I woo d a maiden meek & mild
An I've marryed a woman great wi child

9. "Seven king's daughters has our king wedded
An' seven king's daughters has our king bedded
But he's cutted the paps frae their breast bane,
An' sent them mourning hame again.
10. "But whan you come to the pallace yate
His mither a golden chair will set,
An' be you maid, or be you nane,
O sit you there 'till the day be dane.
11. "And gin you're sure that you're a maid,
Ye may gang safely to his bed;
But if o' that ye be nae sure,
Then hire some virgin o' your bower."
12. O whan she came to the pallace yate p. 19
His mither a golden chair did set,
An' was she maid, or was she nane,
She sat in it 'till the day was dane.
13. An' she's call'd on her bow'r woman,
That waiting was her bow'r within,
"Five hundred pounds I'll gi' to thee
An' sleep this night wi the king for me."
14. Whan bells was rung, & mess was sung,
And a' man unto bed was gone,
Chil' Brenton, & the bonny maid,
Until ae chamber they were laid.
15. "O speak to me blankets, & speak to me sheets,
And speak to me cods that under me sleeps,
Is this a maid 'at I ha' wedded?
Is this a maid 'at I ha bedded?"
16. "Its not a maid that you had wedded,
But its a maid 'at you ha' bedded,
Your Lady lies in her bigly bow'r,
An' for you she drees mony sharp show'r."
17. O he has taen him thro' the ha'
And on his mother he did ca'
"I am the most unhappy man,
That ever was in christen'd lan';
I woo'd a maiden meek & mild, p. 20
And I've married a woman great wi' child."

18. O stay my son intill this ha
An sport you wi your merry men a
An I'll gang to yon painted bow'r
An see how't fares wi yon base whore
19. The auld queen she was stark & strang
She gard the door flee aff the ban
The auld queen she was stark & steer
She gard the door lye i the fleer
20. O is your bairn to laird or loon
Or is it to your fathers groom
My bairns na to laird or loon
Nor is it to my fathers groom
But hear me mither on my knee
An my hard wierd I'll tell to thee
21. O we were sisters, sisters seven
We was the fairest under heaven
We had nae mair for our seven years wark
But to shape & sue the kings son a sark
22. O it fell on a saturdays afternoon
Whan a our langsome wark was dane
We keist the cavils us amang
To see which shou'd to the green wood gang
23. Ohone alas! for I was youngest
An ay my wierd it was the hardest
The cavil it did on me fa
Which was the cause of a my wae
24. For to the greenwood I must gae
To pu the nut but an the slae
To pu the red rose & the thyme
To strew my mothers bow'r & mine
25. I had na pu'd a flowr but ane
Till by there came a jelly hind greeme
Wi high coll'd hose & laigh coll'd shoone
An he 'peard to be some kingis son
26. An be I maid or be I nane
He kept me there till the day was dane
An be I maid or be a nae
H[e] kept me there till the close of day

18. "O stay my son into this ha',
An' sport you wi' your merry men a',
And I'll gang to yon painted bow'r
An' see how't fares wi' yon' base whore."

19. The auld Queen she was stark & strang,
She gar'd the door, flee off the band;
The auld Queen she was stark & steer,
She gar'd the door lie i' the fleer.

20. "O is your bairn to Laird or Loon,
Or is it to your father's groom."
"My bairn's nae to Laird or Loon,
Nor is it to my father's groom,
But hear me mither o' my knee,
'Till my hard wierd I tell to thee.

21. "O we were sisters, sisters seven,
We was the fairest under heaven;
We had nae mair for our seven years' wark,
But to shape & sew the king's son a sark.

22. "It fell on a Saturday's afternoon,
Whan a' our langsome wark was doone
We kest the kavels us amang,
To see which shou'd to the Green-wood gang.

23. "Ohon! alas! for I was youngest, p. 21
An' ay my wierd it was the hardest,
The cavel it on me did fa',
Which was the cause of a' my woe;

24. "For to the green-wood I must gae,
To pu' the nut but an' the slae;
To pu' the red-rose & the thyme;
To strew my mithers bow'r & mine.

25. "I had nae pu'd a flow'r but ane,
'Till by there came a jelly hind-greem
Wi' high coll'd hose, & laigh coll'd sheen,
An' he seem'd to be some king his son;

26. "And be I maid, or be I nane,
He kept me there 'till the day was dane;
And be I maid, or be I nae,
He kept me there 'till the close o' day.

27. He gae me a lock of yallow hair
An bade me keep it for ever mair
He gae me a carket o' gude black beads
An bade me keep them against my needs
28. He gae to me a gay gold ring
An bade me kep it aboon a thing
He gae to me a little pen kniffe
An bade me keep it as my life
p. 37 29. What did you wi these tokens rare
That ye got frae that young man there
O bring that coffer hear to me
An a the tokens ye sal see
30. An ay she ranked & ay she flang
Till a the tokens came till her han
O stay here daughter your bow'r within
Till I gae parley wi my son
31. O she has taen her thro the ha
An on her son began to ca
What did you wi that gay gold ring
I bade you keep aboon a thing
32. What did you wi that little pen kniffe
I bade you keep while you had life
What did you wi that yallow hair
I bade you keep for ever mair
33. "What did you wi that good black beeds
I bade you keep against your needs"
I gae them to a lady gay
I met i the green wood on a day
34. An I would gi a my fathers lan
I had that lady my yates within
I would gi a my ha's & towrs
I had that bright burd i my bowrs
35. O son keep still your fathers lan
You hae that lady your yates within
An keep you still your ha's & towrs
You hae that bright burd i your bowrs
36. Now or a month was come & gone
This lady bare a bonny young son
An it was well written on his breast bane
Gil Brenton is my fathers name

27. "He gae me a lock o' yallow hair,
An' bade me keep it for evermair;
He gae me a carket o' gude black beeds,
An' bade me keep them against my needs;
28. "He gae to me a gay gold ring,
An' bade me keep it aboon a' thing;
He gae to me a little penknife,
An' bade me keep it as my life."
29. "What did you wi' these tokens rare? p. 22
That ye got frae that young man there?"
"O bring that coffer unto me,
An' a' the tokens ye shall see."
30. And ay She ranked, & she flang,
'Till a' the tokens came 'till her han'.
"O stay here daughter your bow'r within,
'Till I gae parly wi' my son."
31. O she has ta'en her thro' the ha'
An' on her son began to ca',
"What did you wi' that gay gold ring?
I bade you keep aboon a' thing?
32. "What did you wi' that little penknife?
I bade ye keep while ye had life?
What did ye wi' that yallow hair?
I bade ye keep for evermair?
33. "What did ye wi' that gude black beeds?
You shou'd ha' kept against your needs?"
"I gae them 'till a Lady gay,
I met i' the green wood on a day:
34. "And I wou'd gie a' my ha's, & tow'rs
I had that bright bird i' my bow'rs
I wou'd gie a' my father's lan'
I had that Lady by the han'."
35. "O son keep still your ha's & tow'rs p. 23
You ha' that Lady i' your bow'rs
An' keep you still your father's lan'
You'se get that Lady by the han'."
36. Now or a month was come & gone
This Lady bare a bonny young son,
An' 'twas well written on his breast-bane
Chil' Brenton is my father's Name.

A

17. Brown Robin [Child 97]

p. 37 1. The king but an his nobles a
Sat birling at the wine
The king but an his nobles a
sat birling at ye wine
He would ha nane but his ae daughter
To wait on them at dine

2. She's serv'd them butt she's serv'd them ben
Intill a gown of green
But her ee was ay on Brown Robin
That stood low under the rain

3. She's doen her to her bigly bowr
As fast as she cou'd gang
An there she's drawn her shot window
An she's harped & she sang

4. There sits a bird i my fathers garden
An o but she sings sweet
I hope to live an see the day
Whan wi my love I'll meet

p. 38 5. O gin that ye like me as well
As your tongue tells to me
What hour o the night my lady bright
At your bow'r sal I be?

6. Whan my father an gay Gilbert
Are baith set at the wine
O ready ready I will be
To lat my true love in

17. Brown Robin [Child 97]

1. The king but & his nobles a' p. 47
   Sat drinking at the wine,
   He wou'd ha' nane but his ae daughter,
   To wait on them at dine.

2. She's serv'd them butt, she's serv'd them benn,
   Intil a gown o' green,
   But her ee was ay upon Brown Robin
   That steed low under the rain.
3. She's doen her to her bigly bow'r,
   As fast as she cou'd gang,
   An' there she's drawn her shot-window,
   An' she's harped, & she's sang.
4. "There sits a bird i' my father's garden,
   An' o, but he sings sweet,
   I hope to live & see the day,
   Whan wi' my love I'll meet."
5. "O gin that ye like me as well,
   As your tongue tells to me,
   What hour o' the night, my Lady bright?
   At your bow'r shall I be?"
6. "Whan my father & gay Gilbert p. 48
   Are baith set at their wine,
   O ready, ready will I be
   To lat my true love in."

7. O she has birl'd her fathers porter
Wi strong beer an wi wi wine
Untill he was as beastly drunk
As ony wild wood swine
She's stown the keys o her fathers yates
An latten her true love in

8. Whan night was gane & day was come
An the sun shone on their feet
Then out it spake him Brown Robin
I'll be discoverd yet

9. Then out it spake that gay lady
My love ye need na doubt
For wi ae wile I've got you in
Wi anither I'll bring you out.

10. She's taen her to her fathers cellar
As fast as she can fare
She's drawn a cup o the gude red wine
Hung't low down by her gare
An she met wi her father dear
Just coming down the stair

11. I wou'd na gi that cup daughter
That ye hold i your han
For a the wines in my cellar
An gantrees whare the stan

12. O wae be to your wine father
That ever't came oer the sea
T'is pitten my head in sick a steer
I' my bowr I canna be

13. Gang out gang out my daughter dear
Gang out an tack the air
Gang out an walk i the good green wood
An a your Marys fair

14. Then out it spake the proud porter
Our lady wish'd him shame
We'll send the Marys to the wood
But we'll keep our lady at hame

15. There's thirty Marys i my bow'r
Ther's thirty o them an three
But there's nae ane amo them a
Kens what flowr gains for me

7. O she has hir'd her father's porter,
Wi' strong beer, & wi' wine,
Until he was as beastly drunk,
As ony wild-wood swine;
She's stown the key o' her father's yate,
An latten her true love in.

8. Whan night was gone & day was come,
An' the sun shin'd o' their feet,
Then out it spake him Brown Robin,
"I'll be discover'd yet."

9. O out it spake that gay Lady,
"My love ye neednae doubt,
For wi' ae wile I've brought you in,
Wi' another I'll bring you out."

10. She's tae'n her 'till her father's cellar,
As fast as she can fare,
She's drawn a cup o' the gude red wine,
Hang't low down by her gare;
An she met wi' her father dear,
Just coming down the stair:

11. "I wou'd nae gi' that cup daughter p. 49
That I see i' your hand,
For a' the wines in my cellar,
And gan-trees whare they stand."

12. "O wae be to your wine father,
That ever't came o'er the sea,
'T has pitten my head in such a steer,
I' my bow'r I canno' be."

13. "Gang out, gang out my daughter dear,
Gang out & tak' the air,
Gang out & walk i' the good green-wood,
An your Marys sae fair."

14. O out it spake the proud Porter,
Our Lady wish'd him shame,
"We'll send the Marys to the wood,
An' keep our Lady at hame."

15. "There's thirty Marys i' my bow'r,
There's thirty o' them & three,
But there is nae ane amang them a',
Kens what flow'r gains for me."

16. She's doen her to her bigly bowr
    As fast as she could gang
An she has dresst him Brown Robin
    Like ony bowr woman

p. 39 17. The gown she pat upon her love
    Was o the dainty green
His hose was o the saft, saft silk
    His shoone o the cordwain fine

18. She's pitten his bow in her boson
    His arrow in her sleeve
His sturdy bran her body next
    Because he was her love

19. Then she is unto her bowr door
    As fast as she cou'd gang
But out it spake the proud porter
    Our lady wish'd him shame
We'll count our Marys to the wood
    An we'll count them back again

20. The firsten Mary she sent out
    Was Brown Robin by name
Then out it spake the king himself
    This is a sturdy dame

21. O She went out in a may morning
    In a may morning so gray
But she came never back again
    Her auld father to see

16. She's doen her 'till her bigly bow'r,
    As fast as she cou'd gang,

17. The gown she pat upon her love,
    Was o' the dainty green;
The stockings was o' the saft, saft silke, p. 50
    An' his shune o' the cordwain fine.
18. She's pitten her bow in her bosom,
    His arrow in her sleeve,
His sturdy bran' her body next,
    Because he was her love.
19. Then out it spake the proud porter,
    Our Lady wish'd him shame,
"We'll count our Marys to the wood,
    An' we'll count them back again."

20. The firstin Mary she sent out,
    Was Brown Robin by name;
Then out it spake the king himsel'
    "This is a sturdy Dame."
21. O she went out in a May morning,
    In a May morning sae grey,
But she came never back again,
    Her auld father to see.

A

18. The twa Sisters [Child 10]

p. 39 1. There was twa sisters in a bowr
Edinburgh, Edinburgh
There was twa sisters in a bowr
Stirling for ay
There was twa sisters in a bowr
There came a knight to be their wooer
Bonny saint Johnston stands upon Tay

2. He courted the eldest wi glove & ring
Edinburgh Edinburgh
He courted the eldest wi glove and ring
Stirling for ay
He courted the eldest wi glove and ring
But he lovd the youngest above a thing
Bonny saint Johnston stands upon Tay

B

18. The Cruel Sister [Child 10]

1. There was twa sisters in ae bow'r, p. 78
    Edinbrough, Edinbrough;
  There was twa sisters in ae bow'r
    Stirling for ay;
  There was twa sisters in ae bow'r,
  There came a knight to be their wooer;
    Bonny St Johnston stands upon Tay
2. He courted the eldest wi' glove & ring p. 79
    Edinbrough, Edinbrough;
  He courted the eldest wi' glove & ring
    Stirling for ay;
  But lov'd the youngest aboon a' thing
    Bonny St Johnston stands upon Tay

3. He courted the eldest wi brotch & knife
But lovd the youngest as his life
4. The eldest she was vexed sair
An much envi'd her sister fair
5. Into her bowr she could not rest
Wi grief an spite she almos brast
6. Upon a morning fair an clear
She cried upon her sister dear
7. O sister come to yon sea stran
An see our fathers ships come to lan
8. She's taen her by the milk white han
An led her down to yon sea stran
p. 40 9. The younges stood upon a stane
The eldest came an threw her in
10. She tooke her by the middle sma
An dash'd her bonny back to the jaw
11. O sister sister tak my han
An I'se mack you heir to a my lan
12. O sister sister tak my middle
An ye's get my goud & my gouden girdle
13. O sister sister save my life
An I swear I'se never be nae mans wife
14. Foul fa the han that I should tacke
It twin'd me an my wardles make
15. Your cherry cheeks & yallow hair
Gars me gae maiden for evermair
16. Sometimes she sank & sometimes she swam
Till she came down yon bonny mill dam
17. O out it came the millers son
An saw the fair maid swimmin in
18. O father father draw your dam
Here's either a mermaid or a swan
19. The miller quickly drew the dam
An there he found a drownd woman
20. You cou'dna see her yallow hair
For gold & pearle that were so rare
21. You cou'dna see her middle sma
For gouden girdle that was sae braw
22. You cou'dna see her fingers white
For gouden rings that was sae gryte

3. He courted the eldest wi' broach & knife,
But lov'd the youngest as his life
4. The eldest she was vexed sair,
And sair envied her sister fair.
5. Into the bow'r she cou'd nae rest
Wi' grief & spite she almost brest.
6. Upon a morning fair & clear,
She cri'd upon her sister dear;
7. "O sister go to yon sea strand,
An' see our father's ships come in."
8. She's ta'en her by the milke white hand,
An' led her down to yon sea strand.
9. The youngest stood upon a stane,
The eldest came & threw her in.
10. She took her by the middle sma',
And dash'd her bonny back to the jaw.
11. "O sister sister take my hand,
An' I'se mak' you heir to a' my land,
12. "O sister sister tak' my middle, p. 80
An' ye's get my gou'd, & gou'den girdle;
13. "O sister, sister save my life,
An' I swear I'se never be no man's wife."
14. "Foul fa' the hand that I shou'd take,
It twin'd me & my warld's make;
15. "Your cherry cheeks & your yallow hair,
Gars me gang maiden for ever mair."
16. Sometimes she sank, & sometimes swam,
'Till she came down yon bonny mill-dam.
17. O out it came the miller's son,
And saw the fair maid swimming in.
18. "O Father haste & draw your dam,
Here's either a mermaid or a swan."
19. The Miller quickly drew his dam,
And there he found a drown'd woman.
20. You cou'd nae see her yallow hair,
For gou'd & pearle that was sae rare;
21. You cou'd nae see her middle sma',
Her gou'den girdle – it was sae braw;
22. You cou'd nae see her fingers white, p. 81
For the gou'd rings that were sae gryte.

23. An by there came a harper fine
That harped to the king at dine
24. Whan he did look that lady upon
He sigh'd & made a heavy moan
25. He's taen three locks o her yallow hair
An wi them strung his harp sae fair
26. The first tune he did play & sing
Was "farewell to my father the king"
27. The nextin tune that he play'd syne
Was "farewell to my mother the queen"
28. The lastin tune that he play'd then
Was "wae to my sister fair Ellen – "

23. O by there came a Harper fine,
That harped to the king at dine:
24. When he did look that Lady upon
He sigh'd & made a heavy moan.
25. He's ta'en three locks o' her yallow hair,
An' wi' them strung his harp sae fair.
26. The first tune he did play & sing,
Was farewel to my father the king.
27. The next tune that he played seene
Was farewel to my mother the queen.
28. The last tune that he played then
Was woe to my sister fair Ellen.

A

19. Allison Gross [Child 35]

p. 40 1. O Allison gross that lives in yon towr
The ugliest witch i the north country
Has trysted me ae day up till her bowr
An monny fair speech she made to me
2. She stroaked my head & she kembed my hair
An she set me down saftly on her knee
Says gin ye will be my lemman so true
Sae monny braw things as I wou'd you gi
p. 41 3. She show'd me a mantle o red scarlet
Wi gouden flowrs & fringes fine
Says gin ye will be my lemman so true
This goodly gift it sal be thine
4. Awa awa ye ugly witch
Haud far awa an lat me be
I never will be your lemman sae true
An I wish I were out o your company
5. She neist brought a sark o the saftest silk
Well wrought wi pearles about the ban
Says gin you will be my ain true love
This goodly gift you sal comman'
6. She show'd me a cup of the good red gold
Well set wi jewls sae fair to see
Says gin you will be my lemman sae true
This goodly gift I will you gi
7. Awa, awa ye ugly witch
Had far awa & lat me be
For I wou'dna ance kiss your ugly mouth
For a the gifts that ye cou'd gi
8. She's turn'd her right an roun' about
An thrice she blew on a grass green horn
An she sware by the meen & the stars abeen
That she'd gar me rue the day I was born
9. Then out has she taen a silver wand
An she's turn'd her three times roun & roun
She's mutter'd sich words till my strength it faild
An I fell down senceless upon the groun

[No parallel text]

10. She's turn'd me into an ugly worm
    An gar'd me toddle about the tree
An ay on ilka Saturdays night
    My sister Maisry came to me
11. Wi' silver bason & silver kemb
    To kemb my heady upon her knee
But or I had kiss'd her ugly mouth
    I'd rather a toddled about the tree
12. But as it fell out on last Hallow even
    When the Seely court was ridin by
The queen lighted down on a gowany bank
    Nae far frae the tree where I wont to lye
13. She took me up in her milk white han
    An she's stroak'd me three times oer her knee
She changd me again to my ain proper Shape
    An I nae mair maun toddle about the tree

[No parallel text]

A

20. The bonny birdy [Child 82]

p. 42 1. There was a knight in a summers night
Was riding oer the lee Diddle
An there he saw a bonny birdy
Was singing upon a tree Diddle
O wow for day Diddle
An dear gin it were day Diddle
Gin it were day Diddle I were away
For I ha na lang time to stay Diddle

2. Make hast make hast ye gentle knight
What keeps you here so late Diddle
Gin ye kent what was doing at hame
I fear you wou'd look blate Diddle
O wow &c

3. O what needs I toil day & night
My fair body to kill Diddle
Whan I hae knights at my comman
An ladys at my will Diddle
O wow &c

4. Ye lee ye lee ye gentle knight
Sa loud's I hear you lee Diddle
Your ladys a knight in her arms twa
That she lees far better nor the Diddle
O wow &c

5. Ye lee you lee you bonny birdy
How you lee upo my sweet Diddle
I will tak' out my bonny bow
An in troth I will you sheet Diddle
O wow &c

6. But afore ye hae your bow well bent
An a your arrows yare Diddle
I will flee till another tree
Whare I can better fare Diddle.
O wow &c

[No parallel text]

7. O Whare was you gotten & whare was ye clecked
My bonny birdy tell me Diddle
O I was clecked in good green wood
Intill a holly tree Diddle
A Gentleman my nest herryed
An ga me to his lady Diddle.
O wow &c

8. Wi good white bread & farrow cow milk,
He bade her feed me aft Diddle
An ga her a little wee simmer-dale wanny
To ding me sindle & saft Diddle.
O wow &c

9. Wi good white bread & farrow cow milk
I wot she fed me nought Diddle
But wi a little wee simmer-dale wanny
She dang me sair & aft Diddle
Gin she had deen as ye her bade
I wou'dna tell how she has wrought Diddle.
O wow &c

p. 43 10. The knight he rade & the birdy flew
The live lang simmers night Diddle
Till he came till his ladys bow'r door
Then even down he did light Diddle
The birdy sat on the crap of a tree
An I wot it sang fu' dight Diddle
O wow for day Diddle,
An dear gin it were day Diddle
Gin it were day & gin I were away
For I ha na lang time to stay Diddle

11. What needs you lang for day? Diddle
An wish that you were away Diddle
Is no your hounds i' my cellar
Eating white meal an gray? Diddle
O wow &c

[No parallel text]

12. Is nae you[r] steed in my stable,
    Eating good corn an hay Diddle
An is nae your hawk i my perch tree
    Just perching for his prey Diddle
An is nae yoursel i my arms twa
    Then how can ye lang for day Diddle
        O wow for day Diddle
        An dear gin it were day Diddle
        For he thats in bed wi anither mans wife
        Has never lang time to stay Diddle
13. Then out the knight has drawn his sword
    An straiked it oer a strae Diddle
An thro & thro the fase knights
    He gard cauld Iron gae Diddle
An I hope ilk ane sal sae be serv'd
    That treats ane honest man sae Diddle
        O wow &c

Part II:

Ballads in B, C, D and E without Parallels in A

B

21. Clark Colven [Child 42]

p. 5 1. Clark Colven & his gay Lady,
As they walk'd to yon garden green,
A Belt about her middle gimp,
Which cost Clark Colven crowns fifteen.

2. "O hearken well now my good Lord,
O hearken well to what I say,
When ye gae to the walls o' Stream
Be sure ye touch nae well far'd May."

3. "O had your tongue my gay Lady
An' dinna deave me wi' your din,
For I saw never a fair woman
But wi' her body I cou'd sin."

4. He mounted on his berry brown steed,
An' merry merry rade he on
'Till he came 'til the walls o' stream,
An' there he saw the Mermaiden;

5. "Ye wash, ye wash ye bonny May,
And ay's ye wash your sark o' silk."
p. 6 "It's a' for you ye gentle knight,
My skin is whiter than the milk."

6. He's taen her by the milk-white hand,
And likewise by the grass-green sleeve,
An' laid her down upon the green,
Nor of his Lady speer'd he leave.

7. "Ohon! alas!" (says Clark Colven)
"An' ay sae sair's I mean my head;"
And merrily leugh the mermaiden, –
"O even on, till ye be dead" – (*Aside*)

8. “But out ye tak’ your little pen-knife
An’ frae my sark ye shear a gare,
Row that about your lovely head,
And the pain you’ll never feel nae mair.”
9. Out has he taen his little pen-knife,
An’ frae her sark he’s shorn a gare,
Row’d that about his lovely head,
But the pain increased mair, & mair.
10. “Ohon! alas!” (says Clark Colven)
“An’ ay sae sair’s I mean my head;”
An’ merrily leugh the mermaiden, p. 7
“’Twill ay be war ’till ye be dead.”
11. Then out he drew his trusty blade,
An’ thought wi’ it to be her dead;
But she became a fish again,
And merrily sprang into the fleed.
12. He’s mounted on his berry brown steed,
An’ dowy, dowy rade he hame,
’Till he came to his Lady’s bow’r door
An’ heavily he lighted down.
13. “O mither, mither, mak’ my bed,
An’ gentle Lady lay me down;
O brither, brither, unbend my bow,
’Twill never be bent by me again.”
14. His mither she has made his bed,
His gentle Lady laid him down;
His brother he has unbent his bow,
’Twas never bent by him again.

C

22. Thomas Rymer, & Queen of Elfland [Child 37]

p. 1 1. True Thomas lay oer yon'd grassy bank
And he beheld a Ladie gay
A Ladie that was brisk and bold
Come riding o'er the fernie brae
2. Her skirt was of the grass green silk
Her mantle of the velvet fine
At ilka tett of her horses mane
Hung fifty silver bells & nine
3. True Thomas he took aff his hat
And bow'd him law down till his knee
p. 2 All hail thou mighty queen of heaven
For your peer on earth I ne'er did see
4. O no O no true Thomas she says
That name does not belong to me
I am but the queen of fair Elfland
And I'm come here for to visit thee
5. But ye maun go wi me now Thomas
True Thomas ye maun go wi me
For ye maun serve me seven years
Thro weel or wae as may chance to be
6. She turnd about her milk white steed
And took true Thomas up behind
And ay whene'er her bridle rang
The steed flew swifter than the wind
7. O they rade on and farther on
Until they came to a garden green
Light down light down, ye Ladie free
Some of that fruit let me pu' to thee
8. O no O no true Thomas she says
That fruit maun not be touchd by thee
p. 3 For a the plagues that are in hell
Light on the fruit of this countrie
9. But I have a loaf here in my lap
Likewise a bottle of claret wine
And now ere we go farther on
We ll rest a while and ye may dine

10. When he had eaten & drunk his fill
    The Ladie say'd ere we climb yon hill
Lay down your head upon my knee
    And I will show you fairlies three
11. O see not ye yon narrow road
    So thick beset wi thorns & briers
That is the path of righteousness
    Tho after it but few enquires
12. And see not ye that braid braid road
    That lyes across yon Lillie leven
That is the path of wickedness
    Tho some call it the road to heaven
13. And see not ye that bonny road
    Which winds about the fernie brae
That is the road to fair Elfland
    Where you & I this night maun gae
14. But Thomas ye maun hold your tongue p. 4
    Whatever you may hear or see
For gin ae word you should chance to speak
    You will ne'er get back to your ain countrie
15. For forty days and forty nights
    He wade thro red blude to the knee
And he saw neither sun nor moon
    But heard the roaring of the sea
16. He has gotten a coat of the even cloth
    And a pair of shoes of velvet green
And till seven years were past & gane
    True Thomas on earth was never seen

C

23. Fa'se Footrage [Child 89]

p. 11 1. King Easter has courted her for her gowd
King wester for her fee
King Honor for her lands sae braid
And for her fair body

2. They had not been four months married
As I have heard them tell
Until the nobles of the land
Against them did rebel

3. And they cast kaivles them amang
And kaivles them between
And they cast kaivles them amang
Wha shou'd gae kill the King

4. O! some said yea and some said nay
Their words did not agree
Till up it gat him Fa'se Footrage
And sware it shoud be he

p. 12 5. When bells were rung and mass was sung
And a man boon to bed
King Honor and his gay Ladie
In a hie cham'er were laid

6. Then up it raise him Fa'se Footrage
While a were fast asleep
And slew the porter in his lodge
That watch and ward did keep

7. O! four and twenty silver keys
Hung hie upon a pin
And ay as a door he did unlock
He has fasten'd it him behind

8. Than up it raise him King Honor
Says what means a this din
Now whats the matter Fa'se Footrage
Or wha wast loot you in

9. O! ye my errand well shall learn
Before that I depart
Then drew a knife baith lang & sharp
And pierced him thro the heart

10. Then up it gat the queen her sell p. 13
    And fell low down on her knee
O! spare my life now fa'se Footrage
    For I never injured thee
11. O spare my life now Fa'se Footrage
    Until I lighter be
And see gin it be Lad or Lass
    King Honor has left me wi
12. O gin it be a Lass he says
    Well nursed she shall be
But gin it be a Lad bairn
    He shall be hanged hie
13. I winna spare his tender age
    Nor yet his hie hie kin
But as soon as e'er he born is
    He shall mount the gallows pin
14. O! four and twenty valiant knights
    Were set the queen to guard
And four stood ay at her Bower door
    To keep baith watch and ward
15. But when the time drew till an end p. 14
    That she shou'd lighter be
She cast about to find a wile
    To set her body free
16. O! she has birled these merry young men
    Wi strong beer and wi wine
Until she made them a as drunk
    As any wallwood swine
17. O! narrow narrow is this window
    And big big am I grown
Yet thro the might of our Ladie
    Out at it she has won
18. She wander'd up she wand'erd down
    She wander'd out and in
And at last into the very swines stye
    The queen brought forth a son
19. Then they cast kaivles them amang
    Wha shou'd gae seek the queen
And the kaivle fell upon wise William
    And he s sent his wife for him

p. 15 20. O when she saw wise Williams wife
The queen fell on her knee
Win up win up madame she says
What means this courtysie
21. O out of this I winna rise
Till a boon ye grant to me
To change your Lass for this Lad bairn
King Honor left me wi
22. And ye maun learn my gay Gose hawke
Well how to breast a steed
And I shall learn your Turtle Dow
As well to write and read
23. And ye maun learn my gay Gose Hawke
To wield baith bow and brand
And I shall learn your Turtle Dow
To lay gowd wi her hand
24. At kirk or market where we meet
We dare nae mair avow
But dame how does my gay Gose hawke
Madame how does my Dow
p. 16 25. When days were gane and years came on
Wise William he thought lang
Out has he ta'en King Honor s son
A hunting for to gang
26. It sae fell out at their hunting
Upon a summers day
That they came by a fair castle
Stood on a sunny brae
27. O! dinna ye see that bonny Castle
Wi wa's and towers sae fair
Gin ilka man had back his ain
Of it you shou'd be heir
28. How I shou'd be heir of that castle
In sooth I canna see
When it belongs to Fa'se Footrage
And he's nae kin to me
29. O gin ye shou'd kill him Fa'se Footrage
You wou'd do what is right
For I wot he kill'd your father dear
Ere ever you saw the light

30. Gin ye shoud kill him Fa'se Footrage p. 17
There is nae man durst you blame
For he keeps your Mother a prisoner
And she dares no take you hame

31. The boy stared wild like a gray Gose hawke
Says what may a this mean
My Boy, you are King Honors son
And your mother's our lawful queen.

32. O! gin I be King Honor s son
By our Ladie I swear
This day I will that traytour slay
And relieve my mother dear

33. He has set his bent bow till his breast
And lap the castle wa
And soon he's siezed on Fa'se Footrage
Wha loud for help gan ca

34. O! hold your tongue now Fa'se Footrage
Frae me you shanna flee
Syne pierced him thro the ful fa'se heart
And set his mother free

35. And he has rewarded wise William p. 18
Wi the best half of his land
And sae has he the Turtle Dow
Wi the truth of his right hand

C

24. Jellon Grame and Lillie Flower [Child 90]

p. 18 1. O Jellon Grame sat in silver wood
He whistled and he sang
And he has calld his little foot page
His errand for to gang

2. Win up my bonny boy he says
As quick as e'er you may
For ye maun gang for Lillie Flower
Before the break of day

3. The boy hes buckled his belt about
And thro the green wood ran
And he came to the Ladies bower door
Before the day did dawn

p. 19 4. O sleep ye or wake ye Lillie Flower
The red runs ithe rain
I sleep not aft I wake right aft
Wha s that, that kens my name

5. Ye are bidden come to silver wood
But I fear you'll never win hame
Ye are bidden come to silver wood
And speak wi Jellon Grame

6. O I will gang to silver wood
Tho I shou'd never win hame
For the thing I most desire on earth
Is to speak wi Jellon Grame

7. She had no ridden a mile a mile
A mile but barely three
Ere she came to a new made grave
Beneath a green oak tree

8. O then up started Jellon Grame
Out of a bush hard bye
Light down light down now Lillie Flower
For it s here that ye maun ly

p. 20 9. She lighted aff her milk white steed
And knelt upon her knee
O! mercy mercy Jellon Grame
For I'm nae prepar'd to die

10. Your bairn that stirs between my sides
Maun shortly see the light
But to see it weltring in my blude
Wou'd be a piteous sight
11. O shou'd I spare your life he says
Until that bairn be born
I ken fu well your stern father
Wou'd hang me on the morn
12. O! spare my life now Jellon Grame
My Father ye neer need dread
I'll keep my bairn ithe good green wood
Or wi it I'll beg my bread
13. He took nae pity on that Ladie
Tho she for life did pray
But pierced her thro the fair body
As at his feet she lay
14. He felt nae pity for that Ladie p. 21
Tho she was lying dead
But he felt some for the bonny boy
Lay weltring in her blude
15. Up has he ta'en that bonny boy
Gien him to nurices nine
Three to wake and three to sleep
And three to go between
16. And he's brought up that bonny boy
Call'd him his sisters son
He thought nae man wou'd eer find out
The deed that he had done
17. But it sae fell out upon a time
As a hunting they did gay
That they rested them in silver wood
Upon a summer day
18. Then out it spake that bonny boy
While the tear stood in his eye
O! tell me this now Jellon Grame
And I pray you dinna lie
19. The reason that my mother dear p. 22
Does never take me hame
To keep me still in banishment
Is baith a sin and shame

20. You wonder that your mother dear
    Does never send for thee
Lo, there s the place I slew thy mother
    Beneath that green oak tree
21. Wi that the boy has bent his bow
    It was baith stout and lang
And through and thro him Jellon Grame
    He's gar'd an arrow gang
22. Says lye you there now Jellon Grame
    My mellison you wi
The place my mother lies buried in
    Is far too good for thee

C

25. The bonny Earl of Livingston [Child 91]

1. O we were sisters seven Maisry p. 23
   And five are dead wi child
   There is nane but you and I Maisry
   And we ll go maidens mild
2. She hardly had the word spoken
   And turn'd her round about
   When the Bonny Earl of Livingston
   Was calling Maisry out
3. Upon a bonny milk white steed
   That drank out of the Tyne
   And a' was for her Ladie Maisry
   To take her hyne and hyne
4. Upon a bonny milk white steed
   That drank out o the Tay.
   And a was for her Lady Maisry
   To carry her away.
5. She had not been at Livingston p. 24
   A twelve month and a day
   Until she was as big wi bairn
   As any Ladie cou'd gae
6. She call'd upon her little foot page
   Says ye maun run wi speed
   And bid my mother come to me
   For of her I'll soon have need
7. See there is the brootch frae my hause bane
   It is of gowd sae ried
   Gin she winna come when I'm alive
   Bid her come when I am dead
8. But ere she wan to Livingston
   As fast as she cou'd ride
   The Gaggs they were in Maisrys mouth
   And the sharp sheers in her side
9. Her good Lord wrang his milk white hands
   Till the gowd rings flew in three
   Let ha's & bowers and a' gae waste
   My bonny Love's ta'en frae me

p. 25 10. O! hold your tongue Lord Livingston
Let a' your mourning be
For I bare the Bird between my sides
Yet I maun thole here to die
11. Then out it spake her sister dear
As she sat at her head
That man is not in christendoom
Shall gar me die sickena dead
12. O! hold your tongue my ae doughter
Let a' your folly be
For ye shall be married ere this day week
Tho the same death you should die

26. Bonny Bee Ho'm [Child 92]

1. By Arthurs dale as late I went p. 26
   I heard a heavy moan
   I heard a Lady lammenting sair
   And ay she cried ohone
2. Ohon alas what shall I do
   Tormented night and day
   I never loved a Love but ane
   And now he's gone away
3. But I will do for my true Love
   What Ladies wou'd think sair
   For seven year shall come and go
   Ere a kaim gang in my hair
4. There shall neither a shoe gang on my foot
   Nor a kaim gang in my hair
   Nor e'er a coal nor candle light
   Shine in my bower nae mair.
5. She thought her Love had been on the sea
   Fast sailling to Bee Ho'm
   But he was in a quiet cham'er
   Hearing his Ladies moan
6. Be husht be husht my Ladie dear p. 27
   I pray thee mourn not so
   For I am deep sworn on a book
   To Bee Ho'm for to go
7. She has gi'en him a chain of the beaten gowd
   And a ring with a ruby stone
   As lang as this chain your body binds
   Your blude can never be drawn
8. But gin this ring shou'd fade or fail
   Or the stone should change its hue
   Be sure your Love is dead and gone
   Or she has proved untrue
9. He had no' been at Bonny Bee ho'm
   A twelve month and a day
   Till Looking on his gay gowd ring
   The stone grew dark and gray

10. O ye take my riches to Bee Ho'm
    And deal them presentlie
To the young that canna
The auld that that maunna
    And the blind that does not see

p. 28 11. Now death has come into his bower
    And split his heart in twain
So their twa sauls flew up to heaven
    And there shall ever remain

27. Bonny Foot-Boy [Child 252]

1. O! there was a Ladie a noble Ladie p. 28
   She was a Ladie of birth and fame
But she fell in love wi her fathers foot Boy
   I wis she was the mair to blame
2. A word of him she ne'er could get
   Till her father was a hunting gone
Then she call'd on the bonny foot boy
   To speak wi her in her bower alone
3. Says ye ken you are my Love Willie
   And That I am a Ladie free
And there s nae thing ye can ask Willie
   But at your bidding I maun be
4. O the loving looks that Ladie gave
   Soon made the bonny Boy grow bold
And the loving words that Ladie spake
   As soon on them he did lay hold
5. She has ta'en a ring frae her white finger p. 29
   And unto him she did it gie
Says wear this token for my sake
   And keep it till the day you die
6. But shou'd my father get word of this
   I fear we baith will have cause to rue
For to some nunnery I shou'd be sent
   And I fear my Love he wou'd ruin you
7. But here is a coffer of the good red gowd
   I wot my mother left it to me
And wi it you'll buy a bonny ship
   And ye maun sail the raging sea
Then like some Earl or Barons son
   You can come back and marrie me
8. But stay not lang awa Willie
   O! stay not lang across the fame
For fear your Ladie shou'd lighter be
   Or your young son shou'd want a name
9. He had not been o the sea sailling
   But till three months were come and gane
Till he has landed his bonny ship
   It was upon the coast of spain

p. 30 10. There was a Ladie of high degree
That saw him walking up and down
She fell in love wi sweet Willie
But she wist no how to make it known
11. She has call'd up her Maries a
Says hearken well to what I say
There is a young man in yon ship
That has been my Love this many a day
12. Now bear a hand my maries a
And busk me brave and make me fine
And go wi me to yon shore side
To invite that Noble youth to dine
13. O they have buskit that Ladie gay
In velvet pall and jewels rare
A poor man might have been made rich
Wi half the pearles they pat in her hair
14. Her mantle was of gowd sae red
It Glaned as far as ane cou'd see
Sweet Willie thought she had been the queen
And bowd full low and bent his knee
p. 31 15. She's gar'd her Maries step aside
And on sweet Willie sae did smile
She thought that man was not on earth
But of his heart she could beguile
16. Says ye maun leave your bonny ship
And go this day wi me and dine
And you shall eat the baken meat
And you shall drink the spanish wine
17. I canna leave my bonny ship
Nor go this day to dine wi thee
For a' my sails are ready bent
To bear me back to my ain countrie
18. O gin you'd forsake your bonny ship
And wed a Ladie of this countrie
I would make you Lord of a this town
And towns and castles twa or three
19. Should I wed a Ladie of this countrie
In sooth I woud be sair to blame
For the fairest Ladie in fair scotland
Wou'd break her heart gin I gaed'na hame

20. That Ladie may choose another Lord p. 32
    And you another Love may choose
There is not a Lord in this countrie
    That such a proffer could refuse
21. O! Ladie shou'd I your proffer take
    You'd soon yoursell have cause to rue
For the man that his first Love forsakes
    Wou'd to a seceond ne'er prove true.
22. She has ta'en a ring frae her white finger
    It might have been a princes fee
Says wear this token for my sake
    And give me that which now I see.
23. Take back your token ye Ladie fair
    This ring you see on my right hand
Was gien me by my ain true Love
    Before I left my native Land.
24. And tho yours wou'd buy it nine times o'er
    I far more dearly prize my ain
Nor wou'd I make the niffer he says
    For a the Gowd that is in spain
25. The Ladie turn'd her head away p. 33
    To dry the sa't tears frae her eyne
She naething mair to him did say
    But "I wish your face I ne'er had seen."
26. He has set his foot on good ship board
    The Ladie waved her milk white hand
The wind sprang up and fill'd his sails
    And he quickly left the spanish land
27. He soon came back to his native strand
    He lang'd his ain true Love to see
Her father saw him come to land
    And took him some great Lord to be
28. Says will ye leave your bonny ship
    And come wi me this day to dine
And you shall eat the baken meat
    And you shall drink the claret wine.
29. O! I will leave my bonny ship
    And gladly go wi you to dine
And I wou'd gie thrice three thousand pounds
    That your fair daughter were but mine.

p. 34 30. O gin ye will part wi your bonny ship
And wed a Ladie of this countrie
I will gie you my ae daughter
Gin she'll consent your bride to be.

31. O he has blaket his bonny face
And closs tuck'd up his yellow hair
His true Love met them at the yate
But she little thought her Love was there.

32. O will you marrie this Lord daughter
That I've brought hame to dine wi' me
You shall be heir of a my lands
Gin you'll consent his bride to be.

33. She looked o'er her left shoulder
I wot the tears stood in her eye
Says "the man is on the sea sailling
That fair wedding shall get of me."

34. Then Willie has wash'd his bonny face
And he's kaim'd down his yellow hair
He took his true Love in his arms
And kindly has he kiss'd her there

p. 35 35. She's looked in his bonny face
And thro her tears did sweetly smile
Then sayd awa awa Willie
How could you thus your Love beguile.

36. She kept the secret in her breast
Full seven years she's kept the same.
Till it fell out at a christning feast
And then of it she made good game

37. And her father leughd aboon the rest
And sayd my daughter you'r nae to blame
For youve married for love & no for land
So a' my gowd is yours to claim

C

28. Cruel Brother Or The Bride's Testament [Child 11]

1. There was thrice Ladies play'd at the Ba, p. 35
With a hey ho and a lillie gay
There came a knight and playd oer them a
As the primrose spreads so sweetly
2. The eldest was baith tall and fair
With a hey ho and a lillie gay
But the youngest was beyond compare
As the primrose spreads so sweetly
3. The midmost had a graceful mein p. 36
With a hey ho and a lillie gay
But the youngest look'd like beauties queen
As the primrose spreads so sweetly
4. The knight bow'd low to a' the three
With a hey ho and a lillie gay
But to the youngest he bent his knee
As the primrose spreads so sweetly
5. The Ladie turned her head aside
With a hey ho and a lillie gay
The knight he woo'd her to be his bride
As the primrose spreads so sweetly
6. The Ladie blush'd a rosey red
With a hey ho and a lillie gay
And say'd Sir knight I'm too young to wed
As the primrose spreads so sweetly
7. O! Ladie fair give me your hand
With a hey ho and a lillie gay
And I'll make you Ladie of a my land
As the primrose spreads so sweetly
8. Sir knight ere ye my favour win
With a hey ho and a lillie gay
You maun get consent frae a' my kin
As the primrose spreads so sweetly
9. He has got consent frae her parents dear
With a hey ho and a lillie gay
And likewise frae her sisters fair
As the primrose spreads so sweetly

10. He has got consent frae her kin each one.
With a hey ho and a lillie gay
But forgot to spier at her brother John
As the primrose spreads so sweetly
11. Now when the wedding day was come
With a hey ho and a lillie gay
The knight wou'd take his bonny bride home
As the primrose spreads so sweetly
12. And many a Lord and many a knight
With a hey ho and a lillie gay
Came to behold that Ladie bright
As the primrose spreads so sweetly
p. 37 13. And there was nae man that her did see
With a hey ho and a lillie gay
But wish'd himsell bridegroom to be
As the primrose spreads so sweetly
14. Her father dear led her down the stair
With a hey ho and a lillie gay
And her sisters twain they kiss'd her there
As the primrose spreads so sweetly
15. Her mother dear led her thro the closs
With a hey ho and a lillie gay
And her brother John set her on her horse
As the primrose spreads so sweetly
16. She lean'd her oer the saddle bow
With a hey ho and a lillie gay
To give him a kiss ere she did go
As the primrose spreads so sweetly
17. He has ta'en a knife baith lang and sharp
With a hey ho and a lillie gay
And stabb'd that bonny bride to the heart
As the primrose spreads so sweetly
18. She had no ridden half thro the town
With a hey ho and a lillie gay
Until her hearts blude stain'd her gown
As the primrose spreads so sweetly
19. Ride saftly on says the best young man
With a hey ho and a lillie gay
For I think our bonny bride looks pale and wan
As the primrose spreads so sweetly

20. O! lead me gently up yon hill
    With a hey ho and a lillie gay
And I'll there sit down and make my will
    As the primrose spreads so sweetly
21. O! what will you leave to your father dear
    With a hey ho and a lillie gay
The silver shode steed that brought me here
    As the primrose spreads so sweetly
22. What will you leave to your mother dear
    With a hey ho and a lillie gay
My velvet pall & my silken gear
    As the primrose spreads so sweetly
23. What will you leave to your sister Anne p. 38
    With a hey ho and a lillie gay
My silken scarf and my gowden fann
    As the primrose spreads so sweetly
24. What will you leave to your sister Grace
    With a hey ho and a lillie gay
My bloody cloaths to wash and dress
    As the primrose spreads so sweetly
25. What will you leave to your brother John
    With a hey ho and a lillie gay
The gallows tree to hang him on
    As the primrose spreads so sweetly
26. What will you leave to your brother Johns wife
    With a hey ho and a lillie gay
The wilderness to end her life
    As the primrose spreads so sweetly
27. This Ladie fair in her grave was laid
    With a hey ho and a lillie gay
And many a mass was o'er her said
    As the primrose spreads so sweetly
28. But it would have made your heart right sair
    With a hey ho and a lillie gay
To see the bridegroom rive his haire
    As the primrose spreads so sweetly

29. Bonny Baby Livingston [D; Child 222]

f. 8r, a 1. O bonny Baby Livingston
Went forth to view the hay,
And by it came him Glenlion,
Sta bonny Baby away.
2. O first he's tae'n her Silken coat,
And neest her Satten Gown;
Syne row'd her in a tartan Plaid,
And hap'd her round and rown'.
3. He has set her upon his Steed,
And roundly rode away;
And ne'er loot her look back again
The live long Summer's day.

---

29. Bonny Baby Livingston [E; Child 222]

2:135 *1.* *O bonny Baby Livingstone*
Gaed out to view the hay;
And by it cam him Glenlyon,
Staw bonny Baby away.
2. *And first he's taen her silken coat,*
And neist her satten gown;
Syne row'd her in his tartan plaid,
And happ'd her round and roun'.
3. *He's mounted her upon a steed,*
And roundly rade away;
And ne'er loot her look back again
The lee-lang simmer day.

4. He's carried her o'er hills & muirs
   Till they came to a Highland Glen,
And there he's met his Brother John,
   With twenty armed men.
5. O there were Cows, and there were Ewes,
   And Lasses milking there.
But Baby ne'er anse look'd about,
   Her heart was fill'd wi' care.
6. Glenlion took her in his arms,
   And kiss'd her, cheek and chin:
Says, I'd gie a these Cows and Ewes
   But ae kind look to win.
7. O ae kind look ye ne'er shall get
   Nor win a smile frae me;
Unless to me you'll favour shew,
   And take me to Dundee.

---

4. He's carried her o'er yon hich hich hill, 2:136
   Intill a Highland glen,
And there he met his brother John
   Wi' twenty armed men.
5. And there were cows, and there were ewes,
   And there were kids sae fair;
But sad and wae was bonny Baby;
   Her heart was fu' o' care.
6. He's taen her in his arms twa,
   And kist her cheek and chin;
"I wad gi'e a' my flocks and herds
   Ae smile frae thee to win!"
7. "A smile frae me ye'se never win;
   I'll ne'er look kind on thee;
Ye've stown me awa frae a' my kin,
   Frae a' that's dear to me.

8. Dundee Baby! Dundee Baby!
   Dundee you ne'er shall see,
Till I've carried you to Glenlion,
   And have my Bride made thee.

9. We'll stay a while at Auchingaur,
   And get sweet milk and cheese;
And syne we'll gang to Glenlion,
   And there live at our ease.

10. I winna stay at Auchingaur
   Nor eat sweet milk and cheese,
f. 8r, b Nor go with thee to Glenlion
   For there I'll ne'er find ease.

---

8. "Dundee, kind sir, Dundee, kind sir,
   Tak me to bonny Dundee;
For ye sall ne'er my favour win
   Till it ance mair I see."

2:137 *9. "Dundee, Baby! Dundee, Baby!*
   Dundee ye ne'er shall see;
But I will carry you to Glenlyon,
   Where you my bride shall be.

10. "Or will ye stay at Achingour,
   And eat sweet milk and cheese;
Or gang wi' me to Glenlyon,
   And there we'll live at our ease?"

11. "I winna stay at Achingour;
   I care neither for milk nor cheese ;
Nor gang wi' thee to Glenlyon;
   For there I'll ne'er find ease."

11. Than out it spak his Brother John,
    O were I in your place,
I'd take that Lady hame again,
    For a her bonny face.
12. Commend me to the Lass that's kind
    Tho' no so gently born;
And gin her heart I cou'dna gain
    To take her hand I'd scorn.
13. O had your tongue now John, he says,
    You wis na what you say;
For I've lov'd that bonny face,
    This twelve month and a day.
14. And tho' I've loo'd her lang and sair,
    A smile I neer cou'd win;
Yet what I've gat anse in my power,
    To keep I think nae sin.

---

12. Then out it spak his brother John, –
"If I were in your place,
I'd send that lady hame again,
For a' her bonny face.
13. "Commend me to the lass that's kind,
Though nae sae gently born;
And, gin her heart I coudna win,
To take her hand I'd scorn."
14. "O haud your tongue, my brother John, 2:138
Ye wisna what ye say;
For I hae lued that bonny face
This mony a year and day.
15. "I've lued her lang, and lued her weel,
But her love I ne'er could win;
And what I canna fairly gain,
To steal I think nae sin."

15. When they came to Glenlion Castle,
They lighted at the Yate,
And out it came his Sisters three,
Wha did them kindly greet.

16. O they've taen Baby by the hands
And led her o'er the Green,
And ilka Lady spake a word,
But bonny Baby spake nane.

17. Than out it spake her bonny Jean,
The youngest O the three,
O Lady dinna look sae sad
But tell your grief to me.

18. O wherefore should I tell my grief?
Since lax I canna find,
I'm stown frae a my Kin and Friends,
And my Love I left behind.

---

16. Whan they cam to Glenlyon castle,
They lighted at the yett;
And out they cam, his three sisters,
Their brother for to greet.

17. And they have taen her, bonny Baby,
And led her o'er the green;
And ilka lady spak a word,
But bonny Baby spak nane.

2:139 *18. Then out it spak her, bonny Jane,*
The youngest o' the three:
"O lady, why look ye sae sad?
Come tell your grief to me."

19. "O wherefore should I tell my grief,
Since lax I canna find?
I'm far frae a' my kin and friends,
And my love I left behind.

19. But had I paper, pen, and ink,
    Before that it were day,
I yet might get a Letter sent,
    In time to Johny Hay.
20. O she's got paper, pen, and ink,
    And candle that she might see;
And she has written a broad Letter,
    To Johny at Dundee.
21. And she has gotten a bonny Boy, f. 8v, a
    That was baith swift and strang,
Wi Philabeg and Bonnet blue,
    Her errand for to gang.
22. O Boy gin ye'd my blessing win,
    And help me in my need,
Rin wi this Letter to my Love,
    And bid him come wi speed.

---

20. *"But had I paper, pen, and ink,*
    Afore that it were day,
I yet might get a letter wrate,
    And sent to Johnie Hay.
21. *"And gin I had a bonny boy,*
    To help me in my need,
That he might rin to bonny Dundee,
    And come again wi' speed."
22. *And they hae gotten a bonny boy*
    Their errand for to gang;
And bade him run to Bonny Dundee,
    And nae to tarry lang.

23. And here's a chain of good red gowd
    And gowd'n guineas three:
And when you've well your errand done,
    You'll get them for your Fee.

24. The Boy he ran o'er Hill and Dale,
    Fast as a Bird cou'd flee
And e'er the Sun was twa hours height
    The Boy was at Dundee.

25. And when he came to Johny's door,
    He knocked loud and sair
Then Johny to the window came,
    And loudly cryd, Whas there?

26. O here's a Letter I have brought,
    Which ye maun quickly read,
And gin ye woud your Lady save,
    Gang back wi me, wi speed.

2:140 *23.* *The boy he ran o'er muir and dale*
    As fast as he could flee;
And e'er the sun was twa hours hight,
    The boy was at Dundee.

24. *Whan Johnie lookit the letter on,*
    A hearty laugh leuch he;
But ere he read it till an end,
    The tear blinded his e'e.

25. *"O wha is this, or wha is that,*
    Has stown my love frae me ?
Although he were my ae brither,
    An ill dead sall he die.

27. O when he had the Letter read
    An angry man was he:
He says, Glenlion, thou shalt rue
    This deed of villany.
28. O saddle to me the Black, the Black, f. 8v, b
    O saddle to me the Brown;
O saddle to me the swiftest Steed,
    That e'er rade frae the Town.
29. And arm ye well my merry men a'
    And follow me to the Glen;
For I vow I'll neither eat nor sleep;
    Till I get my Love again.
30. He's mounted on a milk-white Steed,
    The Boy upon a Gray;
And they got to Glenlion's Castle
    About the close of day.

---

26. "Gae, saddle to me the black," he says;
"Gae, saddle to me the brown;
Gae, saddle to me the swiftest steed,
That ever rade frae the town."
27. He's call'd upon his merry men a',
To follow him to the glen;
And he's vow'd he'd neither eat nor sleep
Till he got his love again.
28. He's mounted him on a milk-white steed, 2:141
And fast he rade away;
And he's come to Glenlyon's yett,
About the close o' day.

31. As Baby at her window stood,
    The west wind saft did bla
She heard her Johny's well kent voice
    Beneath the Castle wa'.
32. O Baby, haste the window jump,
    I'll kep you in my arm;
My merry men a' are at the yate
    To rescue you frae harm.
33. She to the window fixt her sheets
    And slipped safely down;
And Johny catch'd her in his arms,
    Ne'er loot her touch the ground.
34. When mounted on her Johny's Horse,
    Fou blithely did she say:
Glenlion, you have lost your Bride,
    She's aff wi Johny Hay.

---

29. As Baby at her window stood,
    And the west-wind saft did blaw,
She heard her Johnie's well-kent voice
    Aneath the castle wa'.
30. "O Baby, haste, the window loup;
    I'll kep you in my arm;
My merry men a' are at the yett
    To rescue you frae harm."
31. She to the window fix'd her sheets,
    And slipped safely down;
And Johnie catched her in his arms,
    Ne'er loot her touch the groun'.

35. Glenlion and his Brother John,
    Were birling in the Ha'
When the[y] heard Johny's bridle ring,
    As first he rade awa.
36. Rise Jock, gang out and meet the Priest,
    I hear his Bridle ring,
My Baby now shall be my wife
    Before the Laverocks sing.
37. O Brother, this is not the Priest,
    I fear he'll come o'er late,
For armed men with shining Brands
    Stand at the Castle yate.
38. Haste Donald, Duncan, Dugald, Hugh,
    Haste, take your swords and Spier;
We'll gar these Traytors rue the hour
    That e'er they ventured here.

---

32. Glenlyon and his brother John
    Were birling in the ha',
When they heard Johnie's bridle ring
    As fast he rade awa'.
33. "Rise, Jock; gang out and meet the priest, 2:142
    I hear his bridle ring;
My Baby now shall be my wife,
    Before the laverock sing."
34. "O brother, this is nae the priest;
    I fear he'll come o'er late;
For armed men wi' shining brands
    Stand at the castle yett."
35. "Haste, Donald, Duncan, Dugald, Hugh,
    Haste, tak your sword and spear;
We'll gar these traytors rue the hour
    That e'er they ventured here."

39. The Highland men drew their claymores
And gae a war-like shout;
But Johny's merry men kept the yate,
Nae ane durst venture out.

40. The Lovers rade the live lang night,
And safe gat on their way;
And bonny Baby Livingston
Has gotten Johny Hay.

41. Awa Glenlion, fy for shame!
Gae hide ye in Some Den
You've lett'n your Bride be stown frae you
For a your armed men.

---

36. The Highlandmen drew their claymores,
And gae a warlike shout;
But Johnie's merry men kept the yett,
Nae ane durst venture out.

37. The lovers rade the lee-lang night,
And safe got on their way;
And Bonny Baby Livingstone
Has gotten Johny Hay.

2:143 *38. "Awa, Glenlyon! fy for shame!*
Gae hide you in some den;
You've latten your bride be stown frae you,
For a' your armed men."

D

30. The Baron of Braikly [Child 203]

1. O Inverey came down Deeside whistling and playing, f. 6r
He's landed at Braikly's yates at the day dawing.
2. Says, Baron of Braikly, are ye within?
There's sharp Swords at the yate, will gar your blood spin.
3. The Lady raise up, to the window she went,
She heard her Kye lowing o'er Hill, and o'er Bent.
4. O rise up, John, she says, turn back your Kye,
They're o'er the Hills rinning, they're skipping away.
5. Come to your Bed, Peggie and let the Kye rin,
For were I to gang out, I would never get in.
6. Then she's cry'd on her women, they quickly came ben;
Take up your Rocks, Lassies and fight a like men.
7. Though I'm but a woman, to head you I'll try,
Nor let these vile Highland men steal a our Kye.
8. Then up gat the Baron and cry'd for his Graith,
Says, Lady, I'll gang, tho' to leave you, I'm laith.
9. Come kiss me my Peggie, nor think I'm to blame,
For I may well gang out, but I'll never win In.
10. When the Baron of Braikly rade through the Close
A gallanter Baron ne'er mounted a Horse.
11. Tho' there came wi Inverey thirty and three
There was nane wi bonny Braikly, but his Brother and he.
12. Twa gallanter Gordons did never sword draw.
But against four and thirty, waes me, what was twa?
13. Wi Swords, and wi Daggers they did him Surround,
And they've pierc'd bonny Braikly wi mony a wound.
14. Frae the head of the Dee, to the banks of the Spey,
The Gordons may mourn him, and bann Inverey.
15. O Came ye by Braikly, and was ye in there?
Or saw ye his Peggy dear riving her hair?
16. O I came by Braikly, and I was in there,
But I saw not his Peggy dear riving her hair.
17. O fye on ye, Lady, how could ye do sae?
You open'd your yate to the faus Inverey.
18. She eat wi him, drank wi him, welcom'd him in, f. 6v
She welcomd the Villain that slew her Baron.
19. She kept him till morning, syne bad him be gane,
And show'd him the road that he wou'd na be tane.

20. Thro' Birss and Aboyne, she says lyin in a tour,
    O'er the hills of Glentanor you'll skip in an hour.
21. There is grief in the Kitchen and mirth in the Ha'.
    But the Baron of Braikly is dead and awa.

31. Allan O Maut

1. Now Allan O Maut was ance ca'd Bear, f. 6v
And he was cadged frae Wa to Weer
2. He first grew green, and then he grew white
And a man judg'd than Allan was ripe.
3. Wi crooked Gullies and hafts o tree
They've hewed him down fou doughtily.
4. Syne they've Set Allan up into Stooks,
And casten on him mony pleasant looks.
5. They ve niest taen Allan up i' their arms,
And they have carried him into their Barns.

E

32. Willie and May Margaret [Child 216]

1:135 1. "Gie corn to my horse, mither;
Gi'e meat unto my man;
For I maun gang to Margaret's bower,
Before the nicht comes on."

2. "O stay at hame now, my son Willie;
The wind blaws cald and sour;
The nicht will be baith mirk and late,
Before ye reach her bower."

3. "O tho' the nicht were ever sae dark,
Or the wind blew never sae cald,
I will be in my Margaret's bower
Before twa hours be tald."

1:136 4. "O gin ye gang to may Margaret,
Without the leave of me,
Clyde's waters wide and deep enough;
My malison drown thee!"

5. He mounted on his coal-black steed,
And fast he rade awa';
But ere he came to Clyde's water,
Fu' loud the wind did blaw.

6. As he rode o'er yon hich hich hill,
And down yon dowie den,
There was a roar in Clyde's water,
Wad fear'd a hunder men.

7. His heart was warm, his pride was up;
Sweet Willie kentna fear;
But yet his mither's malison
Ay sounded in his ear.

8. O he has swam through Clyde's water,
Tho' it was wide and deep;
And he came to may Margaret's door,
When a' were fast asleep.

1:137 9. O he's gane round and round about,
And tirled at the pin;
But doors were steek'd, and windows barr'd,
And nane wad let him in.

10. "O open the door to me, Margaret,
O open and lat me in!
For my boots are full o' Clyde's water,
And frozen to the brim."
11. "I darena open the door to you,
Nor darena lat you in;
For my mither she is fast asleep,
And I darena mak nae din.
12. "O gin ye winna open the door,
Nor yet be kind to me,
Now tell me o' some out-chamber,
Where I this nicht may be."
13. "Ye canna win in this nicht, Willie,
Nor here ye canna be;
For I've nae chambers out nor in,
Nae ane but barely three.
14. "The tane o' them is fu' o' corn, 1:138
The tither is fu' o' hay;
The tither is fu' o' merry young men;
They winna remove till day."
15. "O fare ye weel, then, may Margaret,
Sin better manna be;
I've win my mither's malison,
Coming this nicht to thee."
16. He's mounted on his coal-black steed,
O, but his heart was wae!
But ere he came to Clyde's water,
'Twas half up o'er the brae.
17. . . . .
. . . .
. . . . he plunged in,
But never raise again.

E

33. Hugh of Lincoln [Child 155]

1:151 1. Four and twenty bonny boys
Were playing at the ba';
And by it came him, sweet sir Hugh,
And he play'd o'er them a'.

2. He kick'd the ba' with his right foot,
And catch'd it wi' his knee;
And throuch-and-thro' the Jew's window,
He gar'd the bonny ba' flee.

3. He's doen him to the Jew's castell,
And walk'd it round about;
And there he saw the Jew's daughter
At the window looking out.

1:152 4. "Throw down the ba', ye Jew's daughter,
Throw down the ba' to me!"
"Never a bit," says the Jew's daughter,
"Till up to me come ye."

5. "How will I come up? How can I come up?
How can I come to thee?
For as ye did to my auld father,
The same ye'll do to me."

6. She's gane till her father's garden,
And pu'd an apple, red and green;
'Twas a' to wyle him, sweet sir Hugh,
And to entice him in.

7. She's led him in through ae dark door,
And sae has she thro' nine;
She's laid him on a dressing-table,
And stickit him like a swine.

8. And first came out the thick thick blood,
And syne came out the thin;
And syne came out the bonny heart's blood;
There was nae mair within.

1:153 9. She's row'd him in a cake o' lead,
Bade him lie still and sleep;
She's thrown him in Our Lady's draw well,
Was fifty fathom deep.

10. When bells were rung, and mass was sung,
    And a' the bairns came hame,
When every lady gat hame her son,
    The Lady Maisry gat nane.
11. She's ta'en her mantle her about,
    Her coffer by the hand;
And she's gane out to seek her son,
    And wander'd o'er the land.
12. She's doen her to the Jew's castell,
    Where a' were fast asleep;
"Gin ye be there, my sweet sir Hugh,
    I pray you to me speak."
13. She's doen her to the Jew's garden,
    Thought he had been gathering fruit;
"Gin ye be there, my sweet sir Hugh,
    I pray you to me speak."
14. She near'd Our Lady's deep draw-well, 1:154
    Was fifty fathom deep;
"Whare'er ye be, my sweet sir Hugh,
    I pray you to me speak."
15. "Gae hame, gae hame, my mither dear;
    Prepare my winding sheet;
And, at the back o' merry Lincoln,
    The morn I will you meet."
16. Now lady Maisry is gane hame;
    Made him a winding sheet;
And, at the back o' merry Lincoln,
    The dead corpse did her meet.
17. And a' the bells o' merry Lincoln,
    Without men's hands were rung;
And a' the books o' merry Lincoln,
    Were read without man's tongue;
And ne'er was such a burial
    Sin Adam's days begun.

E

34. Lamkin [Child 93]

1:176 1. It's Lamkin was a mason good,
As ever built wi' stane;
He built lord Wearie's castle,
But payment got he nane.

2. "O pay me, lord Wearie;
Come, pay me my fee."
"I canna pay you, Lamkin,
For I maun gang o'er the sea."

3. "O pay me now, lord Wearie;
Come, pay me out o' hand."
"I canna pay you, Lamkin,
Unless I sell my land."

1:177 4. "O, gin ye winna pay me,
I here sall mak a vow,
Before that ye come hame again,
Ye sall ha'e cause to rue."

5. Lord Wearie got a bonny ship,
To sail the saut sea faem;
Bade his lady weel the castle keep,
Ay till he should come hame.

6. But the nourice was a fause limmer
As e'er hung on a tree;
She laid a plot wi' Lamkin,
Whan her lord was o'er the sea.

7. She laid a plot wi' Lamkin,
When the servants were awa';
Loot him in at a little shot window,
And brought him to the ha'.

8. "O, whare's a' the men o' this house,
That ca' me Lamkin?"
"They're at the barnwell thrashing,
'Twill be lang ere they come in."

1:178 9. "And whare's the women o' this house,
That ca' me Lamkin?"
"They're at the far well washing;
'Twill be lang ere they come in."

10. "And whare's the bairns o' this house,
That ca'me Lamkin?"
"They're at the school reading;
'Twill be night or they come hame."

11. "O, whare's the lady o' this house,
That ca's me Lamkin?"
"She's up in her bower sewing,
But we soon can bring her down."

12. Then Lamkin's tane a sharp knife,
That hang down by his gaire,
And he has gi'en the bonny babe
A deep wound and a sair.

13. Then Lamkin he rocked,
And the fause nourice sang,
Till frae ilkae bore o' the cradle
The red blood out sprang.

14. Then out it spak the lady, 1:179
As she stood on the stair,
"What ails my bairn, nourice,
That he's greeting sae sair?

15. "O still my bairn, nourice;
O still him wi' the pap!"
"He winna still, lady,
For this, nor for that."

16. "O, still my bairn, nourice;
O, still him wi' the wand!"
"He winna still, lady,
For a' his father's land."

17. "O, still my bairn, nourice;
O, still him wi' the bell!"
"He winna still, lady,
Till ye come down yoursel."

18. O, the firsten step she steppit,
She steppit on a stane;
But the neisten step she steppit,
She met him, Lamkin.

19. "O mercy, mercy, Lamkin! 1:180
Ha'e mercy upon me!
Though you've ta'en my young son's life,
Ye may let mysel be."

20. "O, sall I kill her, nourice?
Or sall I lat her be?"
"O, kill her, kill her, Lamkin,
For she ne'er was good to me."

21. "O scour the bason, nourice,
And mak it fair and clean,
For to keep this lady's heart's blood,
For she's come o' noble kin."

22. "There need nae bason, Lamkin;
Lat it run through the floor;
What better is the heart's blood
O' the rich than o' the poor."

23. But ere three months were at an end,
Lord Wearie came again;
But dowie dowie was his heart
When first he came hame.

1:181 24. "O, wha's blood is this," he says,
"That lies in the châmer?"
"It is your lady's heart's blood;
'Tis as clear as the lamer."

25. "And wha's blood is this," he says,
"That lies in my ha'?"
"It is your young son's heart's blood;
'Tis the clearest ava."

26. O, sweetly sang the black-bird
That sat upon the tree;
But sairer grat Lamkin,
When he was condemn'd to die.

27. And bonny sang the mavis
Out o' the thorny brake;
But sairer grat the nourice,
When she was tied to the stake.

35. The Birth of Robin Hood [Child 102]

1. O Willie's large o' limb and lith, 2:44
   And come o' high degree;
   And he is gane to Earl Richard,
   To serve for meat and fee.
2. Earl Richard had but ae daughter, 2:45
   Fair as a lily flower;
   And they made up their love-contract
   Like proper paramour.
3. It fell upon a simmer's nicht,
   Whan the leaves were fair and green,
   That Willie met his gay ladie
   Until the wood alane.
4. "O narrow is my gown, Willie,
   That wont to be sae wide;
   And gane is a' my fair colour,
   That wont to be my pride."
5. "But gin my father should get word
   What's past between us twa,
   Before that he should eat or drink,
   He'd hang you o'er that wa.
6. "But ye'll come to my bower, Willie,
   Just as the sun gaes down;
   And kep me in your arms twa,
   And latna me fa' down."
7. O whan the sun was now gane down, 2:46
   He's doen him till her bower;
   And there, by the lee licht o' the moon,
   Her window she lookit o'er.
8. Intill a robe o' red scarlet
   She lap, fearless o' harm;
   And Willie was large o' lith and limb,
   And keppit her in his arm.
9. And they've gane to the gude green wood;
   And ere the night was deen,
   She's born to him a bonny young son,
   Amang the leaves sae green.

10. Whan night was gane, and day was come,
And the sun began to peep,
Up and raise the Earl Richard
Out o' his drowsy sleep.

11. He's ca'd upon his merry young men,
By ane, by twa, and by three;
"O what's come o' my daughter dear,
That's she's nae come to me?

2:47 12. "I dreamt a dreary dream last night,
God grant it come to gude!
I dreamt I saw my daughter dear
Drown in the saut sea flood.

13. "But gin my daughter be dead or sick,
Or yet be stown awa,
I mak a vow, and I'll keep it true,
I'll hang ye ane and a'."

14. They sought her back, they sought her fore,
They sought her up and down;
They got her in the gude green wood,
Nursing her bonny young son.

15. He took the bonny boy in his arms,
And kist him tenderlie;
Says, "though I would your father hang,
Your mother's dear to me."

16. He kist him o'er and o'er again;
"My grandson I thee claim;
And Robin Hood in gude green wood,
And that shall be your name."

2:48 17. And mony ane sings o' grass, o' grass,
And mony ane sings o' corn;
And mony ane sings o' Robin Hood,
Kens little whare he was born.

18. It wasna in the ha', the ha',
Nor in the painted bower;
But it was in the gude green wood,
Amang the lily flower.

Notes

1. "Rose the red & White Lilly" (Child 103A)

This is the longest ballad in Mrs Brown's repertoire. The story is unusually complex, involving six characters: two couples, an evil stepmother who separates them and a king who reunites them. Two sisters, Rose the Red and White Lilly, are happily in love with the two sons of their stepmother. The stepmother spoils their pleasure by sending her sons away. Devastated, the two sisters decide to leave their home, Barnsdale. Disguised as Sweet Willy, Rose the Red sets out for the king's court to be near her lover, Bold Arthur, while White Lilly disguises herself as Roge the Round and follows her lover, Brown Robin, who now lives in the greenwood. Before parting, they agree that each will blow a horn in case of need in order to call for the other's assistance.

One day Brown Robin discovers Roge the Round. He breaks into her bower and a child is conceived. Nine months later White Lilly is desperately in need of a bower woman. She blows her horn, which Sweet Willy hears at court and she immediately comes to her sister. Brown Robin fights the intruder but is dismayed when he discovers he has wounded a woman and the sisters' identity is revealed to him. At the king's court rumour has it that one of Robin's men has given birth to a son. Curious, the king sets out to the greenwood along with Bold Arthur, who seeks a missing foot page. Bold Arthur calls his foot page to him with a blast on his horn. His foot page answers the call yet refuses to tell the king who lives in the bower. On entering they are amazed to find White Lilly nursing her son. Rose the Red kneels down and tells the whole story upon which Bold Arthur recognises her. When Brown Robin returns from hunting he is afraid of the king, who however reassures him by inviting him to live at the castle. Setting the child on his knee he declares his intention of making him his bowman when he grows up. The king takes care of both couples by dressing the ladies in appropriate clothing and a joyful marriage takes place. In A, Rose the Red laughs to think of what the stepmother would say if she saw them then.

The three full versions of this ballad are all Scottish, the Brown version being the first known. This greenwood narrative has a slight connection with the Robin Hood cycle of ballads through its mention at verse 12 of Barnsdale in Yorkshire where some of them are set. This connection might have been established by the tune; it bears close resemblance to Christie's "Birth of Robin Hood" (Child 102; see Brown 35).

A (pp. 1–5; ff. 10r–13r)

There are 59 verses in Jamieson's numbering as against the 58 here. RJ 12

= 11.5–12.2; RJ 13 = 12.3–13.6, so that RJ 14 corresponds to 15. Jamieson has also skipped the number between 25 and 27, so that his 25 = 24.1–25.4.

B (pp. 37–46)

20.1 "nae" inserted (TG). 26.4; "dread" has been overwritten by "dried" (TG); 55.1: the first "it" corrected to "in" (TG).

Music

Bronson 103.1. "Slow". Since this tune is very similar to the one she uses for Brown 8 "Lady Elspat", it is therefore very likely that Mrs Brown also sang Brown 35, "The Birth of Robin Hood" (Child 102) to this tune. Two variants are recorded from the north-east of Scotland and Bronson gives the following conjectural, more singable, tune along with the original that he printed above:[1]

2. "Jack the little Scot" (Child 99A "Johnie Scot")

Johney (or Jack) is a knight serving at the English court. Not long after his arrival, word is quickly spread that the king's daughter is pregnant by him. The king is enraged and threatens to put his daughter in prison. Johney flees to his home at Pitnachton in Scotland, and sends a boy to the princess asking her to come to him there. However, she is in prison and sends the boy back to tell Johney the situation. He sets out to free her and advances on London at the head of five hundred men. The king at first thinks it is a friendly visit by the Duke of Albany or King James, but he soon realises that it is Johney and threatens to hang him. The Scots then point out that they will defend Johney. When the king mentions that he has an exceptional Italian fighter in his court, Johney offers to take the Italian on in single combat. If he wins, he

1 I am grateful to Katherine Campbell for having fitted the words of the first stanza to each of Bronson's tunes.

is to receive the king's daughter. He kills the Italian with his sword and the wedding is immediately arranged. In A Johney refuses the gold and silver offered as dowry, saying he only desires the lady.

A (pp. 5–8; ff. 13r–15v)
"Scot" in the title is spelt "Scott" in the heading of the following pages and in the narrative.

B (pp. 11–16)
5.4 "A wot" was first written, and "A" has been deleted and "I" written before it by TG, who apparently made the same change in 5.2 though the deleted letter is not visible. 7.1–2 "See Gil Maurice." (JR). 14.4 is followed by a division line.

Music
Bronson 99.10. "Slow". Mrs Brown's is "the best as well as the earliest" tune for this rather scarce ballad (Bronson,"Professor Child" 191). There are two minor rhythmic inconsistencies at the beginning and the end of the tune but this could reflect RES's confusion about how to transcribe Mrs Brown singing rallentando first and then holding the A before trilling the G-sharp. Here is Bronson's conjectural reading of the tune:

Munro (222) has commented on Sophia Scott's conjecture below:

> 'John the Scott' [...] stays in 3/4 time but adds some dotted rhythms which lend a somewhat mazurka-like flavour, and the awkward emphasis on the sharp 7th note of the scale is avoided by a simple downward leap of an octave from the 6th of the scale (bar 3), which contrasts nicely with the preceding two bars of rising melody.

3. "Willy o Douglass dale" (Child 101A)

This is a sentimental story of secret love. Willy is a handsome Scottish lord who has taken service at the English court. He longs for the king's daughter and manages to meet her when she goes to the greenwood. She immediately falls in love with him and shortly afterwards they become lovers. When she realises she is pregnant, she fears that Willy will be killed once her condition becomes known. Willy offers to take her to Scotland and make her his lady. They agree to go away together and one night she leaps over the castle wall and he catches her in his arms. In the greenwood she follows him weeping and he builds a fire and makes a bed for her to lie on. When she is about to give birth, she asks Willy to sound his hunting horn, saying that, if her father is in the wood, he will hear it and come to her. Willy is not prepared to help her to appeal to a man of her family in this way and refuses, and shortly afterwards, while he is absent hunting, the lady bears a son. Willy finds a young shepherdess feeding her flock and they persuade her to become the child's nursemaid and they all three take ship to Scotland where the king's daughter becomes Lady of Douglass-Dale.

This is a rare ballad, all the versions of which come from north-east Scotland. It is worth noting that the collection of Glenbuchat Ballads, made c. 1818 but only published in 2007, edited by David Buchan and James Moreira, includes two versions (*Glenbuchat* 63–71). See also GD 1010.

A (pp. 8–10; ff. 15v–17v)
"Douglass dale" in the title is spelt with a single "s" in the following headings. An asterisk at the title "Willy o Douglass dale" connects to the note on the facing page: "See Blind Harry, Vol. 2, p. 157 line 4". This reference is correct for *The Metrical History of Sir William Wallace, Knight of Ellerslie, by Henry, commonly called Blind Harry* (3 vols, Perth: R. Morison junior for R. Morison and Son, 1790). The line referred to is "Schyr Wilzham lang off Douglacedaill was Lord" which is Bk. IX, line 1548 in this edition, and Bk. X, line 857 in a modern edition (ed. McDiarmid). The note is written in ink on top of 14 rubbed-out pencilled long lines of verse which are almost indecipherable. Mention is made here of a few words that can be made out in case they may lead to future identification. The first two lines end with "light" and "beauty bright", "had" occurs earlier in line 1, and line 4 includes "in secresie".
9.6 Underneath "An low laid is my pride" are written in pencil the numbers 1 5 6 4 2 3 – making this read "An my pride is low laid". This change is part of a larger revision intended to create a complete 4-line stanza with an ade/aid rhyme based on 9.5–6. The two lines to be added before them were written in pencil and partially erased on the facing page: "Dowy my heart that ance was blythe / As goudspink in the shade".

14.2 “An lions gaed to their dens” is underlined in pencil and opposite is written faintly in pencil “An the wolf [to the] wood was boun.” This revision both replaces the exotic lions and supplies a rhyme for “down” at 14.4.

B (pp. 51–57)

12.4 is followed by a division line.

Music

Bronson 101.1. “Slow”. Only two tunes survived, yet there is little connection between them. The rhythm is problematic in “Willie o Douglas Dale”. The initial up-beat was probably prolonged by Mrs Brown, the mid-pause abbreviated and extra time taken at the end of the first phrase (see Bronson 1: 507). This might look like a confusing, mixed rhythm from a classical point of view but, just as oral formulas distinguish oral from written discourse, a slow “free rhythm with no discernible beat” (Johnston, *Music and Society* 94) is the hallmark of oral recitation.

4. “Young Bekie” (Child 53C “Young Beichan”)

Young Bekie serves at the French court and falls in love with the king’s daughter, Burd Isbel. He is thrown into prison and calls for help. Burd Isbel secretly sets him free and ensures his escape, and gives him a number of gifts including a horse and a leash of hounds, of which one is called Hector. They vow to marry before three years have passed but, before the end of a year, Young Bekie finds that he has to marry a duke’s daughter in order to avoid losing all his land. The helpless hero bewails not being able to contact Burd Isbel, but the Belly Blind steps in, awakens Burd Isbel from her sleep and informs her that this is Young Bekie’s wedding day. Instructed by the Belly Blind, Burd Isbel takes two of her maids along with her and the three women dress themselves richly and go down to the seashore where they board a boat that, steered by the spirit, magically transports them to where Young Bekie’s wedding celebrations are taking place. The porter hurries to the wedding party and informs them of the three fine ladies at the gates.

With tears in his eyes, Young Bekie runs instantly to Burd Isbel and kisses her, and the hound she gave him recognises her. Young Bekie sends the duke's daughter back home and marries Burd Isbel instead.

"Young Bekie" and Brown 5 "Young Beichan" are versions of the same ballad, which is a widely known one. Mrs Brown's "Young Bekie" is unique in including a supernatural helper.

A (pp. 11–13; ff. 18v–21r)

10.3–4 "A leash o hounds o ae litter / An hector called one." "See Warton's Eng. Poetry, Vol. 2. p. 221, Note *m*." (f. 18v): Jamieson's reference is to the 3-volume *History of English Poetry* by Thomas Warton (London: printed for J. Dodsley et al., 1770), and Warton's note is to the two milk-white greyhounds that run beside a beautiful lady on horseback identified as Fame in the poem by Stephen Hawes called "The Passetyme of Pleasure, or the Historie of Graunde Amoure and La Bal Pucel" (1506).

28.3–4 "An they hae girdles about their middles / Wou'd buy an earldome". "See Way's Fabliaux, V. 2, p. 337, in ~~the Lay of~~ Launfal Miles,

> 'The paytrelle of her palfraye
> 'Was worth an erldome stout & gay,
> 'The best in Lumbardye.'" (RJ)

34.3–4 "For at ilka word the Lady spake / The hound fell at her feet".

> "Vid 'Throug Karlyon rood that lady,
> Twey whyte greyhoundys ronne her by &.'
> Launfal Miles *ut sup*." (RJ)

Jamieson's source is *Fabliaux or tales, abridged from French manuscripts of the XIIth and XIIIth centuries, by M. Le Grand, selected and translated into English by the late Gregory Lewis Way, Esq. With a preface, notes and appendix, by G. Ellis* (London: printed by W. Bulmer for R. Faulder, 1802). His quotations are both at 2.337 and are of lines 959–61 and 965–6 of the tail-rhyme lay called "Launfal Miles" or "Sir Launfal".

B (pp. 30–36)

14.3 "Belly-blind" glossed as "a guardian spirit" (TG). Stanza 18 is inserted (TG). AFT has noted at the foot of the page containing this addition: "Professor Gordon's handwriting". 20.2, 24.2 TG's revision is so heavily written when he twice gives the letter "i" in hail that the original is unclear but it looks as if the word had been spelt "haul". 25.3 "Sae" altered from "She" (TG).

Music

Bronson 53.112. "Brisk". Many tunes are on record, but Mrs Brown's, again, is the oldest.

5. "Young Bicham" (Child 53A "Young Beichan")

Young Bicham was born in London. When he set off on his travels to see the world, he is captured and imprisoned by a savage moor who treats him cruelly. The moor's daughter, Shusy Pye, bribes her father's men and sets him free. Young Bicham promises to return and marry her before seven years have passed and sails back to London. Longing to see Young Bicham, Shusy Pye grows impatient and follows him. Arriving at his gates, she is told that it is Young Bicham's wedding day. She asks to speak to the groom and the porter informs the wedding party about the fine lady. Realising who is at his gates, Young Bicham cries out her name and hurries to meet her and kisses her tenderly. Shusy Pye fears she has been forsaken and should try to forget Young Bicham, but he declares that he must marry his first love and sends the bride home with a double dowry as compensation.

This and Brown 4 "Young Bekie" are both versions of Child 53 "Young Beichan", a widespread ballad (in chapbooks and oral tradition) which continued to be sung in north-east Scotland. GD 1023 has nineteen versions. See also Glenbuchat 136 "Young Bonwell". A close variant is Child 53B "Young Brechin" from the Glenriddell manuscript of the Society of Antiquaries (vol. 8, pp. 80–83).

A (pp. 13–15; ff. 21v–23r)

6. "The gay goss hawk" (Child 96A "The Gay Goshawk")

This ballad has high tragic potential. The goshawk is a magical bird which can speak and sing and it functions as a messenger between a Scottish squire and an English lady, who are in love. Before flying off, the bird asks the squire how to recognise the lady to which he replies that she is the fairest lady in England. As instructed, the bird sings on a birch tree near the lady's bower, and attracts her attention. It then both gives her a letter that it plucks from among its feathers and also tells her that her lover can wait no longer. She tells the bird to bid her lover make preparations for the wedding feast and puts her plan to join him into action. She asks her father for a boon and he says he will grant her anything except the Scottish squire. She then asks to be buried in Scotland, drinks a sleeping draught and is seemingly dead the next morning. Her family prepares her funeral and she is carried to Scotland and is taken from church to church as she had requested. At the fourth church, the squire meets the funeral party and asks to look upon the dead. The lady smiles at him and speaks, asking immediately for bread and wine to break her long fast. She then mocks her brothers, bidding them go home and tell how she has bested them.

We may note that the bird messenger lies at the interface between oral and literate culture. Since it can speak, it is perfectly capable of conveying the message itself but here it also carries a written letter from the lover tucked into its plumage. The speaking bird is at the root of the narrative idea, and the speaking has not been supplanted when a written message was introduced. All the seven known full texts of this ballad are from Scotland. The Brown version does not include an episode found elsewhere in which the young woman's family is shown to be suspicious of her sudden death and tests her by dropping molten gold or lead on the body.

A (pp. 15–17; ff. 23r–25r)
In 1.3 and 11.4: "hell" should read he'll". In 1.2 the hawk is "he", in 7.3 "she".
B (pp. 24–29)
6.4 is followed by a division line. 9.3 "my shot window" glossed as "a drawing window" (TG).

Music
Bronson 96.1. "Slow". For Child 96 only one other tune (from Christie's *Traditional Ballad Airs* 2: 124) is known but, although the two tunes both come from the same north-eastern tradition, they seem to be unconnected.

7. "Brown Adam" (Child 98A)

This story is set in the greenwood, where a lady's loyalty is put to the test by a false knight. The protagonist is a banished smith, living in solitude with his lady. No reason is given for his banishment. One day, Brown Adam goes hunting and sends two birds home, promising to return home in the morning. On returning he stands a bit apart, watching how the knight tries to seduce his lady. The knight tempts the lady with a golden ring and a purse full of gold. She refuses each time, asserting her love to Brown Adam. Only when the knight threatens the lady with his sword, does Brown Adam intervene. He attacks the would-be seducer, forcing him to leave behind his bow and sword, and slashes his right hand so severely that he also leaves behind four of his fingers.

The opening of the story is rather obscure since little context is given. In the three versions known, which are all Scottish, either the hammer or the anvil used by Brown Adam is said to be of gold, so that we are led to imagine something grander than the day-to-day work of a smithy.

A (pp. 17–19; ff. 25r–27r)
B (pp. 8–10)

Music
Bronson 98.1. "Briskish". Mrs Brown's tune "Brown Adam" is one of two known variants. As it stands in RES's notation, however, there is "something radically wrong with the timing … It cuts quite against the metrical scheme of the common ballad stanza, allowing for only three real stresses in the first and third lines, and two in the second and fourth" (*TT* 2: 482). Here is Bronson's attempt to produce a more singable form:

8. "Lady Elspat" (Child 247)

The heroine is not very active at the beginning of the narrative but later plays a decisive role. Sweet William and Lady Elspat have exchanged vows and she plans to meet him that night at the back of her mother's castle to elope with him. Unfortunately a page overhears them and informs Lady Elpat's mother, who, disapproving of their union because the suitor is not wealthy enough, has Sweet William bound and brought in front of the lord justice. She falsely accuses him of having broken into her castle and stolen her jewels. Lady Elspat defends Sweet William with the truth, and the judge finds him innocent and sets him free. The judge then turns out to be Sweet William's uncle. He blesses the couple and, in A, he offers them as much of his own land as a fine horse of his can ride round in a summer's day.

The Brown version of this ballad is the only one known. It is interesting to note the dominance of Elspat's mother (cf. the mother's dominance in other ballads such as "Clyde's Waters"), and also the arbitrary power attached to her rank. She tells a bare-faced lie in the presence of her daughter who knows the truth, and we are made to feel that it took considerable spirit for the daughter to stand up to her in this formal setting and hope that the judge will accept her account.

A (pp. 19–20; f. 27r–v)
There are 12 verses in RJ's numbering as against 13 in this edition, since RJ 6 = 6 and 7.
B (pp. 63–65)
4.4 and 7.4 are followed by division lines.

Music
Bronson 247.1. "Slow". Mrs Brown's tune for "Lady Elspat" is similar to that for "Sweet Willie, My luve she lives in Lincolnshire" (Child 256 "Alison and Willie") as sung by the Harris sisters (see Bronson 4.13–14; *Harris Repertoire* 178). There may be also a connection between Mrs Brown's and Christie's tunes of the same name (Bronson 247.2). The tune of "Lady Elspat" was mistakenly given with the text of "King Henry" in the Abbotsford MS and thus in Sophia Scott's manuscript (see discussion in Munro 223). The mistaken tune connection was repeated in *ESPB* 5: 422, but Bronson was able to correct the error. Bronson's conjectural form of the tune runs:

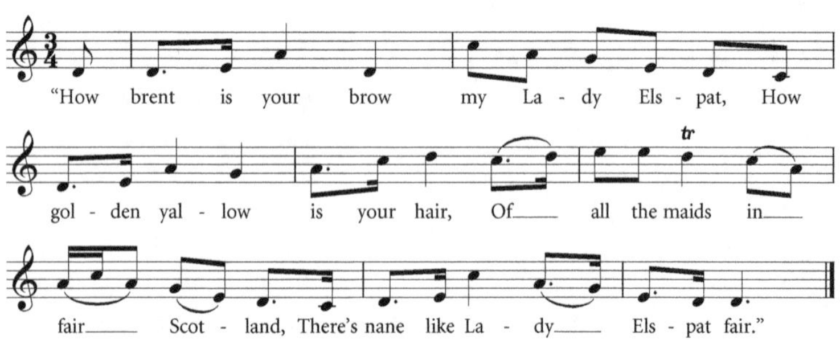

Here also the wrong tune was fitted to the words of "Lady Elspat" by Sophia Scott. She simply doubled the note-lengths to accommodate four lines of words instead of two and, as Munro observes (223), "we have a perfectly good tune! And it fits the words."

9. "Lady Jane" (Child 62E "Fair Annie")

This is a tale of revelation. A woman (later identified as Lady Jane) is living happily out of wedlock with the lord she loves until he confronts her with his decision to marry and asks her to welcome his bride. She agrees to prepare for the wedding. Devastated, she dresses her sons in scarlet red and herself like a maid to greet the couple. The bride asks the lord who the lady is, who has welcomed them, saying that she would like to do her good since she reminds her of her elder sister, Jane, who had been abducted. Visibly agitated and distressed, the lady then serves the wedding party during dinner. At night she takes up her harp to sing the couple asleep. She sings of the Earl of Richmond, who was her father, and the bride recognises that she is her sister. The lord sends the bride back home on one of the seven ships she brought and keeps the other six as a dowry for Lady Jane.

This ballad has Scandinavian (DgF 258), Dutch and German analogues. The Brown version is the oldest recorded in Britain apart from an 8-verse fragment published by Herd in 1769. In most of the Scottish versions, the bride warmly gives her new-found sister most of the wealth she brought as dowry and this fits well with her character as shown earlier. In the Brown version the lord arbitrarily and abruptly keeps six of the bride's seven ships when he sends her home and this idea is present with a fuller conversational context in Peter Buchan's version (Child J).

A (pp. 20–21; ff. 27v–28r)

The following are underlined and alternatives written above: "An leugh amo" (11.2) now reads "And smil'd upon" and "gay" (18.1) now reads "sad". Two asterisks indicate that there were notes or insertions at the end of 8.3 and between 14 and 15 but these are not present. There is no interleaf at this point and it can be assumed that a leaf is missing.

For 10.4 RJ has the following footnote in *PB* 2: 373 when he prints the ballad verbatim: "'To keep her colour fine', i.e. to preserve her complexion; to keep her from betraying the secret emotions of her heart by changing countenance."

10. "Burd Ellen" / "Lord John and Bird Ellen" (Child 63 "Child Waters" Bb)

The ballad begins with a moral warning to ladies not to leave their father's house to follow young men, and Burd Ellen declares that she will not accept the advice and will follow Lord John. Disguised as a page she runs behind Lord John, who is riding home. When they come to the River Clyde, she attempts to swim across and, when she is in danger of drowning, Lord John takes her up on his horse. It is when Burd Ellen is in the river that it is revealed that she is pregnant; she speaks to her unborn child saying that Lord John is indifferent to them both. Lord John mentions the castle where they are going and assures Burd Ellen that she will be poorly treated there but she remains firm in her resolve to follow him. When they arrive, Lord John is welcomed by a large company but his supposed page leads his horse to the stable. During dinner, Burd Ellen cannot eat and Lord John's mother comments that the page looks more like a woman great with child than a serving man. When Lord John sends Burd Ellen to feed the horses, she gives birth in the stable. Lord John's mother hears her moans and alerts Lord John who hurries to the stable and forces his way in to Burd Ellen and the baby boy she has just borne. He orders his son to be taken care of and comforts Burd Ellen, declaring his intention of marrying her. In C, Burd Ellen blesses the day she followed him.

This ballad is mainly known in the Scottish and Scandinavian traditions (DgF 267; TSB D396). The earliest form occurs in the Percy Folio MS c. 1625, and the Brown version was the next recorded. In the early twentieth century, it was still possible to record versions in north-east Scotland (see GD 1229A, from Alexander Robb, and 1229B, from Bell Robertson) and in America. Coffin and Renwick point out that "the American texts follow the Child B [i.e. Mrs Brown's] tradition" (see Coffin/Renwick 64).

A (pp. 22–24; ff. 28v–30r)

Jamieson published this version at *PB* 1: 113–25, omitting, however, the warning at the beginning – he moves the first two stanzas to the notes.

The following phrases are underlined in the manuscript and an alternative written above, but only the first of the alterations was brought into *PB*: "i my father house" (6.1) reads now "wi my bower woman"; "Betide me well betide me wae" (14.3) was first changed to "Yet hap me well or hap me wae" and then the alteration was crossed out again; 26.4 "for love has follow'd me" underlined and "I got in the North Countrie" written above:

The paired lines at 16.1–2 and 18.1–2 had the following revisions squeezed in after them.

> The food that [*PB* sic] love is fed upon
> Is neither bread nor bran;
> O nay, O nay, Lord John, whate'er
> I eat, Or meat or corn,"

These revisions are printed in *PB*, which includes a footnote to the first of the lines reading (*PB* 1: 121*):

> " 'The food,' &c. originally,
> 'O, I shall eat the good white bread,
> And your dogs shall eat the bran,' &c
> These lines are again repeated in the beginning of stanza 21 [st. 18 in A]."

At the end of the last verse (36), one of Jamieson's manicules appears and a matching one is to be found on the facing page referring to this text:

> 37 She heavit up her droopin head; –
> O but her face was wan!
> And the smile upon her wallowt lip,
> Wad meltit heart o' stane!
> 38 O blissins on thy couth, Lord John!
> Well's me to see this day!
> For mickle hae I dane and dreed;
> But well does this repay!
> 39 And O, be to my bairnie, kind,
> As I hae lovit thee! –
> Back in his tremblin arms she sank,
> And cald death closed her ee!

In *PB* these verses are bracketed as an interpolation and Jamieson makes special note of them in his introduction:

> Whether the catastrophe is rendered more affecting by the three stanzas which I have added at the end; or whether I may expect praise or blame for having sacrificed poetical justice to what appeared to me to be natural probability, is what I cannot determine: different readers will probably be of different opinions; and such as prefer the piece in its original state, may have their full gratification in this, as in every other case in this miscellany, by passing over such lines as are marked not authentic.
> (*PB* 1: 113–14)

Jamieson has a manicule between stanzas 14 and 15 and three bracketed verses appear at this point in *PB*. These verses were probably written on a missing leaf that came between pp. 22 and 23.

C (pp. 39–46)

1.4 "men" inserted; 15.4, 16.4 "Lord John" written in pencil above "a man" (unidentified hand); 25.3 "mair" is written above to clarify this word in the text which had been poorly written; 25.3 "I trow" written in pencil above "wi bairn" (same hand as wrote "Lord John", noted above); 26.2 "a" inserted; 29.1 "bonny" added; 30.1 "the" added; 34 Brackets to the right of the text indicate that this is a six-line stanza.

11. "Lady Maisry" (Child 65A)

Lady Maisry is courted by many Scottish noblemen, but she rejects them all and declares that she is in love with an English lord. Her father's kitchen boy overhears this and takes word to her brother that she is pregnant. The brother visits Lady Maisry and demands to know who the father is. Lady Maisry informs him that it is Lord William and that she is betrothed to him. Her brother is enraged and demands that Lady Maisry give up Lord William but she refuses. He calls for his men to prepare a fire, in which his sister is to burn. Lady Maisry asks a boy to run as fast as possible to tell Lord William of her plight and, when the boy delivers his message, Lord William immediately rides to the rescue. Lady Maisry is already in the fire when he arrives; she hears his approach but he is too late to save her. Her final words are that, if her hands had been unbound, she would have saved his son by throwing him out of the blaze. Lord William vows to take a bitter revenge on her family by burning them all and then to leap into a fire himself.

In this fairly widespread ballad, the emphasis in accounts of the family's outrage may fall rather on the fact that the young woman is with child before marriage than on the identity of the father, who may or may not be English. The Brown version has a strong Scotland versus England divide, like that in Brown 6 "The Gay Goss Hawk", where also the lovers are indifferent to nationality.

A (pp. 24–27; ff. 29v–33r)
St. 9 was revised to the stanza given below on the facing page which is numbered 9:

A malison licht on the tongue
  Sic tidings bears [*PB* tells] to me;
But gin it be a lie you tell,
  You sall be hangit hie.

The revised form was included in the version published at *PB* 1: 75–79, without bracketing.

B (pp. 71–77)
13.3 "My" inserted. At st. 21, a pencilled note by JR runs "Vide Gil Mor-/ris", and JR has also indicated that "whan" should be read before "he" in 22.1 and has pointed out by underlining and marginal crosses the difference between "broken" at 23.1 and "brunt" at 24.1. St. 22 has been bracketed by RES to indicate that it is a six-line stanza.

Music

Bronson 65.1. "Slow". Mrs Brown's is the earliest record and is unrelated to the other Scottish copy, Motherwell's variant.

12. "Fair Anny" / "Love Gregor" (Child 76 "The Lass of Roch Royal" D)

There are considerable differences between these two variants. In "Fair Anny" in Brown A, Fair Anny's family provide their daughter with everything she needs; only her love and the father of her son, Gregor, is absent. Her father gives her a ship to travel to him and she arrives at night with her son in her arms. It is stormy and the heroine has to wait a long time before her love's treacherous mother answers the door. Pretending to be Gregor, she demands evidence of the young woman's identity, saying she suspects she is a witch or warlock or a mermaid. Anny speaks of two tokens she exchanged with Gregor, but the apparent voice of Gregor says he has another love. Heartbroken, Anny returns to the ship. Meanwhile Gregor starts from his sleep, having dreamt of Anny being turned away from his door. After hearing the truth from his mother, he hurries after her, only to witness the ship's destruction in a storm. Anny's corpse comes floating towards him with his son in her arms. Gregor plunges into the sea and draws her out by the hair, and, after kissing her, he dies of a broken heart and his soul flies to heaven.

"Love Gregor" in Brown C focuses more on Annie's desires. The beginning is very similar, yet Annie urges the sailors along, emphasising her longing. She is more vividly pictured waiting for Gregor to answer the door. It is not mentioned, that the mother pretends to be Gregor until the next morning, which highlights the heroine's perspective. The false claim of having another love and Annie's return to her ship are not present, and instead of Gregor's dream of seeing her waiting at the door there is a foreshadowing of her death. Although Gregor hastens to the shore, he does not plunge into the water but instead the waves deposit the bodies of Annie and her son at his feet. This narrative ends with Gregor's curse on his evil mother.

This ballad, well-known in oral and broadside tradition, was recorded in Scotland in the eighteenth century and has been quite widely sung in a variety of forms, including those that became current in America (for popularity and diversification in America see Coffin/Renwick 73–75; 234–35). Only Brown contains the mother's suggestion that the heroine may be a supernatural creature.

A (pp. 27–29; ff. 33r–34r)

On the page facing the opening of this ballad (marked for insertion with a poorly formed manicule) Robert Jamieson gave the following note, in which "Robt" is both inserted and deleted. The Mr Scott mentioned twice in the quotation is Walter Scott and not Robert Eden Scott. Jamieson's version in A was taken down between 1781 and 1783; Walter Scott's version in C in 1800:

> The various readings in Fair Anny were taken from Mr. ~~Robt~~ Scott's copy, dictated also by Mrs Brown, at a distance of near twenty years, when it was much less fresh in her memory than when she dictated mine. Mine is much superiour to Mr Scotts original Copy.

The following variations written in ink were incorporated in the version from MS A called "Fair Annie of Lochroyan" at *PB* 1: 36–44. 3.1 "Her" and "shoe'd" underlined, with "Yr" and "will shoe" written above; 4.1 "will" inserted between "brother" and "kemb'd"; 4.3 "And" written above "But" and "will" above "maun" which is underlined. 12.3 "fair" underlined and "your" written above. 16.4 "But ay the best was mine" underlined and written above: "And I can shew thee thine". 17.1 "And" replacing "For". At 11.3 and 12.1: "wile warlock" is underlined; "–?f she says" written and deleted above the second. The following suggested revisions written in pencil are not found in the *PB* text. 31.1 "cherry" underlined and "blae, blae" written above; 31.3 "ruby" underlined and "ance sweet" written above. A manicule indicates an insertion before st. 22 and a lost leaf probably contained the two extra verses "inserted from memory" which occur here in *PB* (see 1: 36, 41).

C (pp. 5–10)

3.1 "father" inserted; 8.3 "sair" inserted; 9.3 "blaws" inserted; 18.2 "The the", with the repeated word deleted; 19.3 "night" inserted; 21.1 "d" of "yon<u>d</u>" superscript; 22.1 the first "Annie" inserted.

13. "Kempion" (Child 34B "Kemp Owyne")

A lady, turned into a fiery beast by her stepmother, is doomed to live on the East-muir rock until Kempion, the king's son, comes and kisses her three times. Word reaches him. Unafraid, Kempion sets out in a boat accompanied by his brother Segramour. When they are nearing their destination, Kempion says he fears the savage beast might set the whole land or more on fire and asks Segramour to keep the boat afloat. He himself approaches the rock and leans over to kiss the lady. After the first and second kisses she goes away and returns in the same state, but after the third kiss she returns as a beautiful woman. Kempion recognises his own true love and asks who transformed her. She tells him, and he (see below) lays a spell on the stepmother turning her into a four-footed dragon-like creature that will have to live in a certain wood until St Mungo comes over the sea. In B, the transformed stepmother expresses the fear that that will never happen.

As Child's title shows, the name "Kempion" is a composite, and the "kemp" or hero has the name of the knight "Sir Owain" found in Arthurian romance, although not with this adventure. There are only a few versions of this ballad and a parallel form recorded in Northumberland called "The Laidley Worm of Spindleston Heughs", which Child includes as an appendix. "The Laidley Worm" throws some light on the ending for it is made explicit there that it is the hero who puts the spell on the stepmother. Although the often light punctuation in B does not indicate this, it seems probable that the lady's speech stops at the end of 16.4 and that verses 17 and 18 are spoken by Kempion.

A (pp. 29–31; ff. 34r–36r)

The numbering begins with the second verse, which is marked "2". An asterisk at 7.4 "The fiery beast ha gane to see" indicates the following pencilled text on the facing page:

An Kempion an Segramour,
  This fiery beast they now could see.

10.2 "An he has gien her kisses ane" has the numbers 1 4 5 7 6 2 3 written underneath in pencil, making it read: "An kisses ane he has her gien", probably with a view to providing a rhyme with "seen" at 10.4. 15.3 "wolf" underlined and "an Ouph" written above; 15.4 "fish intill" underlined and "mermaid in" written above; 16.1 "wolf" underlined and "Ouph" written above' 16.2 "fish" and the "to" of "into" underlined and "mermaid" written above to give "mermaid in".

B (pp. 58–62)

18.2 "St Mungo"

Music

Bronson, sole tune. "Slow". Mrs Brown's tune is the only one known for this ballad and it was first printed (in a lower key) in 1959. It is a "striking pentatonic melody" (*TT* 1: 322) that has no parallels.

14. "King Henry" (Child 32)

After hunting the deer and slaying a fat buck, King Henry is alone in his hunting lodge when a gigantic female of fearsome appearance comes in. She is evidently naked for King Henry's first response is to give her his mantle to cover herself with. She demands food, and, although it hurts King Henry's heart, he sacrifices his horse, his greyhounds and his goshawks to satisfy her enormous hunger. She eats them all up skin and bone, and, thirsty, demands drink served in his horse's hide. He fulfils her next wish by preparing a bed of heather, and then, very reluctantly, agrees to her request to lie with her that night. In the morning, he finds that she has turned into a beautiful woman but he has his doubts about how long this shape will last. She assures him that she will be beautiful all his life for, although other knights she had approached had fulfilled her wishes in part, only he had granted all she desired.

The well-known loathly lady theme is also found in the ballad Child 31: "The Marriage of Sir Gawain", from the mid-seventeenth-century Percy Folio MS, and in Chaucer's "Wife of Bath's Tale". The full "King Henry" story is only found in Brown although Walter Scott drew on another fragment of it in the *Minstrelsy of the Scottish Border*.

A (pp. 31–33; ff. 36r–38r)

Stanza 8 has been misnumbered and thus the verse numbers after it no longer correspond to those in this edition. Jamieson published an adapted form of this ballad at *PB* 2: 194–201, saying in his introductory note: "*The interpolations will be found inclosed in brackets; the genuine text was taken from* MRS BROWN'S *recitation*." All the bracketed portions, consisting of five cases of two lines and two blocks of verses, are found as additions in the manuscript. A one-word revision at 8.3 where "skin" is underlined and "flesh" written above (in pencil) is included in *PB* but not bracketed. A change that was not taken up is "capull's" which was written in below "horses" at 13.5. The lines: "It's meat, it's meat that I ma'n hae; / An sith nae better be," occur three times (before 7.5, 9.5 and 11.5); and "Drink, gi'e me [gi'e me *inserted*] drink, she says, and sith / Nae ither boot hae ye," (before 13.5) are squeezed into the text. Asterisks indicate the insertion points of new material before 16.3 "O God" and 17.1 "Whan night". The new material, of respectively two lines and seven stanzas, is given on the facing page, and the passage also includes the six lines of st. 16. After st. 15 read thus:

Tak' aff your claiths now king Henry
  An lye down by my side
An ye sall be the groom sae gay,
  An I sall be the bride.

O God forbid says king Henry
  That ever the like betide
That ever the fiend that wons in hell
  Shou'd streak down by my side.

What I can do, as I have done,
  I yet will try for thee;
But [~~sicean a grim~~] sic an ugsome ghaist as thou
  Nae bride can be to me.

A boon, a boon, now, King Henry
  Grant me a boon I pray;
For never did a curteis Knicht
  Yet say a Lady nay.

Be thou the groom an I the bride,
  As thou art a leal Knicht.
I wad gie half my lands, Lady,
  Or bed wi sic a wicht.

Yet [*PB* But] sith thou will nocht be gain-said,
  I will do mair for thee
Nor a' the Knichts intill my Court
  I ~~wat~~ wad do ~~for~~ to pleasure me.
    [to pleasure *inserted*;
    PB I wat wald do for me.]

To sink or swim, or fecht or fa,
  They wad whate'er they dow;
But thee to clip, nae ane o' them
  For me wad mird, I trow.

Yet as I am leal-hearted Knicht,
  My fame I winna stain;
Nor ever [v *inserted*] deny a Lady's boon,
  Albe I grant wi pain.

Syne he has doff'd his claithing fine,
  Streekit down by her side;
An King Henry was the groom sae gay;
  The Lady was the bride.

Whan Nicht was gane, &c, &c. as Verse 17.

The last verse is followed by a double asterisk referring to the following text on the facing page which is marked in the same way:

And as you've done as husbands shoud,
  That wish their ladies fair,
(For ay her face is sweet and kind
  Whase heart is licht o' care;)

Ye ay sall bless the curtesie
  My beauty that has won;
And sae sall every Knicht that chears
  His dame as ye hae done.

B (pp. 66–70)
12.4, 13.6, 15.4 and 16.6 are followed by division lines.

Music
Bronson, sole tune. "Slow".

The text of "King Henry" was mistakenly matched in the Abbotsford manuscript with the tune of "Lady Elspat" (see note to Brown 8 above). Variants of the correct tune given here have been noted for "Young Benjie" (Child 86) in Alexander Campbell's *Albyn's Anthology* (1816); "Geordie" (Child 209) in George R. Kinloch's *Ancient Scottish Ballads* (1827) and for "Love Robbie" (Child 97) in William Christie's *Traditional Ballad Airs* (1876) (see *TT* 1: 319; 1: 479; 2: 408).

15. "Sweet Willy" / "Willie's Lady" (Child 6 Aa/Ab "Willie's Lady")

As the differing titles indicate, the emphasis is slightly different in the two variants since in "Willie's Lady" but not in "Sweet Willy" the male protagonist follows his wife's directions about offering gifts. The story begins with a young man seeking and bringing home a bride from afar. Because the mother does not approve of the match she prevents the wife from giving birth by the exercise of black magic. The witch and the wife are never directly opposed, although the main conflict takes place between them. The young man approaches his mother with elaborately described gifts from his lady, asking her to relieve his wife. In A Willy offers a girdle and a steed, and in B Willie offers a cup, a steed and a girdle and here the wife tells Willie to offer the latter two gifts. All attempts fail. Each time the witch wishes the wife to die and her son to remarry. Each time the young man stubbornly refuses to give up his wife and the wife laments. The circle is interrupted by supernatural intervention. The belly blin instructs the young man to make a fake wax child and invite his mother to the boy's christening. The witch, falling for the trick, reveals how her charms can be broken, and the young man then breaks them and his wife can bear their child. In B, two passages that can taken as understood because they are repetitions are indicated simply by "&c." There is also another passage not indicated by "&c." which is implied by the narrative, which occurs at the point where the two-verse instruction about making a child of wax is not matched by the following out of the instruction, although the witch's response shows that the action has been taken.

The Brown version of this very interesting treatment of a widespread motif was the only one available to Child but another version, called "Simon's Lady", also from north-east Scotland, was supplied at a later date by Bell Robertson (GD 346). This ballad is also widespread in Scandinavia (DgF 84 and 85; TSB A40).

A (pp. 33–34; ff. 37v–39r)
In Jamieson's verse numbering, 8 = 8.1–4 and 9 = 8.5–9.4.
4.2 "Hings fifty silver bells an ten" has an asterisk referring to this note on the facing page:

> See, among other instances, in the Songs of Jayadeva, in the As. Researches.
> "See, how he ties round her waist a rich girdle illumined with Golden bells, which seem to laugh as they tinkle, at the inferiour brightness of the leafy Garlands which lovers hang on their bowers to propitiate the God of desire."

And afterwards,

> "– he – tied on her wrists the loosened bracelets, on her ancles the beamy rings, and round her waist the Zone of bells ~~which~~ that sounded with ravishing melody." (RJ)

A section entitled "Gítagóvinda; or, The Songs of Jayadéva" is to be found at 3: 185–207 in the 5-volume set of *Asiatic Researches; or, transactions of the Society instituted in Bengal, for inquiring into the history and antiquities, the arts, sciences, and literature, of Asia produced by the Asiatic Society of Bengal* (London: printed for J. Sewell et al., 1799). The passages quoted by Jamieson are at 3: 197, 206–07.
18.1 There is a pencil note on the facing page attached to "witch knots" by a small cross: "Enchanted knots are tied by Witches in Scotland on many occasions. They were known to the Greeks (see Ulysses buying Wind) & are at present in use among the Laplanders &c. We find them also mentioned

in the last chapter except one of The Koran. See Sale's Kora[n.] Ed. 1734, p. 508." (RJ) Jamieson's source is *The Koran* translated and introduced by George Sale (London: printed by C. Ackers for J. Wilcox, 1734).

Jamieson gives two copies of this ballad in *PB*, one directly from the Anna Brown text at 2: 367–70 as Appendix No. 1 "Sweet Willy" and an adapted version called "Sweet Willie of Liddesdale" at 2: 178–86. It should be noted that "Willie of Liddlesdale" (see No. 26 in the Cowie manuscript) is no variant of Brown 15 "Sweet Willy", but Jamieson's own imitation. The adapted version in *PB* includes as verses 14–16 the three verses given on the facing page, beginning opposite st. 9. After st. 9 read:

O mither! and woman's heart ye bear,
Tak ruth upon a mither's pine;
Tak ruth on your ain flesh and blood,
Nor lat her sakeless bairnie tine:

And it shall live your oy to be,
To chear your eild in mony a stead;
And sain wi bennisons your truff,
Whan in the mools your banes are laid.

Awa, awa, for never she
Or imp or oy to me sall hae;
But they sall die and turn to clay;
And ye sall wed anither may.

11.2 "She spake ay in a good time" is underlined and there is a cross at the end of 11.4. A substitution, apparently motivated by the desire to rhyme, is written in pencil on the facing page:

In good time ay she gae warnin
Ye to the market-place ma'n hie,
And there a loaf o' wax ye buy;

This wording is not found in either of the *PB* versions.

B (pp. 1–4)

1.1 "fame" glossed as "the sea" (TG); 3.1 "has" inserted; 6.3 and 14.3 are preceded by division lines. 6.2 and 14.3 "Belly-blind" glossed as "a good spirit" (TG). 15.1 "ye" inserted; 17.3 "kaims" glossed as "combs" (JR); 19.4, connected with "etc.": "These lines should be repeated at full length – for they are very fine" (JR).

Music

Bronson, sole tune. A "slow", highly monotonous tune with no parallels. "Willie's Lady" appears to be *zersungen* for it will be difficult for any singer to fit "tetrameter couplets to five bars of music" (*TT* 1: 104); here the opening grace-notes might help to adjust hypermetrical lines to the tune. The conjectural reading suggests a 2/4 timing.

16. "Gil Brenton"/ "Chil Brenton" (Child 5A)

The young king, Gil Brenton, is not the protagonist; his wife and his mother dominate the action. His mother acts rationally, revealing the wife's true identity and counterbalances her son's actions, which are governed by desire. Gil Brenton has wooed and won a wealthy lady from beyond the sea, and she is being escorted to his palace by a boy who observes her unhappiness. She tells him that she is sad because she is going to be Gil Brenton's bride and asks him about the customs of the country. He reveals that the king has had seven brides already and that he had cut off their breasts and sent them back home. He tells her she will be expected to sit all day in a golden chair set out by the king's mother and warns her not to sleep with the king unless she is a maid. When the lady arrives, she sits in the golden chair, and, following the boy's advice, bribes her waiting woman to spend the night with the king. The king asks his blankets, sheets and pillows to tell him whether the woman he has married and is lying with is a maid, and they reply that the woman he is lying with is indeed a maid but that the woman he has married is not and is pregnant. Gil Brenton is grief-stricken and goes to tell his mother, who then storms into his lady's room and demands to know who the father of her child is. The lady tells her that she is one of seven sisters, and that, when they drew lots to determine who was to go into the greenwood, the lot fell on her and that, while she was gathering flowers, a fine young man came along and took her maidenhead. He gave her a lock of yellow hair, a necklace of black beads, a gold ring and a pen-knife. Gil Brenton's mother demands to see the tokens and, recognising them as gifts from herself to her son, goes to ask him what he has done with her gifts. Saying he has given them to a lady met in the greenwood, he expresses his desire for that lady, and his mother reveals that she is the woman whom he has married. Less than a month later, she bears a son and he has his father's name written on his breast.

This intricate ballad has only been collected in Scotland with the exception of a fragment from the London area (*ESPB* 5: 207), but it has analogues in Scandinavia (DgF 274; TSB D421), and even the detail of a speaking blanket reporting on the chastity or otherwise of the woman occupying the bed is to be found there. The chair set out for the lady to sit on is also a chastity test in Child C but the point has been lost in the Brown version. The seven sisters taking seven years to make a shirt for the prince and then drawing lots to go to the greenwood are mysterious elements that add to the resonance of the ballad but are not fully explicable within its context.

A (pp. 34–37; ff. 38v–41r)
37 numbered two-line verses. 3. "There was twal' & twal' wi' beer & wine / And twal' & twal' wi' muskadine".
B (pp. 17–23)
2.1 "twal' "glossed as "twelve" (JR).

Music
Bronson 5.1. "Slow". Mrs Brown's tune has some affinity with Christie's tune in *Traditional Ballad Airs* (1876) and thus, in order to overcome the rhythmic problems, Bronson's conjectural reading adopts Christie's triple time (1: 101).

The most significant difference between Mrs Brown's "Chil Brenton" and Christie's is the fact that hers has no interlaced refrain; Christie has "A-bowing down, a bowing down" and "Any aye the birks a-bowing". For Brown 18 "The Twa Sisters" an interlaced refrain was recorded but, since manuscripts A and B have no such lines for Brown 16, it is highly unlikely that Mrs Brown sang it that way (as Bronson suggests in *TT* 1: 101). The ballad has already 36 verses and this would have added considerably to the length of the performance. The difficulty here of having six-bar lines (with twelve accents) for tetrameter couplets (of eight accents) can be overcome by chanting, rather than singing the ballad.

17. "Brown Robin" (Child 97A)

This story involves a secret love affair, deception and disguise. While the king is carousing with his nobles, his daughter serves at table, but her eyes keep wandering to Brown Robin, who is standing outside in the rain. She goes to the window of her chamber and sings an indirect invitation to Brown Robin and, when he responds, she arranges to let him in later that night. After making the porter drunk, she steals the keys for her father's gate, and her lover passes the night in her chamber. Another ruse is required to get him out again the next morning. She draws a cup of red wine in the cellar and, when her father finds her there, she pretends that her head is spinning with drink. He sends her and her maids out for a walk in the fresh air. Only the porter is suspicious, demanding to count the maids going out and coming back. Disguised as a bower-woman, Brown Robin is the first to pass outside right under the eyes of her father, who observes how sturdy the maid looks. She hides his bow, arrow and sword in her own clothing and leaves, never to return again.

The four full versions of this ballad, all from north-east Scotland, differ in their endings. In Child B, the porter follows the lovers into the greenwood and shoots Brown Robin dead, and in Child C, the porter realises that one of the supposed waiting-women is a man, threatens to reveal the secret and is bribed to remain silent but is in a position to locate the lovers when the father wants his daughter back, and the story ends with the father's blessing on his daughter's wedding to Robin. The happy outcome for the lovers achieved in the Brown ballad, and in GD 1932A from Bell Robertson, follows the logic of the story which stresses the girl's initiative in opposition to parental authority.

A (pp. 37–39; ff. 41r–43r)
1.4 "ye wine" – "e" of "ye" is superscript.
B (pp. 47–50)
1.1–2 These two lines are bracketed and an attached note by RS reads: "Repeated again to the Tune". 3.4 "r" in "harped" inserted; 18.1 In "her bow" the word "her" is underlined and "his" is written in pencil in the margin (different hand).

Music
Bronson 1. "Slow". It is unusual that Mrs Brown repeats the first two lines of a quatrain instead of the last two and also that it is supposed to be sung slowly for a brisker tempo could be more appropriate (see *TT* 2: 479). Bronson's conjectural version is followed by a facsimile from Sophia Scott's Music Book:

The facsimile is part of a page (reduced) from Sophia Scott's manuscript (Munro 228). The title is written in her hand, and the words and music are probably in that of Anna Jane Clephane. There are errors of transcription in the Abbotsford copy that are repeated here.

18. "The twa Sisters" / "The Cruel Sister" (Child 10Ba/Bb "The Twa Sisters")

This is the story of a murder motivated by envy and the supernatural revelation of the murderer's identity. A knight pays court to the elder of two sisters but actually loves the younger, who is much the more beautiful. The elder sister is jealous of her younger sister and leads her down to the water, ostensibly to watch for the return of their father's ships, but actually to give her the opportunity to push her in. The elder sister leaves the younger sister to drown, despite her pleading. The corpse floats away and eventually reaches a mill dam where it is found by the miller's son. A harper who passes by laments her and strings his harp with three locks of her hair. When he plays before the king at dinner, the harp (in which the identity of the drowned sister survives) accuses her elder sister.

This narrative turns on the widespread "singing bone" motif, in which a part of the body of a murdered person accuses the murderer. The Scots / English ballad treatment dealing with two sisters, which was quite common in Britain and became widespread in America, has close cognates in the Danish, Faroese, Icelandic, Norwegian and Swedish traditions (see DgF 95; TSB A38). The Brown text is one of several Scottish versions that speak of the accusing instrument as a harp (cf. Child G and Crawfurd No. 137 and 2: xxvi (see *Crawfurd Collection*)), by contrast with a more commonly found use of the fiddle in this role.

Jamieson's published version in *PB* (1: 48–58) is based on A and he states in his introduction to "The Twa Sisters" that:

> the whole text is given verbatim, as it was taken from the recitation of the lady in Fifeshire, to whom this publication, as well as Mr Scott's, is so much indebted. [...] the burden was the same as is specified by Mr Scott ("Border Minstrelsy," vol. ii. p. 144) which seems to have belonged to some other ditty; and indeed it is sung with several different burdens. [...] The following copy, in the exact state in which it now appears, was shewn by the editor to Mr Scott, some years before the publication of the Minstrelsy, and before he had any thoughts of adopting it.

As can be seen from the notes below, Jamieson made a number of revisions and additions to the ballad as taken down by Robert Eden Scott both in A and in his printed text, and he normally identified them as his. Other substantive differences between A and *PB* are 4.2 "sair" instead of "much"; 5.2 "moistly" instead of "almos"; 14.2 "o'" instead of "an"; 15.2 "gang" instead of "gae"; 26.1, 27.1, 28.1 "it did play" instead of "he did play", emphasising that the harp caused this tune to be played.

The interlaced refrain (which is printed with each verse) is given (as in *MSB* 2: 145–50) as "(Binnorie, O Binnorie!) / ... / By the bonny mill-dams o' Binnorie" and Jamieson has attached the following footnote:

> (Binnorie, O Binnorie*!): *It may be necessary *euphoniæ gratia* to caution the English reader, that the burden is pronounced Binnōrie, and not Binnôrie, as it is accented in a beautiful little modern ballad bearing that name, which appeared in the Morning Chronicle some time ago.
> (*PB* 1: 50)

Scott adds in *MSB* 2: 144 that this refrain is "the most common and popular; but Mrs Brown's copy bears a yet different burden."

A (pp. 39–40; ff. 42v–44r)
3.1 "However awkward such a circumstance may seem now, it was not so formerly; and such presents made to ladies by their lovers are often mentioned by our old Poets: thus Chaucer, in the Prologue to his Canterbury tales, says of his gallant Frere,

> 'His tippet was ay farsed full of *knives*
> And pinnes for to given payre wives.'

A well-finished pen-knife was in those times accounted a rare and precious trinket." (RJ)
14.3 "Wardles make, Warld's make; or that which constituted made the whole world to me. We find the word assumes the same form in Blind Harry, B. 3. line 125.

> 'Hoys hede, I wait, mycht mar weille pless the king
> Than gold or land, or ony worldly thing.'

See for a different exposition. Ritson's romances, V. 3, p. 197." (RJ)
In the 1790 edition referred to in the note to Brown 3 above, the Blind Harry lines run:

> Hys hede I waite, mycht mar weille, pless ye King,
> Yan gold, or land, or ony wardly thing.
> (Vol. 1, p. 37, Bk III, lines 125–26)

Jamieson's Ritson reference is to the occurrence of "worldly make" in line 85 of "The Knight of Curtesy, and the Fair Lady of Faguell" in Joseph Ritson's *Ancient English Metrical Romances* (London: W. Bulmer for G. and W. Nicol, 1802).
25: "Originally the harp seems to have been strung with hair; 'for we find that scholars continued to have theirs so, untill as late as the beginning of the 15 century, which was the aera when strings of gut came into ~~Public~~ general use.' Camb. Register. Vol. 1, p. 396." (RJ) This is the *Cambrian Register* ([vv. [1]–3, 1795–[1818]. London: E. & T. Williams, 1796–1818) to which Jamieson subscribed, and the discussion here is of the Welsh harp.

Jamieson has the following revisions which were incorporated into his text at *PB* 1: 48–58. The added verses are indicated there by square brackets except for some confusion about the insertion between verses 19 and 20 where the bracketing includes verse 19 as well as the "Sair will" verse and does not include the "And sair" verse.

At 16.2 “down yon bonny” is underlined and “to the mouth o’ yon” written above. The following lines are squeezed in between 19 and 20:

“Sair will [~~be their~~] they be, whae’er they be
“Their hearts that live to weep for thee;
“And sair and lang mat their teen last
“That wrought thee sic a dowy cast.”

The next additional lines are squeezed in between 24 and 25 in extremely small writing:

“O wha sall tell to thy father dear
“The sad an waefu sicht is here
“An wha in thy mithers bower shall tell
“The wierd her [~~darling child~~] dearest bairn befell
“An wha to thy luckless love shall speak
“The tidings will doe his heart [~~micht~~] to break

Similarly, another line, underneath verse 25 reads:

An the harp untoucht to the windis rang,
An heavy and dulefu was the sang.

Jamieson has also added the following four verses at the end of the ballad, introducing them with a note to 28.1, indicated by a manicule, which runs: “Line 28, for ‘lasten,’ which line subjoin:”.

But the lasten tune it play’d sae sma’
Was saft, and sadly sweet o’er a’,
The hardest heart wad bled to hear;
It maen’d wi’ sic a dowie cheir,

“And fareweel, O fareweel to thee,
The dearest youth alive to me,
“Sin I maun bless thy heart nae mair,
May ruing Heaven mees thy care

In “The dearest youth alive”, the word “alive” is underlined and written above it are the words “on life” which are found in *PB*.

B (pp. 78–81)

1.7; 2.7; 3.4 Bonny St

3.2 “eldest was first written, but was corrected by RS to “youngest”. 6.1, 16.1 and 23.1 are indented to mark points of transition.

After text in pencil: “The fragment of a very different copy of this Ballad has been communicated to J. R. by a friend at Dublin” (JR). This note was left by Joseph Ritson who had the use of B in 1793–94.

Music

Bronson 10.79. “Slow”. A great number of tunes are recorded for “The Two Sisters”. Mrs Brown’s version falls into Bronson’s third, entirely Scottish, group that has some of the earliest recordings of Child 10 and has as its characteristic feature “Edinburgh, Edinburgh” in the refrain. Robert Eden Scott’s notation, however, gives trouble as to its timing and again “it needs drastic handling as to timing, if any sense is to be made out of it" (*TT* 1: 144). Bronson's reconstruction retains the Mixolydian mode and the scale of E major. This is his attempt to "restore" it.

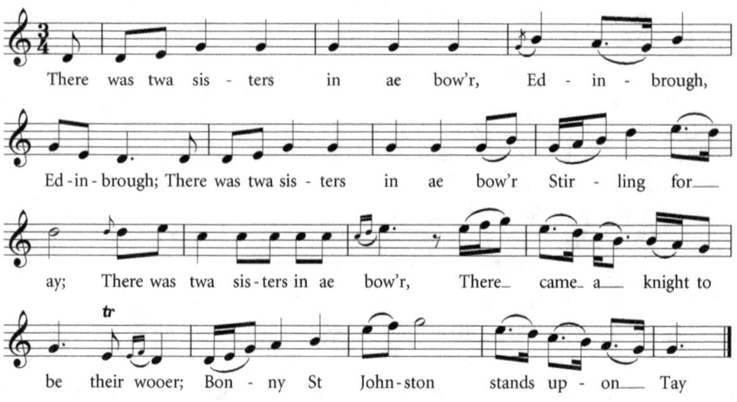

This is only one of two ballads from Mrs Brown, which indicates a refrain, although, surprisingly, "scarcely any of the other versions preserve her elaborate refrain …" ("Professor Child's" 187). "Bonny St. Johnston stands fair upon Tay" is also to be found in Christie's *Traditional Ballad Airs*. In Sophia Scott's Music Book is another, more singable conjecture (Munro 221):

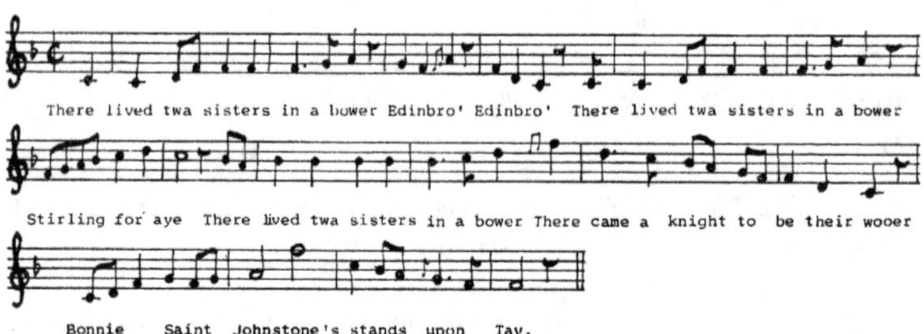

19. "Allison Gross" (Child 35 "Allison Gross")

This ballad has a male first-person narrator. All other characters are female – a witch, the narrator's sister and a fairy queen and the two magic-working characters balance each other in this story of transformation. Allison Gross, who is described as the ugliest witch in the north country, invites the narrator up to her tower and tries to seduce him by offering him rich gifts. When the narrator violently refuses her and calls her an ugly witch, she grows angry and turns him into a dragon that is compelled to circle around a tree. His sister, Maisry, visits him every Saturday night, and combs his head with a silver comb. Eventually, when the fairy court rides by on Hallowe'en, the queen removes the spell and changes him back into his own shape.

The Brown version was the only one known to Child. In recent times, the ballad was sung by the Scottish traveller singer Lizzie Higgins (see *In Memory of Lizzie Higgins – 1929–1993*, Musical Traditions Records, 2006, MTCD 37–38).

A (pp. 40–41; ff. 44r–45r)
12.2 "Seely" underlined and a cross added in pencil, referring to this pencil note on the facing page: "See Fabliaux Vol. 1, p. 114 And Ritson's Antient Songs, Dissert*ation* p. xxxviii for Seely. Fairies are the Oriental Peris –". The following note in ink is written below it: "See also Fabliaux, V. 1. 104 and p. 76, for castles built by the Fairies." For *Fabliaux*, see note to Brown 4.

20. "The bonny birdy" (Child 82)

When a knight is riding along on a summer night, he comes on a bird singing in a tree and the bird tells him that his lady is betraying him with another knight. The knight refuses to believe the bird and threatens to shoot it. The bird then tells the knight how a gentleman took it from its nest and gave it to his lady, instructing her to treat it well. The lady maltreated the bird, who now indicates that the knight himself is the man who gave these instructions and says that it would not have revealed the lady's secret if she had treated it well. The knight rides home and the bird flies along with him and perches and sings in a tree near the lady's bower. The knight surprises the lovers before daybreak and slays the false knight with his sword. A moral comment at the end approves of his action.

The Brown version is unique. The ballad has some similarity to Child 81: "Little Musgrave and Lady Barnard" where it is a page that tells the lord who is out hunting about the liaison and where the lord returns to his castle at daybreak and kills both the lover and the lady with his sword. RJ publishes them both in *PB* (1: 162–69; 170–75). Interestingly he renames the ballad "Lord Randall" (see below) and possibly because of this change, he does not give Mrs Brown as his source. Bronson calls Mrs Brown's "The Bonny Birdy" "a sort of moralized and refined 'Little Musgrave' [...]" and points out that the missing stanzas in her version are equivalent to the ones given in Brown 29 (*TT* 3: 359).

A (pp. 42–43; ff. 45v–46r)
Jamieson published a version of this incorporating his additions at *PB* 1: 162–69 under the name of "Lord Randall". He explains in his preliminary note that he has introduced the name of Lord Randall "for the sake of distinction, and to prevent the ambiguity arising from 'the knight,' which is equally applicable to both" (1: 162).
1.1 "There was a knight in" underlined and "Lord Randall wicht" written above; in 2.1 and in 4.1 "gentle knight" is underlined and "wicht baron" written above. Lines 4.1–2 are replaced by the following text squeezed in above : "O well is he, ye wicht baron, / Has the blear drawn o'er his ee". At 4.3 "But" is added at the beginning of the line. 7.5 "A Gentleman" is underlined and "A baron sae bald" written above. 10.1 "The knight" is underlined and "Ld. Randall" written above. 13.3 "waste" is added after "knights". All these revisions are included in *PB* along with larger additions that are partially enclosed in square brackets. The places where verses were added between 10 and 11 and between 12 and 13 are indicated by manicules and these verses were evidently written on a missing leaf that had come between pages 42 and 43. A line of pencil crosses also indicates a break between 10 and 11.

21. "Clark Colven" (Child 42A "Clerk Colvill")

Clark Colven's lady tells him not to touch any good-looking young woman when he goes to the well of Stream. Scorning her, he rides off merrily on his steed to the well of Stream and sees there a mermaid who is washing a silk shirt. She speaks invitingly to him and he lies with her, and then immediately cries out because of a terrible pain in his head. The mermaid, in an aside, comments that the pain will continue until Clark Colven is dead. Openly, she advises him to cut a piece from her shirt and wrap his head with it to ease the pain. When Clark Colven does this, the pain increases and the mermaid tells him that he will die, and then escapes into the water as a fish before he is able to strike her with his sword. Sadly he rides home, where he asks his family to prepare everything for his imminent death and then dies.

This theme is an international one with many ballad analogues, especially in Scandinavia (DgF 47; TSB A63), although it is represented in the Scots/English tradition by only two other versions, including the one in Herd that Ritson drew attention to (see below). In some parallels, the young man has had a long-lasting liaison with the supernatural woman and it is when he is about to marry and threatens to leave her that she destroys him.

Mrs Brown's version was published by "Monk" Lewis, in *Tales of Wonder*, but not by Scott or Jamieson.

B (pp. 5–7)
6.4 is followed by a division line. 11.4 "fleed" glossed as "flood" in pencil; 13.3, 14.3 "un" of "unbend" inserted. After text: "N.B. The fragment of a different copy of this ballad is printed in the 1st vol. of 'Ancient and modern Scottish songs', &c. Edin. 1776 beginning 'Clerk Colvill and his lusty dame'" (JR).

Music
Bronson 42, sole tune. "Slow". It is extremely difficult to fit the words to the tune. As Bronson points out (*TT* 1: 334):

> The first six bars obviously make provision for two lines of text, of equal length. The repeat would thus accommodate a full quatrain. But there are four bars left over, and these are to be repeated. If this be a second strain, to which the second and alternate stanzas are to be sung, it is very odd that it should be two bars shorter than the first: it has to carry the same length of text.

One solution could be that there was the text of a (nonsense?) refrain left unrecorded but, as Munro points out, if you simply ignore the original repeat marks, it "has no need of Bronson's conjecturally-added refrain" (221). It also seems that the tune is wrongly barred. The tune is closely analogous to "The Duke of Gordon's Daughters" (Child 237).

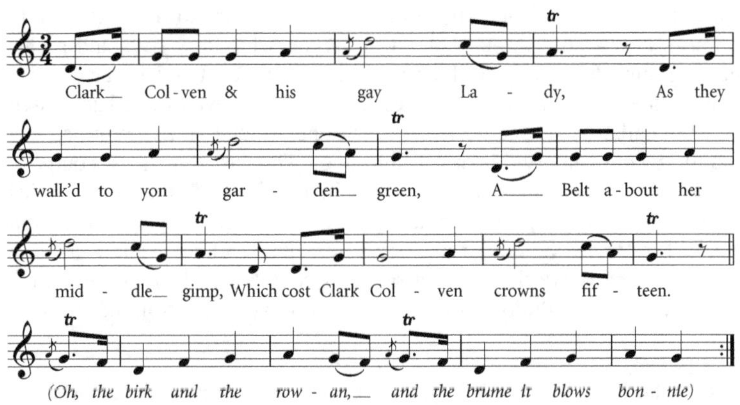

And here is Sophia Scott's much shorter version of the same tune (Munro 222):

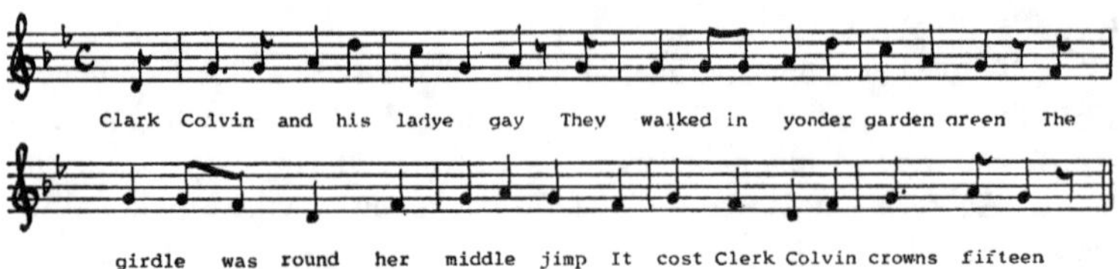

22. "Thomas Rymer & Queen of Elfland" (Child 37A "Thomas Rhymer")

Thomas, lying on a grassy bank, sees a lady wearing a green silk skirt and a velvet mantle come riding on a white horse with silver bells on its mane. He takes her for Mary, Queen of Heaven, but she tells him that she is the Queen of Elfland and that he is to serve her for seven years in Elfland. She takes him up on her horse and they ride more swiftly than the wind and arrive at a garden where Thomas offers to pluck fruit. She warns him not to, saying that the plagues of hell are on it, but supplies bread and wine for Thomas and invites him to lay his head on her lap. When he does so, she shows him three roads: one of righteousness, one of wickedness and a third that leads to Elfland, where they are going. She warns Thomas not to speak since otherwise he will never be able to return to his own country. Thomas now wades through blood in darkness for forty days and nights, hearing only the roaring of the sea. He is given a coat and a pair of green velvet shoes and was not seen on earth again until seven years had passed.

This ballad is a specifically Scottish one which has as its protagonist the thirteenth-century historical figure of Thomas Rymer, a composer of prophetic verses who also features in the fourteenth-century English romance-prophecy called Thomas of Erceldoune (see Lyle, *Fairies and Folk*). The Brown version of the ballad is the earliest known and is the only one with a narrative that gives a sense of completion. It does not include the location in the Eildon Hills that is found in versions from the Borders.

C (pp. 1–4)
The ballad itself is preceded by this note in Anna Brown's hand, which is divided by a line from the text.

> The tradition concerning this ballad is, that Thomas Rymer when young, was carried away by the Queen of Elfland or fairyland, who retain'd him in her service for seven years, during which period he is supposed to have acquired all that wisdom which afterwards made him so famous.

3.1"Thomas" inserted; 6.3 "e'er" of "whene'er" inserted; 8.2 "by" inserted; 10.3 "your" inserted; 10.4 "And I will show you fairlies three" inserted; "fairlies" glossed as "wonders"; 12.2 "Lillie leven" glossed as "flowery Lawn"; 13.4 "re" of "Where" inserted.

Jamieson also has a version of Child 37A in *PB* (2: 7–10): "The following is the copy procured in Scotland for this work before the author knew that he was likely to be anticipated in its publication by Mr Scott. It is an imperfect fragment but it is short" (*PB* 2: 7). His version is taken from C with only minor alterations. A manuscript copy, also with minor alterations, is to be found among Jamieson's papers in the Cowie manuscript (No. 44). As Neilson (132) observes, "concordances of spelling are notable" and, since Jamieson superscribes the words "inquires orig." (11.4), he clearly indicates that he had a written version as his source. The following differences deserve to be noted between the various sources:

	Brown C	Cowie	*PB*
1.1	yon'd grassy	yon grassy	yonder
2.4	Hung	Hang	Hang
3.4	peer	like	like
4.4	I'm; for to visit	I am; to visit	I am; to visit
5.4	or	and	and
6.4	The; swifter	her; faster	Her; swifter
7.3	Light down light down	Licht down, licht down	Light down, light down
9.1	loaf	loaf	laef
9.2	claret	claret	clarry
9.4	may	may	maun
10.1	drunk	drank	drank
10.3	Lay down	Lay down	Lay
11.1	not ye	ye not	you not
11.2	wi	wi	with
11.4	but few enquires	theres few that speers [*with* inquires orig. *written above*]	there's few inquires
12.1	not ye that	not you the	ye not yon
13.1	not ye that	not you the	ye not that
13.2	Which	that	That
13.3	fair Elfland	fair Elfland	Elfland
13.4	night	nicht	night
15.2	blude	blood	blood

23. "Fa'se Footrage" (Child 89 "Fause Foodrage" A)

This tale involves a long time span between a rebellion of nobles resulting in regicide and the restoration of order. A lady is courted by King Easter, King Wester and King Honor and marries King Honor. After they have been married four months, the nobles rebel, and Fa'se Footrage gains access to the royal chamber at night and stabs the king through the heart with a long knife. The queen falls on her knees and begs for mercy until her child is born. Fa'se Footrage decides to have her locked up, heavily guarded by twenty-four knights, and says that if the child is a girl she will be allowed to live, whereas a boy will be hanged. By making the wardens drunk, the queen is able to flee into a pig-sty, where she gives birth to a son. The wardens draw lots for the task of seeking the queen, and the lot falls on Wise William, who sends his wife. When the queen sees Wise William's wife, she proposes exchanging her son for the other's daughter, and arranges how they will keep in touch about the welfare of the children. Years pass before Wise William tells King Honor's son the whole story on a hunting trip one summer's day. The young man does not hesitate but immediately leaps the castle wall, stabs Fa'se Footrage through the heart and sets his mother free. He rewards Wise William with the best half of his land and marries his daughter.

This ballad is known only in the Scottish and Scandinavian traditions (DgF 298; TSB E96). Child gives three versions including the fragment in Harris (No. 29), and a tiny fragment was also recalled by Bell Robertson (GD 1930). In the other versions where the opening is present, it is one of the rejected royal suitors who kills the successful king and this draws the wooing theme more tightly into the narrative than in the Brown version.

C (pp. 11–18)
Title: The "a" in "Footrage" inserted; 1.3 "her" inserted; 2.2 "tell" probably altered from "till"; 3.1 "cast kaivles" glossed as "cast lots"; 7.4 "it" inserted; 19.4 "his" inserted; 24.1 "we" inserted; 29.1 "gin" perhaps altered from "ging"; 33.1 "bow" inserted; 34.3 "ful" apparently written "foul" with the "o" then obliterated.

24. "Jellon Grame and Lillie Flower" (Child 90A "Jellon Grame")

Jellon Grame, who is in the woods, sends a boy messenger to Lillie Flower at night to ask her to come to him. The messenger hints at his fears that she will not return home if she goes to Jellon Grame but she is eager for the meeting and ignores the warning. She sets off on horseback and comes on a freshly dug grave beneath an oak tree. Jellon Grame steps out from behind a bush and tells her that the grave is for her. The lady begs him to spare her life for the sake of his child that she is carrying. He refuses, saying he fears her father would hang him (if he knew about their child). Although the lady swears she will stay in the greenwood with the child (so that her father will not know), Jellon Grame kills her, but he takes pity on the boy lying in her blood and brings him up as his sister's son. One summer's day, while the two of them are out hunting, the boy demands to know why his mother does not take him home. Jellon Grame points out the oak tree where he killed his mother, whereupon the boy kills his father with an arrow from his bow.

There are only six known versions of this ballad including fragments (see GD 198 in addition to Child) and they are all from Scotland. Child B and C begin differently from Brown and have jealousy as the motive for the killing; the lady loves a rival and is carrying his child not that of the killer. The rival can be the killer's brother (Child C and D), and so the boy raised by the killer is actually a nephew, although a brother's, not a sister's, son. The perhaps incongruously light-hearted villain of the first two lines may be a borrowing from the innocent opening of Child 83, "Child Maurice", in which a messenger is sent from silver wood; the Greig-Duncan version from Alexander Robb begins chillingly: "O, Jellon Graeme sat in good greenwood, / And he sharped his broadsword lang."

Jamieson claims that he had a version from Mrs Brown, possibly a fragment of this ballad in 1800. He refers to this ballad in his letter to Scott (29 June 1801; MS 672, f. 9):

> What have you made of "Jellon Graeme?" You have two copies, concluding differently. And you take the other, & leave Mrs Brown's for me! This is a very bold request; but if the other is good also, both might be preserved; and I am very fond of it.

Mrs Brown's version is in C. Jamieson did not include the ballad in *PB* but there is a text in his hand in the Cowie manuscript (No. 45) that is basically a copy of C. The main differences are the following: the name is written as "Graem" instead of "Grame"; 4.3 "richt of" instead of "right aft"; 6.3 "maist" instead of "most"; 7.1 "The ladies" instead of "She had no"; 9.1 the last word of this line is "and" while in C this is the first word of the second line. The version in RJ's hand has 9 stanzas as compared to the 22 stanzas in manuscript C but, since the 9th stanza finishes at the bottom of a page, it is very likely that the rest of the ballad was written on a missing sheet and that Jamieson had more than this fragment.

C (pp. 18–22)

Pencil stanza numbers added in the margins are consistent up to stanza 16 and then erratic. 4.2 The meaning of "The red runs ithe rain" is obscure; the line is emended to "The red sun's on the rain" in *MSB* 2: 23. 13.3 "her" inserted.

25. "The bonny Earl of Livingston" (Child 91C "Fair Maid of Wallington")

Five of seven sisters have already died in childbirth and the two remaining sisters naturally do not want to marry. Nevertheless, Maisry agrees to marry the Earl of Livingston and rides to his home at Livingston. Less than a year later she is about to give birth and sends a messenger to her mother. When her mother arrives, Maisry is already having a caesarean section and is dying while her husband is grieving over his loss of her. Maisry tells him that it is she, not he, who is the main sufferer and must endure her death. The last sister exclaims that no man will cause her to die such a death but the cold-hearted mother informs her sole remaining daughter that she is to be married immediately, even if it means that she will die in the same fashion.

The fairly brief Brown version contains the main incidents of the ballad story, which was sometimes told at greater length as in the earliest known form, Child A, derived from a garland that was probably printed by 1775.

C (pp. 23–25)
7.1 "oa" is written in pencil above the "oo" of "brootch". 11.4 "me" inserted.

26. "Bonny Bee Ho'm" (Child 92A "Bonny Be Hom")

The narrator overhears a lady lamenting and swearing her deep devotion to her absent lover who she thinks has gone to sea and is sailing to Bee Hom. However, he has not yet sailed and hears her lamenting and tries to comfort her although he says he has sworn to make the voyage and must go. The lady then gives him a gold chain that will render him invulnerable, and a ring with a ruby in it that will become discoloured if she dies or is untrue to him. After he has been in Bee Hom for less than a year, when he looks at the ruby he finds that it has grown dark and he takes his leave of the world by distributing his wealth among people in need. The final verse states that the man died and that the souls of the two lovers flew up to heaven and will remain there for ever.

Another version of this slight ballad, Child B, is also from north-east Scotland and comes from Peter Buchan. It tells us that the necessity of going to Bee Hom was to do with fighting traitors there. Bronson suggested that the name might have been a corruption of Bahama (*TT* 2: 418). A similar ballad is also known in England and America as "The Lowlands of Holland" (see Child 92 Appendix).

Depite Brown 26 being only available in manuscript C, it was published not by Walter Scott but by Robert Jamieson who states: "This fragment is given *verbatim* from Mrs Brown's MS" (*PB* 1: 185). Between stanzas 8 and 9 Jamieson inserts "* * * * *" (*PB* 1: 191), thereby indicating a fragmentary state.

C (pp. 26–28)
1.3 "Lady" altered from "Ladie".

27. “Bonny Foot-Boy” (Child 252C “The Kitchie-Boy”)

A noble lady falls in love with her father’s page and seduces him. Knowing that her father will not agree to their union, she gives him the gold her mother left her and tells him to buy a ship in which to sail away and return like a nobleman. After three months Willie arrives in Spain, where a fine lady falls in love with him and offers to marry him and make him a lord. However, she cannot persuade Willie to forsake his first love in Scotland and is left mourning when he sails for home. Seeing his ship arrive, the father takes him for a lord and invites him to dinner. Willie asks to marry his daughter, backing up his request with an offer of nine thousand pounds. The father readily consents, providing his daughter is willing. Since Willie has blackened his face and tucked up his yellow hair, she does not recognise him at first and refuses, but he soon reveals himself to her. Seven years later the truth comes out at a christening feast, and the father happily accepts the situation, expressing pleasure that his daughter has married for love and promising that she will be his heir.

In most versions of this ballad, which is found only in Scotland (Child A–E and GD 1048A–D; see also Harris No. 20), more is made of the disguise motif than in Brown. There is generally a love token given by the lady before the young man’s departure which serves to identify him on his return in a sequence similar to that in Child 17: “Hind Horn”. Child saw in the “Bonny Foot-Boy” “a modern ‘adaptation’ of ‘King Horn’” (*ESPB* 4: 401) and neither Scott nor Jamieson thought it worth including in their collections.

C (pp. 28–35)
3.2 “And” added in margin. 12.4 “th” of “youth” fitted into the line after “you to” had been written; a “th” added and partially erased after “yon” in the previous line seems to be a mistaken first attempt at this correction. 19.4 “her” inserted. Seven brackets indicate that this is a six-line stanza. 24.3 “niffer” glossed as “exchange”. 35.2 Above the end of the line “And thro her tears did sweetly smile” is written in Greek letters: “δακρυοεη γελαςαςα” (AFT?). The quotation is from *Iliad* VI.484 and refers to Andromache smiling through her tears in the scene where she parts from Hector. 37.1 “father” inserted; “d” is written in pencil after “leugh” (AFT?). 37.4 “So a my gowd is at your command” is emended by Anna Brown to “So a my gowd is yours to claim”.

28. “Cruel Brother Or The Bride’s Testament” (Child 11A)

The protagonist is the youngest of three sisters, who is killed by her brother. When a knight comes along asking her to be his bride, she at first refuses because she is too young to marry. When she eventually agrees, she tells him he must ask all her relatives for their consent, but when the knight asks consent, he forgets her brother John. On the wedding day, when the knight is to take his bride home with him, she is being seen off by her relatives. Her brother sets her on her horse and, when she leans down to kiss him, he stabs her mortally. She rides away, bleeding and pale, and then dismounts to make her will. She leaves gifts to her father, mother and two sisters and finally calls down vengeance on her brother by making a gift of the gallows to him to be hanged on and the wilderness to his widow to live in after his death. She is buried and the bridegroom laments her.

This ballad, which was particularly current in Scotland, always takes the form of couplets with an internal refrain, which often mentions flowers. The second title in Brown draws attention to the striking last part of the ballad where the bequests in the murdered person's verbal will culminate in the call for revenge, as in Child 12 "Lord Randal" and Child 13 "Edward". The bride's brother was evidently inhabiting a world where the offence to his honour justified the killing in his eyes.

Mrs Brown's tune for this ballad has not survived but since the one from the Harris repertoire (No. 13), the only early recording from Scotland, has a similar interlaced refrain, this tune could be used for her text as well.

C (pp. 35–38)

2–27 In these stanzas, each abbreviated refrain line given follows on the same line as the preceding line of text after an opening bracket. 2.3 "eldest" was first written but was corrected to "youngest" by RES. 3.3 the "k" of "look'd" is partially deleted. 10.3 "spier at". The word "at" is deleted and "to" is written above. Possibly, on reading over, the "r" of "spier" was misread as the fairly similar letter "k" leading to the revision to "to" under the impression that the preposition should connect with "spiek". The original "at" is given here. 19.3 "bride" added.

29. "Bonny Baby Livingston" (Child 222A)

Glenlion seizes Baby Livingston and carries her off to the Highlands, wrapping her in a tartan plaid. She does not give him one kind look, yet Glenlion is determined to make her his bride although his brother, John, entreats him not to force a marriage. When they arrive at Glenlion Castle, Glenlion's three sisters are kind to the abducted heroine, who at first refuses to speak to them but, when the youngest, Jean, asks her about her grief, tells her about her love, Johny Hay, in Dundee and her desire to get word to him. She does manage to write a letter and a boy messenger runs to Dundee and gives it to Johny who rides to the rescue with a band of armed men. Baby escapes through the window and is caught in Johny's arms. Meanwhile the abductor is carousing in the hall. He hears the sound of a bridle ringing when Johny and Baby ride away but mistakes it at first for the sound of the priest's arrival. Discovering his error, he tries to pursue the couple with his armed men, but they are stopped at the castle gate by Johny Hay's men, while the lovers safely ride through the night. The ballad ends by mocking the villain, whose bride was taken back from him, despite all his supporters.

A number of Scottish ballads deal with abduction and some of these can be related to actual events in the eighteenth century but in this case there is no historical record. There are six known versions of the ballad (including GD 1264) and the Brown version is the only one to have a happy outcome (see also Notes to Brown 20). In the others, the young woman is put to bed with Glenlion and "longs for day" in a verse like one that occurs in "The bonny birdy". Only the next morning can she send a letter to her love in Dundee and he arrives to find her dead.

D "Old Song – Bonny Baby Livingston" (f. 1r–1v)

This text was copied by Andrew Brown and sent by Mrs Brown in a letter to Jamieson, 15 September 1800. "Old Song –" precedes the title.

3.3 "let" deleted before "loot"; 17.1 "Jean" altered from "Jane"; 30.4 "break" deleted before "close".

E (*PB* 2: 135–43)

The heading after the title reads: "*Taken by the Editor from* Mrs Brown's *recitation.*"

30. "The Baron of Braikly" (Child 203Ca)

When Inverey comes down from the Highlands to steal the Baron of Braikly's cattle, the baron's wife, Peggie Gordon, urges her husband to go out and stop the cattle being driven off, and shames him by saying that she and the women will fight if men are lacking. The baron is spurred into action and prepares to go out although he knows that he will never return. He and his brother both fall in an unequal conflict with thirty-four opponents. We are told of the widespread mourning among the Gordons for the two brothers, and the question is asked whether the baron's wife, Peggy, is mourning for him. It is now revealed that, far from being in mourning, she has welcomed Inverey and feasted with him, with the implication that she deliberately connived in her husband's death. Next morning she tells him the best way to go to avoid being taken.

The ballad is clearly a localised one, and Mrs Brown mentions in her letter to Jamieson of 18 June 1801 that she had visited the site. It fits in with the general picture of conflict between the people of settled communities in the lowland areas and the freebooting highlanders, of whom the Gordons of Brackley and the Farquharsons of Inverey could be taken as representatives.

Although events in 1592 and 1666 have been discussed in relation to the ballad, it cannot be tied closely to any specific historical incident.

In *Traditional Ballad Airs*, William Christie (1876) gives a tune, obtained from his father c. 1816 from tradition in Buchan and "epitomizes" (1: 20) his text from Mrs Brown's version as printed in *PB* 1: 102–08.

D

Text copied by Rev. A. Brown and sent by Mrs Brown to Robert Jamieson, 18 June 1801.

1.2 "dawing" – written as "dawning" with "n" deleted.

31. "Allan O Maut"

Allan O Maut describes the process of distilling, whereby the barley or malt is personified (Allan). After the barley has ripened it is cut down and taken inside to be processed further.

This fragment, as Mrs Brown calls her text, is a variant of the "John Barleycorn" tradition. By using folk symbolism, the annual ritual of cutting down the corn king is celebrated at great length in this folk song that was widely known in eighteenth-century Scotland and England. Robert Burns' "John Barleycorn. A Ballad" is based on the same folk-song tradition.

D

Text copied by Andrew Brown and sent by Mrs Brown to Robert Jamieson, 18 June 1801.

32. "Willie and May Margaret" (Child 216B "The Mother's Malison, or, Clyde's Water")

When Willie wants to go and see his love, Margaret, on a stormy night, his mother forbids him, and, when he is determined to go without her leave, she lays her curse on him, saying he will drown in Clyde's water. Willie rides away and swims the river safely, although he has his mother's curse in his mind, and he arrives at Margaret's door. Yet the place remains barred; no one lets him in. He calls to Margaret, and he hears her voice from inside the house telling him that she is not willing to open the door in case she might waken her mother and saying that all the chambers are occupied. He mounts back on his horse with a sore heart and drowns in the Clyde.

This ballad version was one that was taken down by Jamieson from Mrs Brown and is the only one that is shown as incomplete, with two and a half lines missing in the last verse given. It seems quite likely that it lacked more than that and that Mrs Brown would have had knowledge of a narrative that explained that it was not Margaret who turned her lover away, as is made apparent in other versions. Child C from Peter Buchan continues past the point of Willie's being drowned and tells how Margaret woke from a dream in which her lover was at the gates and was refused entry. Her mother tells her that he did actually come, and it is implied that it was the mother who spoke to him (as in the parallel incident in Brown 12A "Fair Anny"), and Margaret goes out into the storm and is also drowned in the Clyde, exclaiming that she and Willie had both had cruel mothers.

The ballad has been widely recorded in Scotland, especially in the north-eastern part (see GD 1231 "Clyde's Waters").

E (*PB* 1: 135–38)
The heading after the title reads: "A FRAGMENT. FROM MRS BROWN'S RECITATION."

33. "Hugh of Lincoln" (Child 155A "Sir Hugh, or, the Jew's Daughter")

A boy called Sir Hugh accidentally kicks a football through a Jew's window. When he sees the Jew's daughter looking out, he asks her to throw the ball down to him but she refuses to give it back unless he comes up to her. Sir Hugh is reluctant but she entices him with an apple to come inside and the boy follows her into a dark inner part of the house where she lays him on a table and kills him with a knife. She wraps his body in lead and deposits it in a deep well which is dedicated to the Virgin Mary. When Sir Hugh does not arrive home his anxious mother searches for him and eventually arrives at the well. When she calls out, the voice of her son replies, bidding her prepare his winding sheet and saying that he will meet her next day at the back of Lincoln. At Sir Hugh's funeral, the bells ring and the books are read aloud of their own accord without human intervention.

The miracle of the finding of Hugh's body is linked with an alleged event used in anti-Jewish propaganda that was set in Lincoln in 1255, but the popularity of the ballad treatment in Scottish tradition and its derivatives in Ireland and America seems most likely to relate to the emotional core of a generalised sense of the vulnerability of a young life and the tenderness of a mother's feelings for her son.

The ballad is very popular in Scotland, England and America (see Coffin/Renwick 107–09; 248–49).

E (*PB* 1: 139–56)
The extensive headnote includes the following comments relating to Mrs Brown and her version:

> The text of the following edition has been given *verbatim*, as the editor took it down from Mrs Brown's recitation; and in it two circumstances are preserved, which are neither to be found in any of the former editions, nor in any of the chronicles in which the transaction is recorded; but which are perfectly in the character of those times, and tend to enhance the miracles to which the discovery is attributed. The first of these is, that, in order that the whole of this infamous sacrifice might be of a piece, and every possible outrage shewn to christianity, the Jews threw the child's body into a well dedicated to the Virgin Mary; and tradition says, that it was "through the might of Our Ladie," that the dead body was permitted to speak, and to reveal the horrid story to the disconsolate mother. The other is, the voluntary ringing of the bells, &c. at his funeral. The sound of consecrated bells was supposed to have a powerful effect in driving away evil spirits, appeasing storms, &c. and they were believed to be inspired with sentiments and perceptions which were often manifested in a very miraculous manner. (*PB* 1: 139)

34. "Lamkin" (Child 93A)

Lord Wearie delays payment to a mason named Lamkin for building his castle and sets out to sea, although Lamkin has sworn that he will have cause to regret his failure to pay. He leaves his lady to look after the castle. A treacherous nurse lets Lamkin into the castle through a shot window while the servants are absent, and he stabs the baby in the cradle. When the baby howls with pain, the lady, alarmed, calls down to the nurse from the top of the stairs and the nurse persuades her that the baby will not be pacified until she comes down to him herself. Stepping down the stairs, she meets Lamkin and begs him to spare her life. Lamkin consults the nurse about what to do. She encourages him to continue his bloody revenge, claiming that the lady never treated her well. Lamkin then asks the nurse for a basin in which to collect the lady's noble blood but she refuses, saying that there is no difference between the blood of the rich and the poor. Lord Wearie returns to find the blood of his wife and son staining his chamber and hall, and Lamkin and the nurse are executed for the murders.

This grim ballad is widely known (see Coffin/Renwick 89–91 and 242–43 for America). Although conflict between the rich and the poor is one of the elements underlying this narrative of bloodthirsty revenge, the horror of the actions is stressed and the narrative operates at a personal rather than a political level.

E (*PB* 1: 176–81)

A footnote attached to the title runs: "This piece was transmitted to the editor by Mrs Brown; and is much more perfect and uniform than the copy printed in the Edinburgh Collection, edited by Mr Herd."

35. “The Birth of Robin Hood” (Child 102A “Willie and Earl Richard’s Daughter”)

Robin Hood’s birth resulted from a secret love affair. Willie, who is identified simply as being of high rank, serves in Earl Richard’s household and falls in love with his only daughter and the two young people become lovers. One summer night when they meet in the greenwood she tells him that she is pregnant and fears that her father will have Willie hanged when he finds out their secret. They escape into the greenwood after she has leapt into his arms from her bower window and that same night she bears a son. Earl Richard finds his daughter missing and orders a search for her. When she is discovered nursing her son in the greenwood, Earl Richard kisses the boy, welcomes him as his grandson and names him Robin Hood.

The opening corresponds closely to that of Brown 3 “Willy o Douglass Dale”, and the connection with the cycle of Robin Hood ballads familiar from medieval times onwards is only a slight one (see also Notes to Brown 1). The last two verses have a relatively independent existence. Their parallels appear at the opening rather than the close of Peter Buchan’s version (Child B) and occur at the end of George Ritchie Kinloch’s version of “Willie o Douglas Dale”. Brown verse 17 and its equivalents in other versions seem closer in wording and mood to the older Robin Hood ballads than the rest of this ballad does.

E (*PB* 2: 44–48)
A headnote begins: “The following ballad was taken down by the Editor from the recitation of Mrs Brown, and is here given without the alteration of a single word.”

Glossary

a, a', *adj*, all, every, 1A 3.4, 25.2, 33.3; 1B 3.4, 25.2, 33.3 etc.
a, a', *n*, all, 1A 17.2, 17.3, 33.5; 1B 17.3, 33.5; 3A 32.2 etc.
a back, *adv*, back, 1A 33.1
a be, *see* **lat a be**
aboon, abeen, *adv*, above, on top of, 1A 13.4; 1B 13.2, 13.4, 19A 8.3; 5A 17.3; 12A 29.2 etc.
ae, a, *adj*, one, only, single, 1A 28.4, 33.5, 44.3; 1B 7.3, 10.3, 33.5 etc.
afore, *conj*, before, 13A 7.5; 13B 7.5; 20A 6.1
aft, *adv*, often, 11A 20.1; 11B 20.1; 20A 8.2, 9.4; 24C 4.3
aiken, *adj*, oaken, 8A 7.2; 8B 7.2
ain, *adj*, own, 1A 14.1, 37.4; 1B 37.4; 2A 12.2, 13.2; 2B 12.2 etc.
amang, amo, amo', *prep*, among, 9A 11.2; 10A 21.4, 30.3; 10C 21.4, 30.3; 15A 16.2 etc.
an, an', *conj*, if, 1B 7.4; 3A 10.1; 3B 10.1
ance, anse, *adv*, once, 3A 3.1; 19A 7.3; 29D 5.3, 14.3; 31D 1.1
ane, *adj*, one, 1B 15.3; 3A 2.4; 4A 28.1; 4B 29.1; 6B 21.4 etc.
ane, *article*, a, an, 11B 6.2; 20A 13.6
ane, an, *pron*, one, 9A 20.2; 20A 13.5
aneath, *prep*, beneath, 15A 17.2, 19.2
atween, *prep*, between, 4A 11.1; 4B 11.1; 7B 4.4; 14A 17.4; 14B 17.4 etc.
aught; **is aught**, owns, 11A 11.1; 11B 11.1
auld, *adj*, old, 16A 19.1, 19.3; 16B 19.1; 19.3; 17A 21.4; 17B 21.4 etc.
auld, *n*, old, 26C 10.4
ava, *adv phr*, of all, 34E 25.4
avisiting; **a visiting**, *prep with verbal n*, visiting, to visit, 2A 25.4; 2B 25.4
avow, *v*, admit, express openly, 23C 24.2
awa, awa', *adv*, away, 1A 39.4, 43.4; 1B 39.4, 43.4; 3A 12.4; 3B 12.4 etc.
awooing, a-wooing, *prep with verbal n*, wooing, 11A 1.2; 11B 1.2
awot, see wot
ay, aye, *adv*, always, 1A 44.2; 1B 24.3, 44.2; 6B 8.3; 9A 14.3; 10A 18.3; etc.
ayont, *prep*, beyond, 1A 17.3; 1B 17.3
ba, ba', *n*, ball, 28C 1.1; 33E 1.2, 2.4, 4.1, 4.2
bad, *v pt*, bade, 5A 8.3
bade, baed, *v pt*, waited, 11A 22.2; 11B 22.2
bairn, *n*, child, 9A 4.4; 10A 9.3, 25.3, 32.4; 10C 6.1, 25.3 etc.; **bairns**, *pl*, 9A 17.3; 33E 10.2; 34E 10.1; **bairn an(d) bairnly like**, 15A 12.1, 14.3; 15B 16.1
baken, *adj*, baked, 10C 17.1, 18.1; 16A 3.1; 16B 3.1; 27C 16.3, 28.3
bale, *n*, harm, misery, 1A 51.4; 1B 51.4

ban, *n*, band, 8A 7.2; 19A 5.2

ban, band, *n*, tie, hinge, 12A 1.4, 3.3; 16A 19.2; 16B 19.2; **bands, ban's**, *pl*, bonds, 8A 11.4; 8B 11.4

banded, *v pp*, secured, 8A 7.2; 8B 7.2

bane, been, *n*, bone, 14A 8.3, 10.3, 12.3; 14B 8.3, 10.3, 12.3 etc.

bann, *v*, curse, 30D 14.2

bare, *v pt*, bore, 3A 24.4; 3B 24.4; 16A 36.2; 16B 36.2; 25C 10.3

bear, *n*, barley, 31D 1.1

beerly; **to make him beerly cheer**, to have a rude feast, 14A 4.2; 14B 4.2

begood, *v pt*, began, 10C 9.4

Belly-blind, Belly Blin('), *n*, benevolent spirit, 4A 14.3, 23.3; 4B 14.3, 24.3; 15A 11.1; 15B 15.1

ben, benn, *adv*, in, towards or in the inner part of a house, 4A 6.2; 4B 6.2; 17A 2.1; 17B 2.1; 30D 6.1

bent, *n*, open ground covered with coarse grass, 30D 3.2

bierly, beirly, *adj*, sturdy, well-built, 4A 29.1; 4B 30.1; 9A 19.1

big wi(') bairn, pregnant, 11A 8.4, 11.2; 11B 8.4, 11.2; 25C 5.3

bigged, bigget, biggit, *v pt*, built 1A 3.1; 1B 3.1; 7A 4.3; 7B 4.3; 8A 6.4, 9.2 etc.

biggin, *n*, building, 11A 24.1; **biggins**, *n pl*, 11A 23.1; 11B 23.1, 24.1

bigly, *adj*, pleasant to live in, handsomely made, 1A 3.1, 45.3; 1B 3.1, 45.3; 6A 19.1, 26.1 etc.

bird, *see* burd

birling, *v pres p*, carousing, 17A 1.2; 29 35.2; 29D 35.2; **birl'd, birled**, *pp*, made drunk, 17A 7.1; 23C 16.1

blaket, *v pp*, blackened, 27C 31.1

blate, *adj*, stupid, easily deceived, 20A 2.4

blude, bluide, bleed, *n*, blood, 1A 31.3, 33.4; 1B 31.3; 8A 4.3; 8B 4.3; 22C 15.2 etc.

bonny, bony, *adj*, good-looking, 1A 23.4, 35.4, 45.2, 47.1, 48.4 etc.; **bonniest**, *superl*, 13B 14.4

book, n, bible, 26C 6.3

bore, *n*, hole, 34E 13.3

born, *v pp*, borne, 9A 15.1, 16.1

borrow, *v*, ransom, release, 4A 4.1, 4.3, 5.1; 4B 4.1, 4.3, 5.1

bound, boun, boon, *adj*, prepared, ready, 9A 13.2; 10A 3.2; 10C 3.2; 23C 5.2; **boun, boon to meat**, prepared to eat a meal, 10A 21.2; 10C 21.2

bouted, *adj*, bolted, sifted, 16A 2.3; 16B 2.3

bowman, *n*, archer, 1A 56.4; 1B 57.4; **bowmen**, *pl*, 2A 28.3; 2B 28.3

bowr woman, bow'r woman, *n*, waiting woman, 1A 24.3; 1B 24.3; 16A 13.1; 16B 13.1

bowr, bow'r, bower, *n*, dwelling, lady's private apartment, 1A 3.1, 3.3, 20.5, 21.1, 22.1, 24.3 etc.; **bowrs, bow'rs**, *pl,* 9A 8.2; 16A 34.4, 35.4; 16B 34.2, 35.2

brae, *n*, steep or sloping bank, hillside, 22C 1.4, 13.2; 23C 26.4; 32E 16.4
braid, *adj*, broad, 22C 12.1; 23C 1.3; **braider**, *compar*, 12C 22.4
brain, *adj*, mad, 3A 10.4; 3B 10.4
brak', **brake**, *v*, broke, 1A 2.2; 1B 2.2
bran, **bran'**, **brand**, *n*, sword, 1A 21.3, 22.3, 56.3; 1B 21.3, 22.3, 57.3 etc.; **brands**, *pl*, 29D 37.3
bran, **brann**, *n*, grain husks, 10A 15.2, 16.2; 10C 15.2; 16.2
brast, **brest**, *v pt*, burst, 12A 32.3; 18A 5.2; 18B 5.2
braw, *adj*, fine-looking, fine, 4A 29.3, 29.4; 4B 30.3, 30.4; 18A 21.2; 18B 21.2 etc.
breast, *v*, spring up on, 23C 22.3
bree, *n*, brow, forehead, 1A 13.4; 1B 13.4
brent, *adj*, smooth, 8A 1.1; 8B 1.1
brigs, **briggs**, *n pl*, bridges, 2A 10.1; 2B 10.1; 11A 21.1; 11B 21.1
bright, *adj*, beautiful, 1A 49.4; 1B 49.4; 9A 1.3, 2.3, 3.1, 8.5 etc.
broad letter, *n*, letter on a broad sheet or a long letter, 29D 20.3
brunt, *v pt*, burnt, 11B 24.1
burd, *n*, lady, 4A 3.2, 13.3, 14.2, 15.1, 30.3, 35.3 etc.; female child 25C 10.3
burd alone, *adj*, completely solitary, 14A 2.2; 14B 2.2
busk, *v*, dress, prepare, 27C 12.2; **buskit**, *pp*, 27C 13.1
but, **butt**, *adv*, out, towards or in the outer apartment of a house, 4A 6.1; 4B 6.1; 17A 2.1; 17B 2.1
but an(d), as well as, and also, 1A 40.2; 1B 40.2; 2A 23.3; 3A 18.4, 19.3, 20.3 etc.
by, **bye**, *adj*, side, 10A 21.3; 10C 21.3
by, *adv*, aside, 5A 4.4
cadged, *n pp*, peddled, 31D 1.2
canna, **canno'**, *v*, cannot, 6A 11.3, 12.3; 6B 12.3; 10A 23.3; 12C 5.4 etc.
carket, *n*, necklace, 16A 27.3; 16B 27.3
casten, *v ptp*, thrown, 11A 29.4; 31 4.2
catch'd, **catchd**, *v pp*, caught, 2A 20.3; 2B 20.3
cauld, **caul**, **cald**, *adj*, cold, 6A 20.4; 6B 20.4; 9A 19.2 etc.
cauld, **caul**, *n*, cold, 10A 9.4; 10C 9.4; 12A 18.4
cavel, **cavil**, *n*, piece of wood used in casting lots, 16A 23.3; 16B 23.3; *pl*, **cavils**, **kavels**, **kaivles**, 16A 22.3; 16B 22.3; 23C 3.1, 3.2, 3.3, 19.1
cham'er, **châmer**, *n*, chamber, 11B 4.2; 23C 5.4; 26C 5.3; 34E 24.2
changed, *v pt*, exchanged, 12A 14.3, 16.3; 12C 13.3
chap, *v*, knock, 11A 22.2; 11B 22.2
chess, *n*, jess, strap, 15A 8.4; 15B 8.2
christen'd, *adj*, Christian, 16A 17.4; 16B 17.4
claiths, **cloaths**, *n pl*, clothes, clothing, 14A 16.1; 14B 16.1; 28C 24.3
clecked, *v pp*, hatched, 20A 7.1, 7.3
clim, **clim'**, *v*, climb, 13A 2.4; 13B 2.4; **clam**, **clam'**, *pt*, 13A 4.4; 13B 4.4

close, **closs**, *n,* courtyard, passageway, 28C 15.1; 30D 10.1
closs, *adj*, close, 12C 7.4; 27C 31.2
cods, *n pl*, pillows, 16A 15.2; 16B 15.2
coll'd, *v pt,* cut, 16A 25.3; 16B 25.3
comber, *n*, comb, 4A 9.2; 4B 9.2
cordwain, n, Cordovan leather, 17A 17.4; 17B 17.4
could, *v aux pt*, did, 1A 36.3
couth, *n*, speech, word, 6A 2.3; 6B 2.3
craig, *n*, rock, 13A 3.4, 9.4, 11.4, 12.1; 13B 3.4, 9.4 etc.; **craigs**, *pl*, 13A 2.4; 13B 2.4, 14.1
crap, *n*, top, 20A 10.5
crawn, *v pp*, crowed, 12C 17.1
cried, **cri'd**, **cryd**, **cry'd**, *v pt*, called, 18A 6.2; 18B 6.2; 29D 25.4; 30D 8.1; **cry'd**, *pp*, 30D 6.1
dane, **doone**, *v pp*, done, 16A 10.4, 12.4, 22.2, 27.2; 16B 10.4, 12.4 etc.
darna, **darna'**, **dar na**, **darena**, *v neg,* dare not, 1B 46.2; 32E 11.1, 11.2, 11.4
dead, *n*, death, 12C 28.2; 21B 11.2; 25C 11.4; 29D 25.4
deal, *v*, distribute, 6A 18.2; 6B 18.2; 26C 10.2; *pt*, **dealt**, 6A 25.2; 6B 25.2
dear, *elliptical for oath* 'dear Lord', 20A 1.6, 10.8, 12.8
deave, *v*, deafen, annoy, 21B 3.2
dee, *v*, die, 2B 4.4, 31.4; 4B 34.4; 6B 12.4, 16.3; 11A 6.2 etc.
dee, *v*, do, 1A 6.2, 9.2; 1B 6.2, 9.2, 25.3, 25.4 etc.
degree, *n*, rank, 27C 10.1
deil, see **doole**
den, *n*, narrow valley, 14A 3.2; 14B 3.2
dight, *adv*, well, in a well ordered way, 20A 10.6
dine, *n*, dinner, 12A 16.2; 17A 1.4; 17B 1.4; 18A 23.2; 18B 23.2 etc.
ding, *v*, strike, 20A 8.4; **dang**, *pt*, 20A 9.4
dinna, *v neg*, do not, does not, 10A 1.3, 12.2; 10C 12.2; 12A 14.1, 16.1; 12C 13.1 etc.
doe, **do**, **dae**, *v r*, betake oneself, go, 4A 16.1; 4B 16.1; 15A 11.3, 12.3; 15B 6.3, 11.1 etc.; **did**, *pt*, 15A 14.1, 15.1; **doen**, **done**, *v pp*, 4A 1.3; 5A 4.3; 6A 14.1, 19.1 etc.
dominee, **domine**, *n*, sir, master, 4A 19.2, 23.2; 4B 20.2, 24.2
doole, **deil**, *n*, grief, 11A 10.2; 11B 10.2
door cheeks, *n pl*, sides of the door, 10C 33.3
doubt, *v*, fear, 17A 9.2; 17B 9.2
dow, **turtle dow**, *n*, dove, 23C 22.3, 23.3, 24.4, 35.3
dowie, **dowy**, *adj*, sad, gloomy, 21B 12.2; 32E 6.2; 34E 23.3
draw, *v*, draw off water from, empty, 18A 18.1; 18B 18.1; **drew**, *pt*, 18A 19.1; 18B 19.1; **drawn**, *pp*, opened, 17A 3.3; 17B 3.3
draw up, *v*, become friendly, enter into love relationship, 11A 14.3; **drew up**, *v pt*, 11B 14.3

draw-well, **draw well**, *n*, deep well from which water is drawn by a bucket on a rope, 33E 9.3, 14.1

dree, *v*, suffer, endure, 13A 2.1, 2.3, 4.1, 4.3; 13B 2.1, 2.3 etc.; **drees**, *pres*, 16A 16.4; 16B 16.4; **dreeid**, **dried**, *pt* 1A 26.4; 1B 26.4

durst, *v*, dare, 23C 30.2; **durst**, *pt*, 29D 39.4; 29E 36.4

eat, *v pt*, ate, 14A 8.3, 10.3, 12.3; 14B 8.3, 10.3, 12.3; 30D 18.1

ee, *n*, eye, 2A 14.2; 2B 14.2; 4A 30.2; 5A 21.1; 8A 11.2; 8B 11.2 etc.; **een**, **eyne**, *pl*, 7A 14.2; 7B 14.2; 15A 12.2, 14.4; 15B 16.2; 27C 25.2

eer, **e'er**, **or**, *adv*, before, 2A 18.3, 27.3; 2B 18.3; 3A 24.3; 3B 24.3; 4A 11.3 etc.

eer, **or**, *prep*, before, 1A 23.3; 1B 23.3

eer, **ee'r**, **e'er**, **ere**, *adv*, ever, 1A 2.2, 26.3; 1B 2.2, 26.2, 43.3, 52.2 etc.

enneugh, *adj*, enough, 12C 14.1

even, *adv*, just, straight, 6A 4.1, 7.1; 6B 4.1, 7.1; 10A 30.3; 10C 30.3 etc.; **even on**, continuously, without ceasing, 21B 7.4

even, *n*, evening, 3A 6.2; 3B 6.2; 4A 36.4; 4B 38.4; **at even**, in the evening, 4A 36.4; 4B 38.4

eyne, see **ee**

faem, **fame**, *n*, foam, sea, 12C 6.2; 15A 1.1; 15B 1.1; 16A 1.1; 16B 1.1; 27C 8.2 etc.

fairlies, *n pl*, strange sights, marvels, 22C 10.4

fan, *conj*, when, 1A 58.3

fa, **fa'**, *v*, fall, 2A 18.4; 2B 18.4; 3A 13.4; 3B 13.4; 7A 1.2; 7B 1.2 etc.; **fan**, **fa'n**, *pp*, fallen, 3A 28.2; 3B 28.2; 5A 15.2; 6A 14.2, 20.2; 6B 14.2 etc.

fare ye weel, farewell, 32E 15.1

farrow, *adj,* in milk, 20A 8.1, 9.1

fare, *v*, go, 17A 10.2; 17B 10.2

fat, *pron*, what, 14B 7.4, 9.3

faus, **fause**, **fa'se**, **fas'e**, **fase**, *adj*, false, 7A 9.3, 11.4; 7B 9.3, 11.4; 12A 9.3, 20.3 etc.

fay, *n*, faith, 1A 36.3; 1B 36.3

fear, *v*, frighten; **fears**, *pres*, 1A 5.3; 1B 5.3; **fear**, *pres subj*, 1A 6.1; 1B 6.1; **fear'd**, *pp*, 32E 6.4

fee, *n*, wages, 2A 1.4; 2B 1.4; *see* **freely feed**

fell, *v*, strike down, destroy, 1A 46.4; 1B 46.4; 14B 11.5; **fell'd**, *pt*, 14B 12.1

fernie, *adj*, covered with ferns, 22C 1.4, 13.2

fill, *n*, full supply, 14A 19.2; 14B 19.2

fin, *v*, find, 1A 39.3

firstin, *adj*, first, 2A 22.1; 2B 22.1; 6A 17.1, 24.1; 6B 17.1, 24.1 etc.

flang, *v pt*, flounced, 16A 30.1; 16B 30.1

flee, *v*, fly, 6A 1.2; 6B 1.2; 10C 34.4; 13A 7.6; 13B 7.6; 16A 19.2 etc.; **flaw**, *pt*, 25C 9.2

fleed, **flude**, *n*, flood, sea, 12A 10.4; 21B 11.4

fleer, *n*, floor, 14A 4.4; 14B 4.4; 16A 19.4; 16B 19.4

flinders, *n pl*, splinters, pieces, 10C 34.4

flowr, **flow'r**, *n*, flour, 16A 2.3, 16B 2.3

forebye, **forbye**, *adv*, to one side, 1A 4.2; 1B 4.2, 11.5

forlorn, **forborn** (*written for* **forlorn**), *adj*, lost, 11B 15.4, 16.4

foul fa, **foul fa'**, may evil befall, curse, 18A 14.1; 18B 14.1

fourthin, *adj*, fourth, 6A 18.3, 25.3; 6B 18.3, 25.3

frae, *prep*, from, 1A 14.2, 31.3, 39.4, 43.4, 54.2; 1B 14.2 etc.

free, *adv*, skilfully, without constraint, 2A 33.2; 2B 33.2

freely feed, *probably* nobly reared one, person of gentle upbringing, 13A 1.1; 13B 1.1

fu, **fu'**, **fou**, *adj*, full, 7A 12.2; 7B 12.2; 14A 1.4; 14B 1.4; 29D 34.2; 32E 14.1 etc.

fu', **full**, **fou**, *adv*, fully, very, 1A 2.1, 52.1; 1B 2.1, 52.1; 4A 11.2; 4B 11.2 etc.

gae, **ga**, **gay**, **gang**, *v*, go, 1A 39.2, 47.3; 1B 39.2, 46.3, 47.3; 2A 6.4 etc.; **gaes**, **gangs**, *pres*, goes, 6A 4.4; 6B 4.4; 35E 6.2; **gaing**, **gain**, *v pp*, going, 1A 31.2; 4A 15.4; 2A 32.2; **gaed**, **gi'd**, **gid**, **ged**, *pt*, 3A 14.2; 3B 14.2; 4A 6.1, 22.1; 4B 6.1 etc.; **gane**, *pp*, 1A 11.2, 12.2, 16.1, 24.1, 35.1 etc.

gain, *v*, be suitable, be effective, 17A 15.4; **gains**, *pres*, 17B 15.4

gallows pin, *n*, peg over which the rope was slung on a gallows, 12C 16.4; 23C 13.4

gallows tree, *n*, gallows, 28C 25.3

gan, *v pt*, began to, did, 23C 33.4;

gantrees, **gan-trees**, *n pl*, gantries, 17A 11.4; 17B 11.4

gar, *v*, make, cause, 1A 4.4; 1B 4.4; 3A 30.3; 3B 30.3; 6A 17.2, 17.4 etc.; **gars**, *pres*, 18A 15.2; 18B 15.2; **gard**, **gar'd**, **gart**, **gar't**, *pt*, 1A 17.4, 57.3; 2A 22.2, 22.4, 23.2 etc.; **gard**, **gar'd**, **gart**, *pp*, 1B 17.4; 5A 2.3; 7A 16.1, 16.2, 16.3; 7B 16.1 etc.; **gard**, **gar'd work**, caused to be made, 6A 23.2; 6B 23.2

gare, *n*, stripe or triangular piece of cloth inserted at the bottom on each side of a shirt or of a robe, 2A 13.2; 2B 13.2; 17A 10.4; 17B 10.4; 21B 8.2, 9.2

ghost, *n*, evil spirit, 14A 4.3; 14B 4.3

gie, **gi**, **gi'**, *v*, give, 1A 28.4; 1B 28.4; 3A 27.4; 3B 27.4; 4A 5.3 etc.; **gae**, **ga**, **ga'**, *v pt*, gave, 1A 18.2; 1B 18.2; 3A 12.2; 3B 12.2; 4A 33.1; 4B 35.1 etc; **gien**, **gi'n**, **gin**, **gane**, *v pp*, 4A 9.1, 10.1, 25.2; 4B 9.1, 10.1, 26.2; 5A 8.1, 14.2 etc.

gimp, *see* **jimp**

gin, *conj*, if, whether 1A 6.1, 7.4, 9.1, 21.1, 28.1, 41.3, 56.3, 59.4 etc.

glaned, *v pt*, *probably written for* **glanced**, gleamed, 27C 14.2

glazen, **glasen**, *adj*, glass, 15A 12.2, 14.4; 15B 16.2

glee, *n*, glove, 16A 5.2, 6.4; 16B 5.2, 6.4

gleed, *n*, glowing fire, 11A 29.3; 11B 29.3

glen, *n*, valley, 29D 4.2, 29.2; 29E 4.2, 27.2
gotten, *v pp*, begotten, 20A 7.1
goud, **gou'd**, **gowd**, *n*, gold, 4A 29.2; 4B 30.2; 5A 7.2, 17.3; 6A 5.4, 6.4 etc.; **lay gowd**, embroider with gold thread, 23C 23.4
gouden, **gowden**, **gowd'n**, *adj*, golden, 10A 8.4; 10C 8.4; 12C 26.2 etc.
gowany, *adj*, daisy-covered, 19A 12.3
graith, *n*, equipment, armour, 30D 8.1
gray meal, *adj n,* sweepings of a meal-mill, 20A 11.4
green cloathing, *n*, unbleached clothing, 1A 13.1; 1B 13.1
greet, *v*, weep, 12C 18.2; **greeting**, *pres p*, 10A 32.4; 10B 31.4; 34E 14.4; **grat**, *pt*, 34E 26.3, 27.3
griesly, *adj*, grisly, 14A 4.3; 14B 4.3
growan, **grow'n**, *v pres p*, growing, 2A 10.3; 2B 10.3
gryte, *adj*, large, 18A 22.2; 18B 22.2
gude, **gueed**, **gueede**, *adj*, good, 16A 5.4, 7.4, 27.3; 16B 5.4, 7.4, 27.3 etc.
guede, *n*, good, 1A 1.4; 12A 11.2
gullies, *n pl*, knives, 31D 3.1
gurious, *adj*, grisly, ugly, 2A 31.2; 2B 31.2
ha, *v,* have, 20A 1.8
ha, **ha'**, **hae**, *prep*, here, 2A 13.1; 2B 13.1; 4A 25.3; 6A 11.1; 6B 12.1
ha, **ha'**, *n*, hall, 9A 16.2; 10A 19.2; 10C 19.2; 11A 4.2, 22.6; 11B 4.2 etc.; **ha's**, *pl*, 4A 5.3; 4B 5.3; 9A 8.2; 25C 9.3
haely, *adj*, holy, 1A 13.5; 1B 13.5, 58.1
hafts, *n pl*, handles, 31D 3.1
Hallow even, n, Hallowe'en, the evening of 31 October, 19A 12.1
hap, *v*, cover, wrap, 14A 5.4; 14B 5.4; **hap'd**, **happ'd**, *pt*, 29D 2.4
haste, *v r*, hurry, 2A 7.4; 2B 7.4
hat, *v pt*, hit, 14A 5.1; 14B 5.1
haud, **had**, *v*, hold, 1A 7.1, 10.1, 47.1; 1B 7.1, 10.1, 47.1; 11A 5.1 etc.
hause bane, *n*, collar bone, 25C 7.1
head, *v,* lead, 30D 7.1
heely, *adv*, slowly, 12A 21.1
heigh, **hey**, *interj*, expression of sorrow or pain, 12A 26.1, 27.1; 12C 22.1, 23.1
herryed, *v pt*, harried, plundered, 20A 7.5
hi, **hi'**, **hie**, **hich**, *adj*, high, 2A 27.4; 2B 27.4; 10C 10.3, 13.2; 11A 9.4 etc.
hind-greem, **hind greeme**, n, young man, 16A 25.2; 16B 25.2
hight, *v pt*, was called, 1A 14.3; 1B 14.3
hings, *v pres*, hangs, 15A 4.2; 15B 12.2
hir'd, *v pp*, *probably written for* **birl'd**, made drunk, 17A 7.1
hose, *n*, stockings, 4A 6.3; 4B 6.3; 10A 33.2; 10C 32.2; 16A 25.3 etc.
hou, **hou'**, **how**, *interj*, cry used to attract attention, 12A 26.1, 27.1; 12C 22.1, 23.1
hunder, *adj*, hundred, 2A 21.3, 28.3; 4A 9.3; 32E 6.4

hunts ha, **hunts ha'**, *n*, hunting lodge, 14A 2.3; 14B 2.3
hye, *v r*, hasten, 12A 19.4; **hied**, *pt*, 10C 32.3; **hied**, *pp*, 10C 28.3
hyne, *adv*, away, far off, 25C 3.4
i, **i'**, *prep*, in, 3A 18.1, 25.4; 3B 18.1, 25.4; 4A 2.1, 21.1 etc.
I'se, *pron, v fut*, I shall, 18A 11.2, 13.2; 18B 11.2, 13.2
ilk ane, *n*, everyone, 20A 13.5
ilka, **ilkae**, *adj*, every, 4A 34.3; 4B 36.3; 8A 4.4; 8B 4.4; 15A 4.1, 8.3 etc.
in, **i**, **i'**, *prep*, on, 16A 19.4; 16B 19.4; 17A 21.1; 17B 21.1
intil, **intill**, **until**, *prep*, in, into, inside, 1B 29.1; 3A 4.2, 20.4, 30.2; 3B 30.2; 7A 6.2 etc.
into, *prep*, in, 1A 45.3; 1B 45.3; 18A 5.1; 18B 5.1
ire, *n*, iron, 3A 17.4; 3B 17.4
ithe, in the, 9A 9.6; 10A 31.3; 24C 12.3
jaw, *n*, wave, 18A 10.2; 18B 10.2
jelly, *adj*, jolly, pleasant, attractive, 14A 2.3; 14B 2.3; 16A 25.2; 16B 25.2
jimp, **gimp**, *adj*, slender, 12A 1.3, 3.3; 12C 1.3, 3.3; 21B 1.3
kaim, **kem**, **kemb**, *n*, comb, 11A 12.2; 11B 12.2; 12A 2.2, 4.2; 12C 2.2, 4.2 etc.; **kaimbs**, **kaims**, *pl*, 15A 16.3; 15B 17.3
kaim, **kemb**, *v*, comb, 12A 2.1; 12C 2.1, 4.1;19A 11.2; **kembing**, **keming**, *pres p*, 11A 10.4; 11B 10.4; **kaim'd**, **kembed**, **kemb'd**, *pt*, 12A 4.1; 19A 2.1; 27C 34.2
kaivle, *see* **cavel**
keeped, **keepit**, *v pt*, lived in, took care of, 3A 8.2, 13.3, 31.1; 3B 8.2, 13.3, 31.1
keist, **kest**, *v pt*, cast, 16A 22.3; 16B 22.3
ken, *v*, know, 1A 19.1, 19.3, 20.1, 20.3; 6A 2.1, 3.1 etc.; **kens**, *pres,* 4B 13.4; 24C 4.4; 35E 17.4; **kent**, *pt*, 1B 19.1, 19.3, 20.1, 34.4; 4A 24.3; 4B 25.3; **kent**, *pp*, 4A 34.1; 4B 36.1
kensnae, *v neg*, does not know, 4A 13.4; **kentna**, *pt*, 1A 34.4; 32E 7.2
kep, **keep**, *v*, catch, 29D 32.2; 34E 21.4; 35E 6.3; **kepit**, **keppit**, **kaped**, *pt*, 3A 13.3; 3B 13.3; 35E 8.4
kin'; **a(') kin(') kind**, every kind, 11A 2.2; 11B 11.4
kirk, *n*, church, 6A 5.2, 7.4, 17.1, 17.3, 18.1, 18.3 etc.
kirkin, *n*, churching, 10A 36.3
kitchy boy, *n*, kitchen boy, 11A 6.1; 11B 6.1
knave bairn, *n*, male child, 1A 23.4; 1B 23.4
kye, *n pl*, cows, 30D 3.2, 4.1, 5.1, 7.2
lad bairn, *n*, male child, 23C 12.3, 21.3
laigh, *adj*, low, 16A 25.3; 16B 25.3
laird, *n*, landowner, 16A 20.1, 20.3; 16B 20.1, 20.3 etc.
laith, *adj*, loath, unwilling, reluctant, 3A 13.4; 3B 13.4; 30D 8.4
lammer, *n*, amber, 34E 24.4
lane; **her lane**, alone, 10C 20.4
lang, *see* **think lang**

langsome, *adj*, wearisome, boring, 16A 22.2; 16B 22.2

lap, *v pt*, leapt, 1A 33.1; 3A 13.2; 3B 13.2; 11A 22.3; 11B 22.4; 23C 33.2 etc.

lass, *n*, young woman, girl 23C 11.3, 12.1, 21.3; 29D 12.1; 29E 13.1; **lasses**, *pl*, 29D 5.2

lassies, *n pl*, young women, 30D 6.2

lastin, *adv*, last, 18A 28.1

lat, *v pt*, let, 3B 13.4; 6A 26.2; 6B 26.2; 12A 23.4, 24.3 etc.; **latten**, *pp*, 4A 7.4; 4B 7.4 etc.; **lat, let a be**, let be, 1A 32.2; 1B 32.2

latna, *v neg*, do not let, 35E 6.4

laverock, *n*, skylark, 29E 33.4; **laverocks**, *pl*, 29D 36.4

lax, *n*, relief, release, 29D 18.2; 29E 19.2

learn, *v*, teach, 23C 22.1, 22.3, 23.1, 23.3

lee, *adj*, blessed, eerie, 35E 7.3

lee, *n*, lie, 4A 34.2; 4B 36.2

lee, *v*, lie, 10A 12.2; 20A 4.1, 4.2, 5.1, 5.2

lee-lang, *adj*, livelong, 29E 37.1

leeler, *compar adj*, truer, 7A 1.3; 7B 1.3

leet, loot, loote, *v pt*, let, 2A 18.4; 2B 18.4; 16A 4.2, 4.4; 16B 4.2, 4.4 etc.; **lett'n, latten**, *pp*, 29D 41.3; 29E 38.3

lemman, *n*, lover, 19A 2.3, 3.3, 4.3, 6.3

leugh, *v pt*, laughed, 1B 34.2, 37.2; 2A 29.2; 2B 29.2; 6B 26.4; 21B 7.3 etc.

leve, *n*, rest, 9A 20.3

licht, *n*, light, 35E 7.3

light, *v*, fall, 11A 9.2; 11B 9.2

light (down), *v*, dismount 22C 7.3; 24C 8.4; **lighted (down)**, *pt*, 11A 27.1; 11B 27.1; 19A 12.3; 24A 9.1; 29D 15.2; 29E 16.2

lighter; **be lighter (of, o')**, give birth (to), have given birth, 15A 2.2, 4.4, 5.1, 8.6, 9.1, 19.4 etc.

limmer, *n*, villain, disreputable woman, whore, 34E 6.1

lingcan, *n*, body, 14A 5.4; 14B 5.4

lith, *n*, small part of the body, 35E 1.1; **lith and limb**, expression denoting small and large parts of the body, 35E 8.3

loo, loo', lee, *v*, love, 3A 23.2; 3B 23.2; 7A 11.1, 13.1; 7B 11.1, 13.1; **lees**, *pres*, 20A 4.4; **loed, lood, loo'd, loud**, *pt*, 1A 2.3, 2.4, 52.3, 52.4 etc.

lookit o'er her window, leaned over the window-sill in her room and looked out, 35E 7.4

loon, loun, *n*, whore, common fellow, 1A 37.3; 1B 37.3; 16A 20.1, 20.3; 16B 20.1, 20.3 etc.

loose, *v*, loosen, 8A 11.4; 8B 11.4; **loosd, loos'd**, *pp*, 15A 16.1, 17.3, 18.1, 19.3; 15B 17.1, 19.1

looted, louted, *v reflex pt*, bowed, bent, stooped, 3A 4.1; 3B 4.1; 13A 10.1, 12.1, 14.1 etc.

mailison, **melison**, **mellison**, *n*, curse, 11A 9.2; 11B 9.2; 24C 22.2; 32E 4.4, 7.3, 15.3
mair, *adj*, more, 1A 3.3, 34.3; 1B 3.3, 34.3; 2A 8.4; 2B 8.4 etc.
mair, *n*, more, 27C 1.4
make, *n*, spouse, mate, 6A 25.4; 6B 25.4
mane, *n*, moan, complaint, lament, 4A 3.4
mary, *n* waiting woman, 17A 20.1; 17B 20.1; **marys**, *pl*, 17A 13.4, 14.3, 15.1, 19.5; 17B 13.4 etc.
maun, **man**, *v*, must, 1A 5.4, 6.2, 8.4, 9.2, 55.3; 1B 5.4 etc.
maunna, **manna**, *v neg*, must not, 26C 10.4; 32E 15.2
mavis, *n*, song-thrush, 34E 27.1
may, *n*, maid, young woman, 1A 38.3; 1B 37.3; 15A 5.2, 5.3, 5.4, 6.1 etc.
mean, *v*, lament, 21B 7.2, 10.2
meat, *n*, food, livelihood, 1A 43.1; 1B 43.1; 2A 1.4; 2B 1.4; 3A 5.4, 27.4 etc.
meed, *n*, mood, 16A 5.3, 7.3; 16B 5.3, 7.3
meickle, **mieckle**, *adj*, much, a lot of, 1A 51.4; 1B 51.4; 2A 8.3, 8.4; 2B 8.3, 8.4 etc.
mell, *n*, mallet, heavy hammer, 14A 6.2; 14B 6.2
mellison, *see* **mailison**
middle, *n*, waist, 14A 5.2; 14B 5.2; 18A 12.1, 21.1; 18B 12.1, 21.1
mind, *v*, remember, 5A 8.3; 12A 14.1, 16.1; 12C 13.1
mirk, *adj*, dark, gloomy, 32E 2.3
mis-shapit, **mis-shap'd**, *v pt*, transformed, changed to an ugly form, 13A 15.6; 13B 15.6
mony, **monny**, *adj*, many, 5A 12.4; 7A 10.2; 14A 19.1; 14B 19.1; 16A 16.4 etc.
morn, *n*; **the morn**, the next day, 24C 11.4
mot, **ma't**, *v*, may, might, 13A 16.4; 14A 5.2; 14B 5.2
muirs, *n pl*, moors, 29D 4.1
muskadine, *n*, strong sweet wine, muscatel, 16A 2.2; 16B 2.2
na, **na'**, **nay**, **nae**, *interj*, no, 1A 47.2; 1B 47.2; 11A 4.4; 11B 4.4; 23C 4.1
nae, **na**, **na'**, **no**, *adv*, not, 1A 7.3, 20.1, 41.3, 46.3; 1B 7.3, 10.3 etc.
nae, **nay**, *adj*, no, 1A 22.2, 30.3; 1B 22.2, 30.3; 3A 16.1, 29.2 etc.
nae, **nae**, *adv*, no, 5A 21.4; 10A 36.2; 11A 5.2, 5.4; 11B 5.2, 5.4 etc.
nae ane, *n*, no one, 6A 21.2; 6B 21.2; 13A 18.1; 13B 18.1; 17A 1.3; 17B 1.3
naething, **naithing**, *n*, nothing, 1A 55.2; 11A 7.4; 11B 7.4; 14A 6.3, 8.4, 12.4
nane, *adv*, none, 9A 4.2; 16A 12.3; 16B 12.4
nane, *pron*, none, neither, 2A 12.4, 34.1; 2B 12.4; 5A 18.3; 8A 1.4; 8B 1.4 etc.
near, *adv*, nearly, almost, 11A 26.1; 11B 26.1
neer, **ne'er**, **nee'r**, **ner**, *adv*, never, 1A 10.3; 2A 20.4; 2B 20.4; 4B 28.4; 6B 2.3; 10C 16.3 etc.

nicht, *n*, night, 32E 1.4, 2.3, 3.1, 12.4, 13.1, 15.4 etc.
niest, **neist**, **neest**, *adj*, next, 12C 27.2; 29D 2.2; 29E 2.2; 31D 5.1
niesten, **neisten**, **nextin**, *adj*, next, 2A 22.3; 2B 22.3; 6A 17.3, 24.3; 6B 17.3, 24.3 etc.
niffer, *n*, exchange, 27C 24.3
nor, *conj*, than 1A 28.2, 3A 16.4, 23.2; 3B 16.4; 4A 2.2; 4B 2.2 etc.
nourice, *n*, child's nurse, 34E 6.1, 13.2, 14.3, 15.1, 16.1, 17.1 etc.; **nurices**, *pl*, 24C 15.2
nouriship, *n*, post of a child's nurse, 3A 30.1; 3B 30.1
o, **o'**, *prep*, of, 1A 7.3, 10.3, 14.3, 14.4, 15.3, 31.3 etc.
o', *prep*, on, 12A 7.1; 27C 9.1; 28C 15.3
oer, **o'er**, *prep*, over, 1A 3.2, 58.3; 1B 3.2; 3A 17.3, 18.3; 3B 17.3 etc.
ohone, **ohon**, *interj*, expression of sadness, 3A 16.3; 3B 16.3; 10A 7.3; 10B 7.3, 8.3; 16A 23.1 etc.
or, *see* **eer**
ot, **o't**, of it, 4A 19.3, 23.3; 4B 20.3, 24.3; 16A 8.3
out-chamber, *n*, room attached to a cottage but entered from the outside by a separate door, 32E 12.3
pall, **pa**, **pa'**, *n*, rich cloth, 16A 4.1; 16B 4.1; 27C 13.2; 28C 22.3
pap, *n*, breast, 10A 9.2; 10B 9.2; 34E 15.2; **paps**, *pl*, 16A 9.3; 16B 9.3; 23C 7.2
paramour, *n*, lovers, 35 2.4; *sense obscure* 16A 2.4, 16B 2.4; **like paramour**, appropriate to lovers, 3A 8.4; 3B 8.4
parley, **parly**, *v*, talk, 16A 30.4; 16B 30.4
peer'd, **'peard**, *v pt*, appeared, 14A 6.3; 14B 6.3; 16A 25.4
philabeg, *n*, kilt, 29D 21.3
pin, *n*, peg, perch, serrated metal rod fixed to a door, 6B 8.2; 9A 12.2; 12A 9.2; 12C 16
pine, *n*, pain, 1A 26.4; 1B 26.4; 10A 23.4; 10B 22.4
pit, *v*, put, 2A 4.3; 4A 17.3; 15A 12.2; 15B 16.2; **pat**, **pit**, *pt*, 2A 18.1; 2B 18.1; 3A 12.1; 3B 12.1; 4A 21.3; 4B 22.3 etc.; **pitten**, *pp*, 4A 25.1; 4B 26.1; 5A 2.2, 14.1; 10A 4.1 etc.
plaid, *n*, blanket-like outer garment, 29D 2.3; 29E 2.3
play(')d o(')er them a('), excelled them all in sport, 28C 1.3; 33E 1.4
play'd you (the) scorn, made you a subject of derision, 6A 28.4; 6B 28.4
pu, **pu'**, *v*, pull, pluck, 11A 17.3; 11B 17.3; 14A 14.3; 14B 14.5; **pu'd**, *pt*, 3A 17.1; 3B 17.1; 14A 16.1; 14B 15.1; 16A 25.1; 16B 25.1 etc.
put the stane, hurl a heavy stone with a thrust from the shoulder in sport, 1A 17.2, 1B 17.2
putting stane, *n*, heavy stone used for hurling, 1A 17.4; 1B 17.4
race, *n*, race-course, 9A 15.4
rae, *n*, roe deer, 1A 40.2; 1B 40.2
raise, *v pt*, rose, 23C 6.1, 8.1; 32E 17.4
rank, *adj*, proud, strong, 15A 3.2, 7.2; 15B 3.2, 6.4, 11.2

ranked, *v pt*, *perhaps* ranted, 16A 30.1; 16B 30.1
read, *v*, tell, 13A 1.3; 13B 1.3; **read**, *pp*, 13A 1.4; 13B 1.4
red, *adj*, sense obscure (see Notes to Brown 24)
reef-tree, **reef tree**, *n*, the main beam or ridge of a roof, 14A 5.1; 14B 5.1
rent, *v pp*, torn, 12A 28.2
ried, *adj*, red, 25C 7.2
rive, *v*, tear, 28C 28.3; **riving**, *pres p,* 30D 15.2, 16.2
rocks, *n pl*, distaffs, 30D 6.2
roddins, *n pl*, rowan berries, 3A 19.1, 20.1; 3B 19.1, 20.1
room, *v*, move, 10A 29.1, 29.2; 10C 29.1
rottons, **rottens**, *n pl*, rats, 4A 8.3; 4B 8.3; 9A 16.3
roundly, *adv*, vigorously, briskly, 29D 3.2; 29E 3.2
routh, *n*, abundance, 14A 1.3; 14B 1.3
row, *v*, convey, 4A 19.4; 4B 20.4; **rowing**, **rowin**, *pres p*, moving easily along in the water, 4A 18.4, 22.4; 4B 19.4, 23.4
row, *v*, wrap, 21B 8.3; 10A 35.4; 10C 36.4 etc.; **row'd**, **rowt**, *pt*, 3A 25.4; 3B 25.4
royal bone, ivory, 4A 10.2, 33.2; 4B 10.2, 35.2
runs, *apparently for* **sun's**, 24C 4.2
saddle bow, *n*, pommel, arched front part of saddle, 28C 16.1
sae, **sae'**, **sa**, *adv*, so, 1A 13.3, 14.2, 20.5, 29.2, 32.4, 42.2 etc.
sair, *adj*, sore, greatly, vehemently, 1A 5.3, 6.1, 8.3, 9.1, 24.3 etc.; **sairer**, *compar*, 34E 26.3, 27.3
sal, **sall**, *v*, shall, 1A 4.4, 7.2, 10.2, 22.4, 26.2, 56.4 etc.
sark, *n*, shirt, 2A 12.1, 13.1; 2B 12.2, 13.1; 16A 22.4; 16B 21.4 etc.
satten, *adj*, satin, 29D 2.2; 29E 2.2
saut, **sat**, **sa't**, *adj*, salt, 1A 20.4; 1B 20.2; 12C 6.2, 7.4; 13A 2.2, 4.2 etc.
sear, *v, written for* swear, 1A 21.4
seely court, *n*, fairy court, 19A 12.2
seen, *adv*, soon, 3A 22.4; 3B 22.4
sen, **sen'**, *v pp*, sent, 6A 9.4; 6B 10.4
shanna, **shanno**, *v neg*, shall not, 12C 16.2; 23C 34.2
shape, *v*, cut to pattern, 16A 21.4; 16B 21.4
shaver, *n*, razor, 4A 9.1; 4B 9.1
shear, *v*, cut, 21B 8.2; **shorn**, *pp*, 21B 8.2
shears, *n pl*, scissors, 25C 8.4
sheave, *n*, slice, 6A 27.1; 6B 27.1
shee, *n*, shoe, 15A 17.3, 19.3; 15B 19.1; 16A 5.1, 6.3; 16B 5.1, 6.3; **sheen**, **shone**, **shoon**, **shoone**, *pl*, 2A 10.4; 2B 10.4; 3A 15.2, 16.2; 3B 15.2, 16.2 etc.
sheet, *v*, shoot, 20A 5.4
shew, *v*, sew, 14A 13.5
shot-window, **shot window**, *n*, small opening in the wall of a house, closed

by hinged shutters, sometimes with a few panes of glass at the top, 6A 8.3; 6B 9.3; 17A 3.3; 17B 3.3

show'r, *n*, pang of pain in childbirth; 16A 16.4; 16B 16.4

sic, **sich**, **sick**, **sicken**, *adj*, such, of such a kind, 10A 26.2; 13A 5.4; 13B 5.4; 14A 19.2; 14B 19.2; 17A 12.3 etc.; **sickena**, such a, 25C 11.4

side, *adj*, long, 3A 9.4; 3B 9.4

simmer-dale, *adj*, from the summer part of the year, 20A 8.3, 9.3

sin, *prep*, since, 32E 15.2

sin syne, *adv*, since then, 12A 14.4

sindle, *adv*, seldom, 20A 8.4

slackèd, **slack'd**, *v pt*, slackened, 2A 10.4; 2B 10.4; 11A 21.4

slae, *n*, sloe, 16A 24.2; 16B 24.2

sma, **sma'**, *adj*, small, slender, 1A 7.2, 10.2; 1B 7.2, 10.2; 18A 10.1, 21.1 etc.

sooth, *n*, truth, 13A 15.1, 13B 15.1; 23C 28.2; 27C 19.2; **in sooth**, *n*, truly, 23C 28.2, 27C 19.2

sought, *v pp*, asked in marriage, 11A 3.1; 11B 3.1

southin(g) lands, England, 6A 16.3, 28.3; 6B 16.3, 28.3

span, *v*, encircle with the hand, 14A 5.2; 14B 5.2

speer, **spear**, *v*, ask, 1A 22.2; 2A 12.4; 2B 12.4; **speer'd**, *pt*, 21B 6.4

sta', *n*, stall, 10A 19.4; 10C 19.4

sta, **staw**, *v pt*, stole, 29D 1.4; 29E 1.4

stan, *v*, stand, 15A 15.3; 17A 11.4

stap, *n*, step, 10A 7.1, 8.1, 9.1

stapping, **stappin**, *v pres p*, stepping, 14A 4.4; 14B 4.4; **stappit**, **steppit**, *pt*, stepped, 10A 7.1, 8.1, 9.1; 10C 7.1, 8.1, 9.1 etc.

stark, *adj*, strong, 16A 19.1, 19.3; 16B 19.1, 19.3

steekd, *v pp*, shut in such a way as to prevent entry, 32E 9.3

steer, *adj*, vigorous, 16A 19.3; 16B 19.3

steer, *n*, turmoil, whirl, 17A 12.3; 17B 12.3

stickit him like a swine, stabbed him as if slaughtering a pig, 30E 7.4

still, *v*, quiten, pacify, 34E 15.1, 15.2, 15.3, 16.1, 16.2, 16.3 etc.

stooks, *n pl*, shocks, 31D 4.1

stown, **stow'n**, *v pp*, stolen, 4A 7.3; 4B 7.3

strae, *n*, straw, 20A 13.2

straiked, *v pt*, stroked, 20A 13.2

stran, **strand**, *n*, beach, shore, 4A 18.2, 22.2; 4B 19.2, 23.2; 12C 7.4; 12A 6.2 etc.

strawn, *v pp*, strewn, sprinkled, 1A 3.2, 1B 3.2

streak, *v*, lie stretched out, 14A 16.6; 14B 16.6

streen, *see* **the streen**

study, *n*, anvil, 7A 2.2; 7B 2.2

sue, *v*, sew, 16A 21.4

syne, **seene**, *adv*, then, 18A 27.1; 18B 27.1; 23C 34.3; 29D 2.3, 9.3; 29E 2.3 etc.

tae, *adj*, one, 6A 23.3; 6B 23.3

taiken, *n*, token, 12A 13.3

tak, **tak'**, **tack**, **tacke**, *v*, take, 2A 16.1; 2B 13.1, 16.1; 3A 22.1; 3B 12.3, 22.1 etc.; **ta'en**, **taen**, **take**, **tane**, *v pp*, taken, captured, 3A 25.1, 25.3; 3B 25.1, 25.3; 5A 1.3, 13.1 etc.; **taen**, **ta'en**, **tane**, *vr pp*, betaken oneself, gone, 4A 20.1; 4B 1.3, 21.1; 6B 19.1; 15A 1.1; 15B 1.1 etc.

tane, **teen**, *n*, the one, 1A 2.3, 14.3, 52.3; 1B 2.3, 14.3, 52.3; 32E 14.1

tate, **tet**, **tett**, *n*, small tuft or bundle of hair, 15A 8.3; 15B 8.1; 22C 2.3

taul, **taul'**, **tau'l**, **tauld**, *v pt*, told, 2A 18.2; 2B 18.2; 8A 8.3; 8B 8.3; **tauld**, *pp*, 9A 19.4

teather, **taether**, *adj*, tether, 14A 6.1; 14B 6.1

than, *adv*, then, 29D 11.1; 31D 2.2; 35D 2.2; **or than**, or else, 4A 12.4; 4B 12.4

that, *demonstrative adj*, those, 16A 33.1; 16B 33.1

the streen, *adv*, last night, 6A 9.2; 6B 10.2

think lang, *v*; **thinking lang**, *pres p*, wearying, 4A 16.4, 20.4; 4B 16.4, 21.4; **thought lang**, *pt*, 2A 6.2; 2B 6.2; 7A 5.2; 7B 5.2; 23C 25.2

thirdin, **thirden**, *adj*, third, 2A 23.1; 2B 23.1; 6A 18.1, 25.1; 6B 18.1, 25.1

this, *demonstrative adj*, these, those, 1A 15.1; 1B 15.1; 3A 8.3; 3B 8.3; 4A 11.1; 4B 11.1 etc.

thole, *v*, have to bear, 25C 10.4

throuch-and-thro', *prep*, right through, 33E 2.3

tide, *n*, mood, 16A 7.1; 16B 7.1

till, **'till**, **til**, **ti'**, *prep*, to, 1A 15.4, 27.4, 29.1, 29.4, 42.4; 1B 15.4 etc.

tirled, **tirl'd**, *v pt*, made a rattling noise with a metal ring, 12A 9.2; 32E 9.2

tither, *adj*, other, 6A 23.4; 6B 23.4

tither, *n*, the other, 1A 2.4, 14.4, 52.4; 1B 2.4, 14.4, 52.4; 32E 14.2, 14.3

tocher, *n*, dowry, 2A 33.2; 2B 33.2, 9A 19.4, 20.4

toddle, *v*, move slowly in an ungainly way, 19A 10.2; **toddled**, *pt*, 19A 11.4

took travailing, **travelling**, **traveling**, *v pt*, went into labour, 1A 24.2; 1B 24.2; 3A 21.4; 3B 21.4

tour, *n*, circular route, 30D 20.1

traivail, *n*, labour, 10A 30.2

tree, *n*, wood, pole, gallows, 5A 2.2; 31D 3.1; 34E 6.2

trow, **true**, *v*, believe, think, 1A 37.3, 49.3; 1B 37.3, 49.3; **I trow**, certainly, 12C 19.4

truth, *n*, troth, marriage vow, 23C 35.4

trysted, *v pp*, enticed, 19A 1.3

twa, **twa'**, **twae**, *numeral*, two, 3A 8.3; 3B 8.3; 4A 11.1, 16.3, 20.3, 28.2 etc.

twain, *n*, two, 10C 10.4; 12A 28.2; 26C 11.2

twal, **twal'**, **twall**, *adj*, twelve, 16A 2.1, 2.2, 2.3, 2.4, 3.1, 3.2 etc.

twin'd, *v pt*, separated, 18A 14.2; 18B 14.2
wa, wa', *n*, wall, 1A 32.2; 1B 32.1; 3A 13.2; 3B 13.2; 9A 16.4; 10A 29.2, etc.; **frae wa to weer**, *possibly* from wall to hedge, 31D 1.2
wad, *v*, would, 7A 1.3; 32E 6.4, 9.4
wae, *adj*, sad, woeful, 13A 16.4; 13B 16.4; 32E 16.2
wae, *n*, woe, ill, suffering, 1A 47.4; 1B 47.4; 8A 3.4; 8B 3.4; 10A 10.2 etc.; **wae (be) to**, a curse on 8A 3.1; 8B 3.1; 18A 28.2; 18B 28.2
waes me, wae, woe is me, *interj*, alas, 1A 33.2; 1B 33.2; 30D 12.2
waits, *v*, awaits, 2A 13.4; 2B 13.4
walls, *n pl*, wells, 21B 2.3, 4.3
wallwood, *n*, wild-wood, 23C 16.4
wan, *see* **win**
wanny, *n*, wand, switch, 20A 8.3, 9.3
war, *compar adj*, worse, 1A 6.3, 9.3; 1B 6.3, 9.3; 21B 10.4
wardles make, warld's make, *n*, match or partner in all the world, 18A 14.2; 18B 14.2
ware, *v*, employ, 1A 22.4; 1B 22.4
wark, *n*, work, 16A 22.3; 16B 22.3
wasna, *v neg*, was not, 35E 18.1
wast, *v pt*, was it, 23C 8.4
wat, *v pp*, wetted, 10A 8.4; 10C 8.4
wat, *v, see* **wot**
we's, *pron v fut*, we shall, 4A 29.4; 4B 30.4
wee, *adj*, small, tiny, 20A 8.3, 9.3
weed, *n*, garment, 10C 4.3
weel, *adv*, well, 34E 5.3
weel, *n*, good, 10C 6.2, 22C 5.4
weet, *n*, rain, 11A 20.2; 11B 20.4
weird, wierd, *n*, fate, destiny, 13A 1.3, 17.1; 13B 1.3, 17.1; 16A 21.4, 24.2 etc.
well far'd, *adj*, good-looking, 21B 2.4
well-kent, *adj*, well known, 29D 31.3; 29E 29.3
wend, *v*, go, 14A 1.1; 14B 1.1
what needs, there is no need for, 1A 25.2
what'n, *adv*, what kind of, 9A 9.1
white bread, *n*, white bread, not oat or barley cakes, 10A 15.1, 16.1, 22.2, 23.2; 10C 15.1, 16.1 etc.
white meal, *n*, oatmeal as distinct from barley meal, 10A 17.1, 18.1; 20A 11.4
white money, *adj n*, silver money, 8A 13.2
wi, wi', *prep*, with, 1A 3.2, 30.4, 32.4, 34.3, 39.2, 55.4; 1B 3.2, 30.4, 32.4 etc.
wide, *v*, wade, 10A 5.4
wight, *n*, person, 13A 3.1; 13B 3.1; 15A 6.3, 10.3; 15B 6.1, 10.3

wile, *adj*, vile, 11A 17.4; 12A 11.3, 12.1; 12C 10.3, 11.1; 13A 15.5 etc.

win, won, *v,* get, 2A 20.4; 2B 20.4; 3A 12.4; 3B 12.4; **won, wan**, *pt*, 3A 32.2; 12C 19.4; 23 17.4; 25C 8.1; **win up, won up**, rise, stand up, 5A 15.3; 10A 32.1; 23C 20.3; 24C 2.1

winna, winna', *v neg*, will not, 1A 28.4, 47.2; 1B 28.4, 47.2; 11A 11.3; 11B 11.3 etc.

wis, *v*, know, 29D 13.2; **wisna**, *neg*, 29E 14.2; **wist**, *pt*, 27C 10.4; **I wis**, indeed, 27C 1.4

within, *adv*, inside, indoors, 4A 29.4; 4B 30.4

without, *adv*, outside, out of doors, 4A 29.3; 4B 30.3

won, wone, *v*, live, dwell, 13A 17.6; 13B 17.6; **wons, wiends**, *pres*, 1A 44.4; 1B 44.4; 14A 6.4, 16.5; 14B 6.4, 16.5; **won'd**, *pt*, 1A 51.2

wone, wones, *v pt*, taken, captured, 11A 23.2, 24.2; 11B 23.2, 24.2

wont, *v pt*, was accustomed, 3A 9.2, 9.4; 3B 9.2, 9.4; 19A 12.4; 35E 4.2, 4.4; **had wont**, *v pp*, were accustomed, 5A 2.4

worm, *n*, dragon, serpent, 19A 10.1; **wormies wood, worme's wood**, *n*, dragon's forest, 13A 17.6; 13B 17.6

wot, wat, *v*, know; **I wot, I wat, awot, a wot**, *pron v*, I know, truly, 2A 5.2, 5.4; 2B 5.2, 5.4; 3B 20.4; 5A 4.2 etc.

worry, *v*, seize by the throat, 9A 16.4

wou'dna, *v neg*, would not, 19A 7.3

wow, *interj,* expression of astonishment or surprise, 20A 1.5, 2.5 etc.

wrought, *v pt*, did, caused, 1A 51.4; 1B 51.4; **wrought**, *v pp*, acted, 20A 9.6

wyle, *v*, beguile, deceive, 33E 6.3

yare, *adj*, ready, prepared, 20A 6.2

yate, *n*, gate, 4B 25.1; 11A 27.1 ; 11B 27.1; 16A 10.1; 16B 10.1 etc.; **yates**, *pl*, 4A 27.1; 4B 28.1; 5A 16.1; 11B 22.1; 16A 34.2, 35.2 etc.

yeard fast, yerd fast, *adj*, firmly set in the ground, 10A 11.2; 10C 11.2

yon, yon', *adj*, that, 1A 41.4, 45.3, 45.4; 1B 41.4, 45.4; 2A 11.1 etc.

you's, you'se, ye's, *pron v fut*, you shall, 1B 7.3, 10.3; 6B 15.4; 12A 20.4; 16B 35.4; 18A 12.2 etc.

Bibliography

Primary Sources

Aberdeen Public Library (APL)

Walker 10632, 10633. James Walker Collection. Sederunt Books of the Aberdeen Musical Society. 2 vols. 1748–95.

Aberdeen University, Special Libraries and Archives (AUL)

MS 500. Papers relating to cause between George Skene, Skene, Aberdeenshire and William Forbes, Disblair, Aberdeenshire, 1719–40.

MS 3107/1–9. Papers of Thomas Gordon (d. 1797), regent, King's College. 3 boxes.

Advocates Library, Abbotsford (Adv.)

N 3 Abbotsford Library Catalogue. Scottish Songs, 1795.

British Library, London (BL)

Add. 35043 Original Piieces and Arrangements for Violin or Flute, by John Channing, 1694–1697.

MS 45926, vol. 3, ff. 109–10, Letter from Robert Eden Scott to Robert Jamieson, 19 November 1803.

Edinburgh University Library (EUL)

La.III.473. Popular Ballads, written from Recitation, by Jamieson, with some relative letters, 4to. David Laing Papers.

La.IV.Chi. Letters of F. J. Child to David Laing, Edinburgh. David Laing Papers.

La.IV.25.47, f. 121 Music: Herd. David Laing Papers.

Houghton Library, Harvard University

MS Am 1319/*53m–101. Murdoch, James Barclay. Correspondence.

MS Am 1922–1922.2, No. 152. Curtis, William George. Letter to Francis James Child, 4 Dec. 1880. Francis James Child Papers.

MS Am 2349, 10: 51–53. Letters to Francis James Child 17 Jan. 1881, enclosing a copy of part of a letter from James Burrill Curtis dated 4 Jan. 1881, and 26 Jan. 1881. English and Scottish Popular Ballads Research Material.

MS Eng 1486. Transcripts and notes concerning the "Brown manuscript" of Scottish popular ballads (1793–1920)

(1) Ritson, Joseph. Scotish Ballads: AMs transcript [1793 Jan. 19 – 1794 July 17].

(2) Jamieson – Brown Ms – transcript, 1874.
(3) Lord Woodhouselee's grand-daughter's manuscript: Scottish songs and ballads, probably before 1830: MS transcript, ca. 1881.
(4) Watts, Mary S., transcriber. The Brown ballad manuscript of Alexander Fraser Tytler; AMs transcript, 1881.
(5) Kittredge, George Lyman. Notes on the MS of Ballads in the hand of Joseph Ritson (a transcript of William Tytler's Brown Ms.): AMs, Cambridge, 1920.

Mitchell Library, Glasgow
308889 Cowie manuscript.

National Archives of Scotland, Edinburgh (NAS)
RD4/277/766. Rev. Dr. Andrew Brown's Will, registered 1 May 1805.
CC1/6/74. Bond of Caution for Mrs Rachel Forbes or Scott, 1811.

National Library of Scotland, Edinburgh (NLS)
Acc 2369. Two Ballad Mss of Mrs Brown of Falkland from the Originals at Aldourie Castle (Microfilm: Mt MSS 29; MS 1550).
Acc 3639. Tytler, Alexander Fraser Tytler, Lord Woodhouslee, Photocopies of correspondence of 1772–1812, 2 vols, n.d.
Acc 3640. Photocopies of Acc 10611 (1–2).
Acc 10611 (1). William Tytler Brown manuscript.
Acc 10611 (2). Alexander Fraser Tytler Brown manuscript.
Acc 11737. Tytler, Alexander Fraser. Lord Woodhouselee, Senator of the College of Justice, Commonplace books, diaries, books or etchings, sketch books (of late 18th – early 19th century).
Adv.Ms.22.4.10 Dr Robert Anderson: Original Letters (1760–1830).
MS 672. Letters addressed to Archibald Constable, with a few written by him, arranged roughly in alphabetical order of the correspondents, 1788–1827.
MS 911. Scott, Walter. Miscellanous Papers and Notes.
MS 1001 Miscellaneous Papers (v) Papers of Dr. Robert Anderson, 1799–1808, n.d.
MS 1809. Small Collections of Letters and Papers of the Nineteenth Century, with a few of the eighteenth Century.
MSS 2084–2085. MacFarlane MS., compiled by David Young, c. 1740.
MS 3874 Letters to Sir Walter Scott (1796–1803).
MS 3875 Letters to Sir Walter Scott (1804–06).

Nygard, Personal Communication
Holger Nygard. "Reminiscence of Conversation re. Mss find [with] Mrs Christian Fraser-Tytler, July 3, 1979."

Register House, Edinburgh

OPR 168. Old Parochial Register of the Parish of Old Machar, Aberdeenshire.

OPR 722. Parish Registers, 1611–1855, Parish Church of Tranent, Church of Scotland, East Lothian.

Society of Antiquaries of Scotland Library, Edinburgh

Glenriddell manuscript. Volume 8 (1789) of a "Collection of Scottish Antiquities." Selected and compiled by Robert Riddell of Glenriddell (1755–94).

Virginia Historical Society, Richmond (VHS)

Mss 1 P4686. Peyton Family Papers, 1760–1919. Section 5.

Secondary Sources

Alison, Rev. Archibald. "Memoir of the Life and Writings of the Honourable Alexander Fraser Tytler, Lord Woodhouselee." *Transactions of the Royal Society of Edinburgh* 8 (1818): 515–63.

Andersen, Flemming G. *Commonplace and Creativity: The Role of Formulaic Diction in Anglo-Scottish Traditional Balladry*. Odense: Odense University Press, 1985.

——— and Thomas Pettitt. "Mrs Brown of Falkland: A Singer of Tales?" *Journal of American Folklore* 92 (1979): 1–24.

Anderson, Peter John. *Officers and Graduates of University & King's College Aberdeen*. Aberdeen: New Spalding Club, 1893.

———. *Roll of Alumni in Arts in University and King's College of Aberdeen 1595–1860*. Aberdeen: Printed for the University, 1900.

Anon. "Art. III. – *Minstrelsy of the Scottish Border*. 2 vols. 1802." *Monthly Review* 42 (1803): 21–33.

Anon. "Art. III. – *Popular Ballads and Songs*. By Robert Jamieson, A. M. and F. A. S. 2 vols. London, Cadell and Davies. 1806." *Monthly Review* 52 (1807): 19–31.

Anon. "Art. 16. Tales of Wonder." *British Critic* 16 (Dec. 1800): 681.

Anon. "Memoirs of William Tytler, Esq; of Woodhouslee." *The Scots Magazine* 63 (March 1801): 154–56.

Anon. "Short Characteristical Notices of the Late William Tytler, Esq. of Woodhouslee." *The European Magazine* 23 (May 1793): 329–32.

Anon. "Tales of Wonder." *The Monthly Magazine; or British Register* 11.1 (1801): 605–606.

Apology for the Tales of Terror. Kelso: Ballantyne, 1799.

Apology for the Tales of Terror. Ed. Douglass H. Thomson. <*www.walter-scott.lib.ed.ac.uk/works/poetry/apology/home.html*>

Barczewski, Stephanie L. "Joseph Ritson (1752–1803)", *Oxford Dictionary of National Biography*, Oxford University Press, 2004 [accessed 3 Sept. 2009: <*http://www.oxforddnb.com/view/article/ 23685*>].

Bronson, Bertrand H. "Mrs Brown and the Ballad." *The Ballad as Song*. Berkeley: Univ. of California Press, 1969. 64–78.

———, "Professor Child' s Ballad Tunes." *California Folklore Quarterly* 1.2 (1942): 185–200.

———, ed. *The Traditional Tunes of the Child Ballads*. 4 vols. Princeton, N.J.: Princeton Univ. Press, 1959–72. [=*TT*]

Brown, Douglas (rev. from Francis Espinasse). "Anderson, Robert (1749–1830)", *Oxford Dictionary of National Biography*, Oxford University Press, 2004 [accessed 3 Sept. 2009: <*http://www.oxforddnb.com/view/article/497*>].

Buchan, David. *The Ballad and the Folk*. London: Routledge and Kegan Paul, 1972.

———, "Oral Tradition and Literary Tradition: The Scottish ballads." *Oral Tradition and Literary Tradition: A Symposium*. Ed. H. Bekker-Nielsen et al. Odense: Odense University Press, 1977.

Child, Francis James, ed. *The English and Scottish Popular Ballads*. 5 vols. Boston: Houghton, Mifflin and Co, 1882–98. [= *ESPB*]

———. "Old Ballads. Prof. Child's Appeal." *Notes and Queries* Ser. 4, Vol. 11 (4 January 1873): 12.

Cholmondeley, R. H. *The Heber Letters 1783–1832*. London: The Batchworth Press, 1950.

Christie, William, ed. *Traditional Ballad Airs: Arranged and Harmonised for the Pianoforte and Harmonium, from Copies Procured in the Counties of Aberdeen, Banff, and Moray*. 2 vols. Edinburgh: Edmonston and Douglas, 1876–81.

Churchill, W. A. *Watermarks in Paper in Holland, England, France, etc. in the XVII and XVIII centuries and their interconnection*. Amsterdam: Menno Hertzberger and Co., 1935.

Constable, Thomas. *Archibald Constable and his Literary Correspondents: A Memorial*. 3 vols. Edinburgh: Edmonston and Douglas, 1873.

The Correspondence of Thomas Percy and Robert Anderson. Ed. W. E. K. Anderson. *The Percy Letters* Vol. 9. New Haven: Yale University Press, 1988.

Couper, Sarah (rev. from A. J. G. Mackay). "Tytler, William (1711–1792)", *Oxford Dictionary of National Biography*, Oxford University Press, 2004 [accessed 3 Sept. 2009: <*http://www.oxforddnb.com/view/article/27969*>].

Creffield, C. A. (rev. from J. M. Rigg). "Scott, Robert Eden (1769–1811)", *Oxford Dictionary of National Biography*, Oxford University Press, 2004 [accessed 3 Sept. 2009: <*http://www.oxforddnb.com/view/article/24909*>].

Dobie, M. R. "The Development of Scott's 'Minstrelsy.'" *Edinburgh Bibliographical Society Transactions* 2 (1938–45): 67–87.

Donaldson, William. "Gordon, Anna (1747–1810)", *Oxford Dictionary of National Biography*, Oxford University Press, 2004 [accessed 3 Sept. 2009: <*http://www.oxforddnb.com/view/article/55496*>].

Du Toit, Alexander, "Tytler, Alexander Fraser, Lord Woodhouselee (1747–1813)", *Oxford Dictionary of National Biography*, Oxford University Press, 2004 [accessed 3 Sept. 2009: <*http://www.oxforddnb.com/view/article/27965*>].

Ewen, Graham. "Allanaquoich." *Cairngorm Club Journal* 20 (1999): 324–35.

Fabliaux or tales, abridged from French manuscripts of the XIIth and XIIIth centuries, by M. Le Grand, selected and tr. into English verse, by the late Gregory Lewis Way, Esq. With a preface, notes, and appendix, by G. Ellis. London: W. Bulmer, 1802.

Ferguson, J. De Lancey, ed. *The Letters of Robert Burns*. Second edition by G. Ross Roy. 2 vols. Oxford: Clarendon Press, 1985.

Fowler, David C. "An Accused Queen in 'The Lass of Roch Royal' (Child 76)." *Journal of American Folklore* 71 (1958): 553–63.

———. *A Literary History of the Popular Ballad*. Durham, N.C.: Duke University Press, 1968.

Friedman, Albert B. *The Ballad Revival: Studies in the Influence of Popular on Sophisticated Poetry*. Chicago: Univ. of Chicago Press, 1961.

———. "The Oral-Formulaic Theory of Balladry – a Re-rebuttal." *The Ballad Image*. Ed. James Porter. Los Angeles: University of California Press, 1983.

Geertz, Clifford. *Local Knowledge*. New York: Basic Books, 1983.

The Glenbuchat Ballads, compiled by Robert Scott. Ed. David Buchan and James Moreira. [Jackson]: University Press of Mississippi, 2007.

Greig, Gavin. *Folk Song in Buchan*. Peterhead: P. Scrogie, 1906.

The Greig-Duncan Folk Song Collection. Ed. Patrick Shuldham-Shaw and Emily B. Lyle, with Peter Hall, Andrew R. Hunter, Adam McNaughtan, Elaine Petrie, Sheila Douglas and Katherine Campbell. 8 vols. Aberdeen and Edinburgh: Aberdeen University Press and Mercat Press, 1981–2002. [= *GD*]

Grundtvig, Svend et al. *Danmarks gamle Folkeviser*. 12 vols. Copenhagen: Samfundet til den danske Literaturs Fremme and Universitets-Jubilæts danske Samfund, 1853–1976. [= *DgF*]

Guthke, Karl S. "Die erste Nachwirkung von Herders Volksliedern in England: unveröffentlichte Dokumente zu den Tales of Wonder." *Archiv für das Studium der Neueren Sprachen* 193 (1957): 273–84.

———. "Gruppenbild ohne M. G. Lewis: Neues zu Walter Scotts Übersetzungen von Goethes Balladen." *Archiv für das Studium der neueren Sprachen und Literaturen* 241 (2004): 1–17.

Harry, Keith William. "The Sources and Treatment of Traditional Ballad-Texts in Sir Walter Scott's *Minstrelsy of the Scottish Border* and Robert Jamieson's *Popular Ballads and Songs*." 2 vols. Ph.D. Thesis, Aberdeen University, 1975.

Harvey Wood, Elizabeth Harriet (rev. from T. W. Bayne). "Jamieson, Robert (1772?–1844)", *Oxford Dictionary of National Biography*, Oxford University Press, 2004 [accessed 3 Sept. 2009: <*http://www.oxforddnb.com/view/article/14641*>].

———. "Letters to an Antiquary: The Literary Correspondence of G. J. Thorkelin, 1752–1829." 2 vols. Ph.D Thesis, University of Edinburgh, 1972.

———. "Scott and Jamieson: The Relationship between the Two Ballad-Collectors." *Studies in Scottish Literature* 9 (1971–72): 2–3, 71–96.

Hecht, Hans. *Songs from David Herd's Manuscripts*. Edinburgh: Hay, 1904.

Herd, David. *Ancient and Modern Scottish Songs, Heroic Ballads*. 2 vols. Edinburgh: Wotherspoon, 1776.

Hewitt, David, "Scott, Sir Walter (1771–1832)", *Oxford Dictionary of National Biography*, Oxford University Press, 2004 [accessed 3 Sept. 2009: <*http://www.oxforddnb.com/view/article/24928*>].

Honko, Lauri, ed. *Thick Corpus, Organic Variaton and Textuality in Oral Tradition*. Studia Fennica Folkloristica 7. Helsinki: Finnish Literature Society, 2000.

Hustvedt, Sigurd B. *Ballad Books and Ballad Men*. Cambridge, Mass.: Harvard Univ. Press, 1930; New York: Johnson Reprint, 1970.

———. *Ballad Criticism in Scandinavia and Great Britain during the Eighteenth Century*. New York: American-Scandinavian Foundation, 1916; New York: Kraus Reprint, 1971.

Jamieson, Robert, ed. *Popular Ballads and Songs, from Tradition, Manuscripts, and Scarce Editions; with Translations of Similar Pieces from the Ancient Danish Language, and a Few Originals By the Editor*. 2 vols. Edinburgh: Printed for Archibald Constable and Co. Edinburgh: Cadell and Davies, and John Murray, London. 1806. [= *PB*]

———. "To the Publisher of the Scots Magazine." *Scots Magazine* (Oct. 1803): 698–701.

Johnson, David. *Music and Society in Lowland Scotland in the Eighteenth Century*. 1972. 2nd ed. Edinburgh: Mercat Press, 2003.

———, "Musical Traditions in the Forbes Family of Disblair, Aberdeenshire." *Scottish Studies* 22 (1978): 91–93.

Johnston, George P. "The First Book Printed by James Ballantyne: Being an Apology for Tales of Terror; With Notes on Tales of Wonder and Tales of Terror." *The Edinburgh Bibliographical Society* 3 (1893–94): 1–13.

Jonsson, Bengt R., Svale Solheim, and Eva Danielson, eds. *The Types of the Scandinavian Medieval Ballad: A Descriptive Catalogue*. Oslo: Universitetsforlaget, 1978. [=TSB]

Kekäläinen, Kirsti. "Apects of Style and Language in Child's Collection of English and Scottish Popular Ballads." Diss. Helsinki, 1983.

Kittredge, G. L. "A Lost Manuscript." *Harvard Library Notes* 3 (January 1921): 58.

Lamont, Claire. "James Boswell and Alexander Fraser Tytler." *The Bibliotheck* 6 (1971): 1–16.

Lewis, Matthew G. *Tales of Wonder.* London: W. Bulmer, 1801.

Lyle, Emily, ed. *Andrew Crawfurd's Collection of Ballads and Songs.* 2 vols. Edinburgh: Scottish Text Society, 1975–96.

———, Kaye McAlpine and Anne Dhu McLucas, eds. *The Song Repertoire of Amelia and Jane Harris.* Edinburgh: Scottish Text Society, 2002.

———. *Fairies and Folk: Approaches to the Scottish Ballad Tradition. B·A·S·E 1.* Trier: WVT Wissenschaftlicher Verlag Trier, 2007.

Mackenzie, Henry. "II. A Short Account of the Life and Writings of William Tytler, Esq; of Woodhouselee, F. R. S. Edin." *Transactions of the Royal Society of Edinburgh* 4.1 (1798): 17–34.

Maxwell, Richard (rev. from T. W. Bayne), "Leyden, John (1775–1811)", *Oxford Dictionary of National Biography*, Oxford University Press, 2004 [accessed 3 Sept. 2009: *<http://www.oxforddnb.com/view/article/16630>*].

Minstrelsy of the Scottish Border. 3 vols. Kelso and Edinburgh: Ballantyne, 1802–1803. [= *MSB*]

Montgomerie, William. "A Bibliography of the Scottish Ballad Manuscripts 1730–1825: Part I – Scottish ballad manuscripts, and the libraries where they are deposited." *Studies in Scottish Literature* 4 (1966): 3–28.

———. "A Bibliography of the Scottish Ballad Manuscripts 1730–1825: Part III – David Herd's Manuscript." *Studies in Scottish Literature* 4 (1967): 194–227.

———. "A Bibliography of the Scottish Ballad Manuscripts 1730–1825: Part V – The Glenriddell Ballad Manuscript and An Old Lady's Complete Set of Ballads." *Studies in Scottish Literature* 6 (1969): 91–104.

———. "A Bibliography of the Scottish Ballad Manuscripts 1730–1825: Part VI – Mrs. Brown's Manuscripts." *Studies in Scottish Literature* 6 (1969): 60–75.

———. "A Bibliography of the Scottish Ballad Manuscripts 1730–1825: Part VII – Mrs. Brown's Manuscripts (continued)." *Studies in Scottish Literature* 7 (1970): 238–54.

———. "Bibliography of the Scottish Ballad Manuscripts 1730–1825." Doctoral Dissertation, University of Edinburgh, 1954.

———. "Sir Walter Scott as Ballad Editor." *Review of English Studies* 7 (1956): 158–63.

Munro, Ailie. "'Abbotsford Collection of Border Ballads': Sophia Scott's Manuscript Book with Airs." *Scottish Studies* 20 (1976): 91–108; repr. in *The Persistent Scholar: Essays in Honour of Emily Lyle*. Ed. Frances

J. Fischer and Sigrid Rieuwerts. Trier: WVT Wisenschaftlicher Verlag Trier, 2007. 212–230.

Neilson, George. "A Bundle of Ballads. [An annotated catalogue of a collection of transcripts in the possession of C[harles] R. Cowie. With remarks identifying Robert Jamieson as the collector [1910]]". *Essays and Studies: By Members of The English Association* 7. Oxford: At the Clarendon Press, 1921. 108–42.

Nichols, John Bowyer, ed. *Illustrations of the Literary History of the Eighteenth Century, Consisting of Authentic Memoirs and Original Letters*. 8 vols. London: Nichols and Sons, 1858.

Niles, John DeWitt. "Context and Loss in Scottish Ballad Tradition." *Western Folklore* 45.2 (1986): 83–109.

———. "'Lamkin': The Motivation of Horror." *Journal of American Folklore* 90 (1977): 49–67.

Nygard, Holger Olof. "Mrs. Brown's Recollected Ballads." *Ballads and Ballad Research: Selected Papers of the International Conference on Nordic and Anglo-American Ballad Research (University of Washington, Seattle, May 2–6, 1977)*. Ed. Patricia Conroy. Seattle: University of Washington, 1978. 68–87.

Oberon, A Poem, From the German of Wieland. By William Sotheby, Esq. In Two Volumes. London: Cadell and Davies, 1798.

Ogilvy, Skene. *A Sermon, occasioned by the death of Robert Eden Scott, Esq. M.A., Professor of Logic and Moral Philosophy in the University and King's College of Aberdeen*. Aberdeen: Chalmers, 1811.

Percy, Thomas. *Reliques of Ancient English Poetry, Consisting of Old Heroic Ballads, Songs, and Other Pieces of Our Earlier Poets Together with Some Few of Later Date*. [1765] Ed. Henry B. Wheatley. 3 vols. London: Swan Sonnenschein, 1891.

Percy Letters. See *The Correspondence of Thomas Percy ...*

Pettitt, Thomas. "Mrs. Brown's 'Lass of Roch Royal' and the Golden Age of Scottish Balladry." *Jahrbuch für Volksliedforschung* 29 (1984): 13–31.

Ramsay, Allan. *The Tea-Table Miscellany: A Collection of Choice Songs, Scots and English.* 4 vols. 1723–37. Reprinted from the fourteenth edition. In 2 vols. Glasgow: Crum, 1871.

Reppert, James Donald. "F. J. Child and the Ballad." Ph.D. Thesis, Havard, 1953.

Rieuwerts, Sigrid. "Allan Ramsay and the Scottish Ballads." *Aberdeen University Review* 58. 1, No. 201 (Spring 1999): 29–41.

———. " 'Anonymity Runs in Their Blood:' Frauen und Dichtung im 18. und frühen 19. Jahrhundert." *Frauen in Kultur und Gesellschaft: Ausgewählte Beiträge der 2. Fachtagung Frau/Genderforschung in Rheinland-Pfalz*. Tübingen: Staufenburg Verlag, 2000. 149–59.

———. "Boundaries of Cultural Experience in Ballads: Singer and Scholar." *Ballads and Boundaries: Narrative Singing in an Intercultural Context.*

Ed. James Porter. University of California, Los Angeles: Department of Ethnomusicology & Systematic Musicology, 1995. 374–76.

———. "'The Genuine Ballads of the People': F. J. Child and the ballad cause." *Journal of Folklore Research* 31.1–3 (1994): 1–34.

———. *In the Footsteps of Herder: Robert Jamieson of Morayshire*. 2 vols. [forthcoming]

———. " 'It is mainly through women everywhere …' Zur Tradierung von englisch-schottischen Volksballaden durch Frauen." *Gender – Culture – Poetics: Zur Geschlechterforschung in der Literatur- und Kulturwissenschaft – Festschrift für Natascha Würzbach*. Ed. Andrea Gutenberg and Ralf Schneider. Trier: WVT Wissenschaftlicher Verlag Trier, 1999. 473–83.

———. *Kulturnarratologie: Die Geschichte einer Geschichte*. Trier: WVT Wissenschaftlicher Verlag Trier, 2006.

———. "Percy, Thomas." *Encyclopedia of Folklore and Literature*. Ed. Mary Ellen Brown and Bruce Rosenberg. Denver: ABC-CLIO, 1998. 495–97.

———. "The Voice of the Scottish Muse on the Shores of the Frozen Baltic: Robert Jamieson, Sir Walter Scott and Riga." *Singing the Nations: Herder's Legacy*. Ed. Dace Bula and Sigrid Rieuwerts. B·A·S·I·S 4. Trier: WVT Wissenschaftlicher Verlag Trier, 2007. 47–56.

Ritson, Joseph. *Scotish Songs*. 2 vols. London: J. Johnson, [1794].

Robson, Michael. "Sir Walter Scott's Collecting of Ballads in the Borders." *Transactions of the Hawick Archaeological Society* (1974): 3–33.

Ruff, William. "Sir Walter Scott and Bishop Percy." *Notes and Queries* (Nov. 4, 1933): 308–309.

Scott, Hew. *Fasti Ecclesiæ Scoticanæ: The Succession of Ministers in the Church of Scotland from the Reformation*. New edition. Vol. 5: *Synod of Fife, and of Angus and Mearns*. Edinburgh: Oliver and Boyd, 1925.

Scott, Walter. *The Letters of Sir Walter Scott*. Ed. Herbert Grierson. 12 vols. London: Constable, 1932–37. [= *SL*]

———. *Minstrelsy of the Scottish Border*. Revised and edited by T. F. Henderson. 4 vols. Edinburgh: Oliver and Boyd, 1932.

Shenstone, William, ed. *The Scots Musical Museum Originally Published by James Johnson. With Illustrations of the Lyric Poetry and Music of Scotland by William Shenstone*. Hatboro: Folklore Associates, 1962. Shorter, Alfred H. *Paper Mills and Paper Makers in England, 1495–1800.* Hilversum: Paper Publications Society, 1967.

Shorter, Alfred H. *Paper Mills and Paper Makers in England, 1495–1800*. Hilversum: Paper Publications Society, 1967.

Solbach, Marianne. "Die Balladen der Mrs. Brown aus Falkland." Diss., Bonn, 1953.

Thomson, George. *Select Collection of Original Scottish Airs for the Voice*. 5 vols. London: Preston, 1793–1818.

Tytler of Woodhouselee, William. "A Dissertation on the Scottish Musick." *The History of Edinburgh* by Hugh Arnot. Edinburgh: W. Creech, 1779; repr. *Transactions of the Society of Antiquarians of Scotland* 1 (1792): 469–98.

Walker, Alexander. *Disblair, 1634–1884; or, An old oak panel and something thereon*. Aberdeen: Edmond & Spark, 1884.

Walker, William. "Auld Lang Syne: The Authorship of the Old Aberdeenshire Version." *Aberdeen Daily Journal* (July 16, 1921).

Wilson, W. E. "The Making of the 'Minstrelsy.' Scott and Shortreed in Liddesdale." *The Cornhill Magazine* New Series 73 (Sept. 1932): 266–82.

Zug, Charles G. "Sir Walter Scott, Robert Jamieson and the New 'Minstrelsy.'" *Music & Letters* 57.4 (1976): 398–403.

Index of Titles and First Lines

All forms of the titles of Brown ballads are included in this index. In the case of first lines, where there are parallel texts and their first lines do not differ substantively, only the first version is listed. The number for each text is shown in bold, followed by a reference to the page numbers of the full text. The ballad titles as given in the source text appear in small capitals.

Index of People and Places